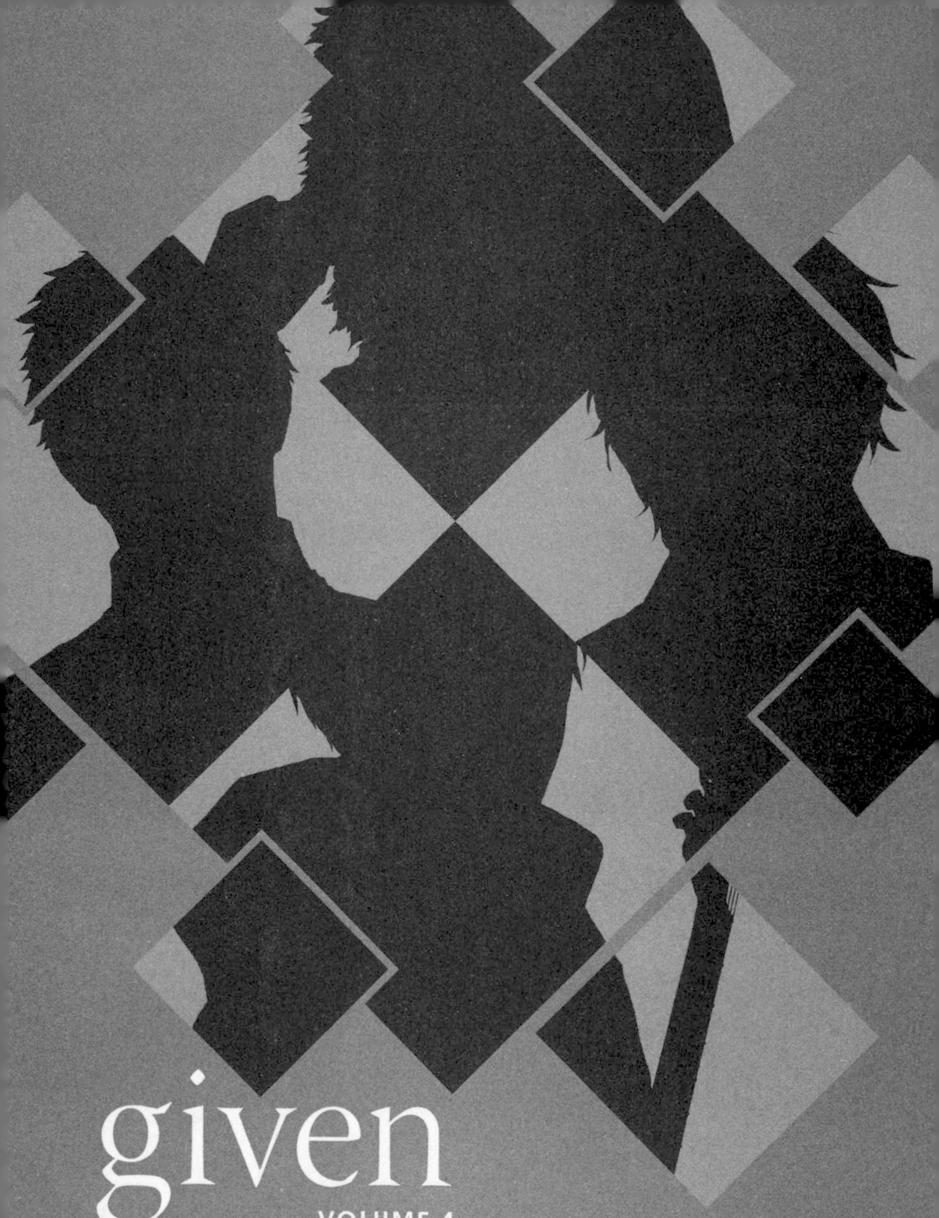

given

VOLUME 4

NATSUKI KIZU

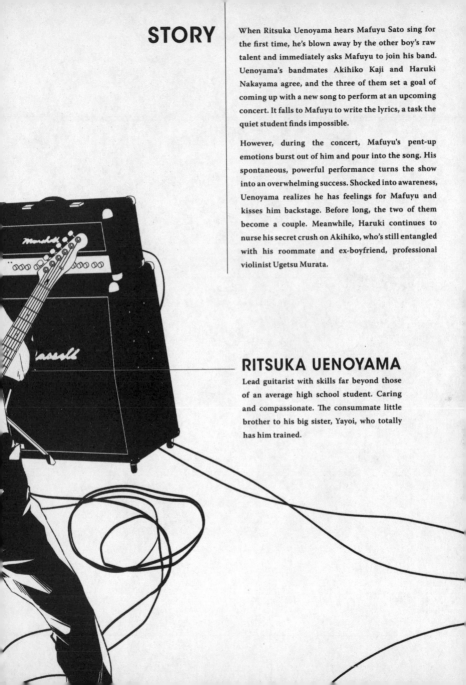

STORY

When Ritsuka Uenoyama hears Mafuyu Sato sing for the first time, he's blown away by the other boy's raw talent and immediately asks Mafuyu to join his band. Uenoyama's bandmates Akihiko Kaji and Haruki Nakayama agree, and the three of them set a goal of coming up with a new song to perform at an upcoming concert. It falls to Mafuyu to write the lyrics, a task the quiet student finds impossible.

However, during the concert, Mafuyu's pent-up emotions burst out of him and pour into the song. His spontaneous, powerful performance turns the show into an overwhelming success. Shocked into awareness, Uenoyama realizes he has feelings for Mafuyu and kisses him backstage. Before long, the two of them become a couple. Meanwhile, Haruki continues to nurse his secret crush on Akihiko, who's still entangled with his roommate and ex-boyfriend, professional violinist Ugetsu Murata.

RITSUKA UENOYAMA

Lead guitarist with skills far beyond those of an average high school student. Caring and compassionate. The consummate little brother to his big sister, Yayoi, who totally has him trained.

MAFUYU SATO

High school classmate of Uenoyama's. Has an impressive singing voice. Attached to Uenoyama ever since he fixed Mafuyu's broken guitar.

HARUKI NAKAYAMA

Graduate student. The band's bassist. He's extremely good-natured and kind.

AKIHIKO KAJI

University student. The band's drummer. A bit of a playboy who's popular without ever trying.

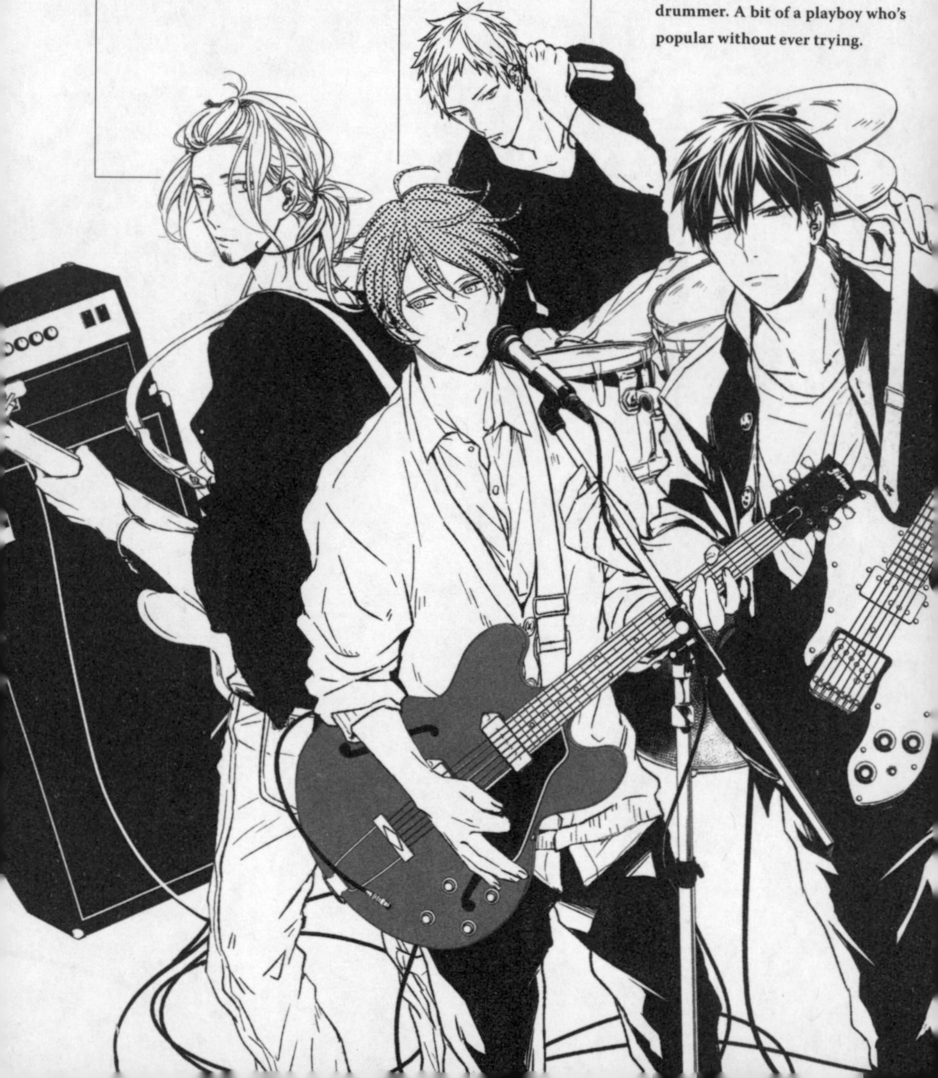

chapter 17 | given

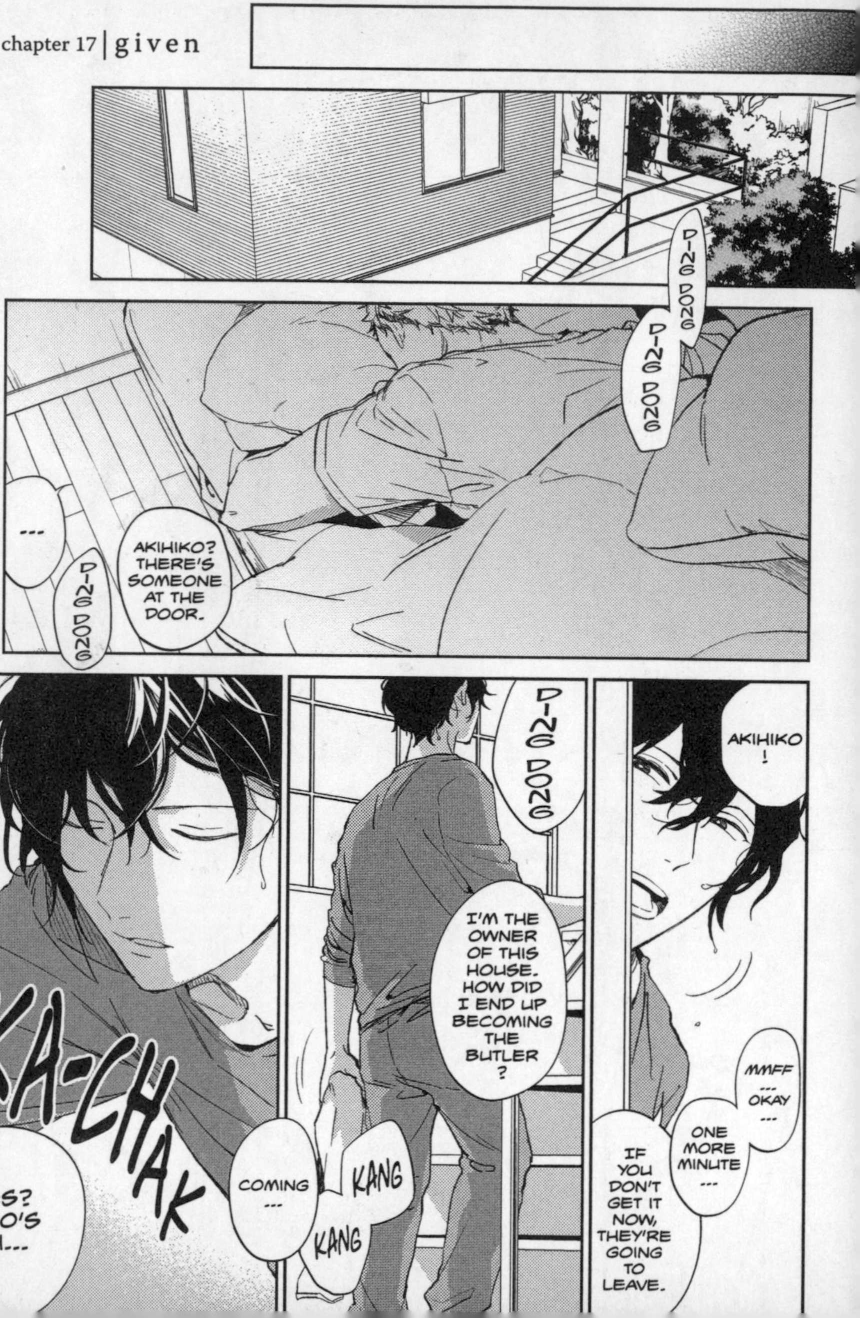
DING DONG
DING DONG
DING DONG
AKIHIKO? THERE'S SOMEONE AT THE DOOR.
...
DING DONG
AKIHIKO!
MMFF ... OKAY ...
ONE MORE MINUTE ...
IF YOU DON'T GET IT NOW, THEY'RE GOING TO LEAVE.
DING DONG
I'M THE OWNER OF THIS HOUSE. HOW DID I END UP BECOMING THE BUTLER?
KANG
KANG
COMING ...
KA-CHAK
YES? WHO'S TH...

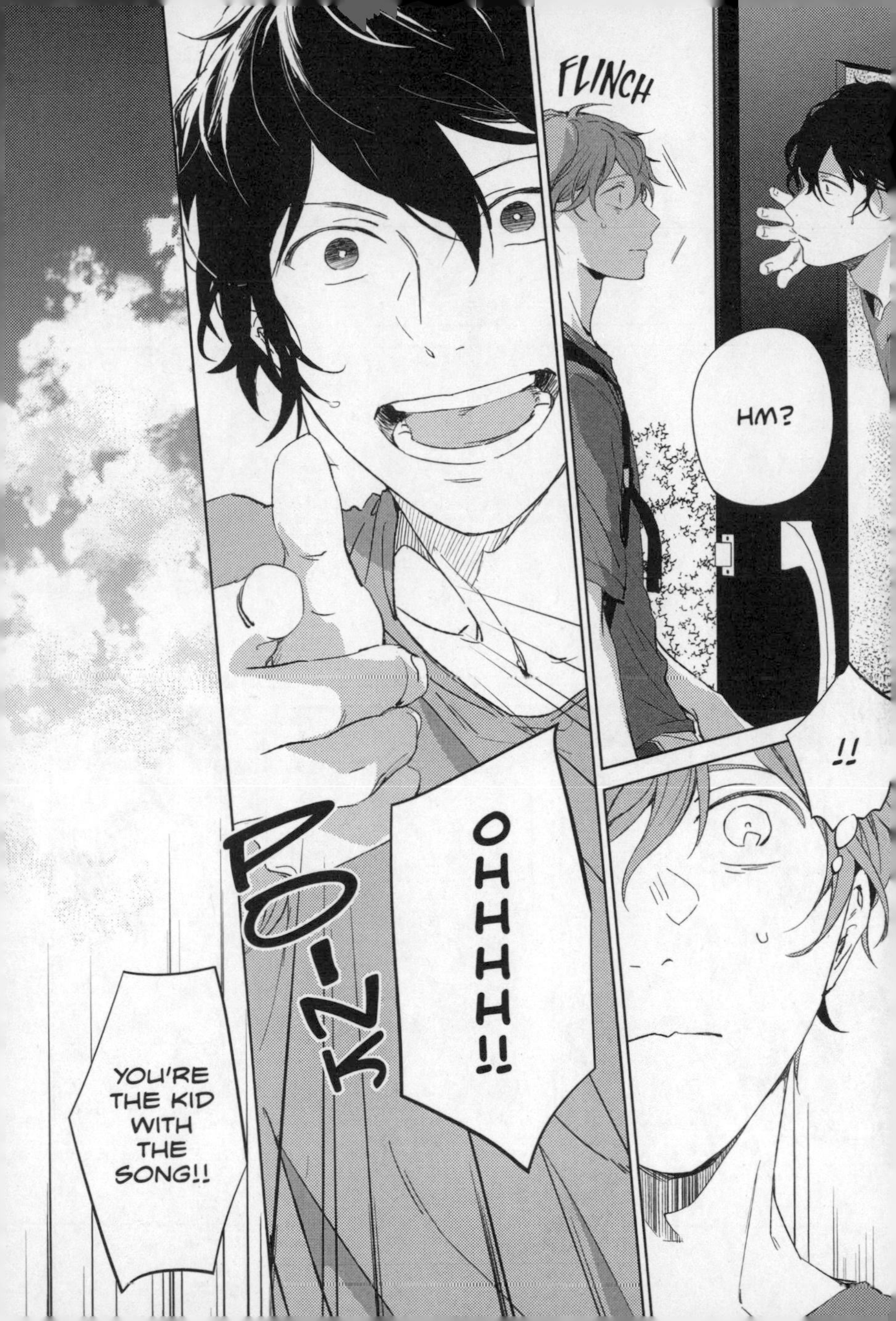
HM?
FLINCH
!!
OHHHH!!
POINK
YOU'RE THE KID WITH THE SONG!!

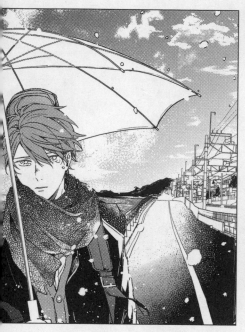
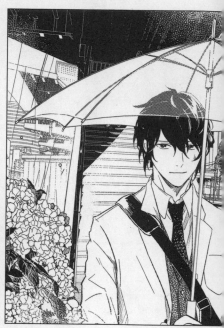

given

chapter 17

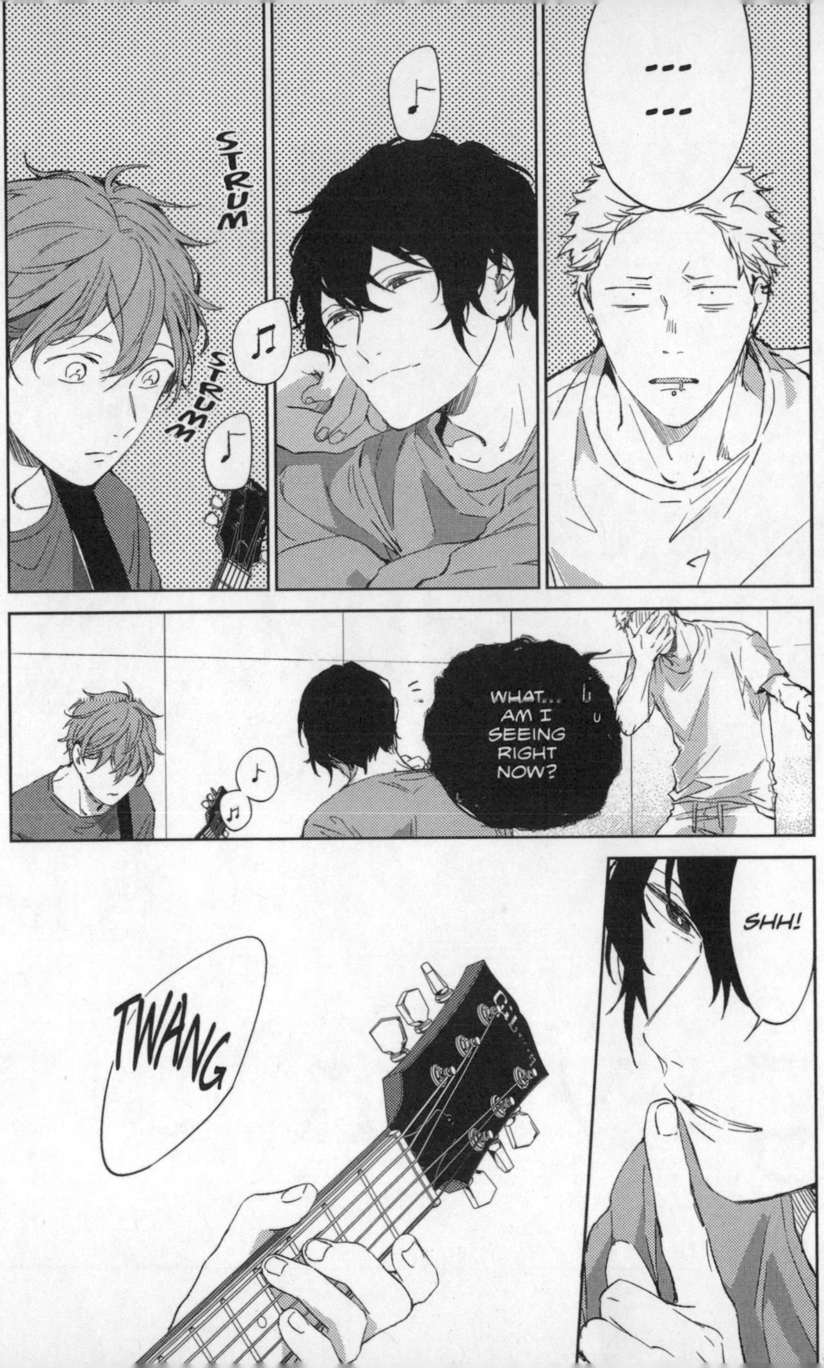
...
...
STRUM
STRUM
WHAT... AM I SEEING RIGHT NOW?
SHH!
TWANG

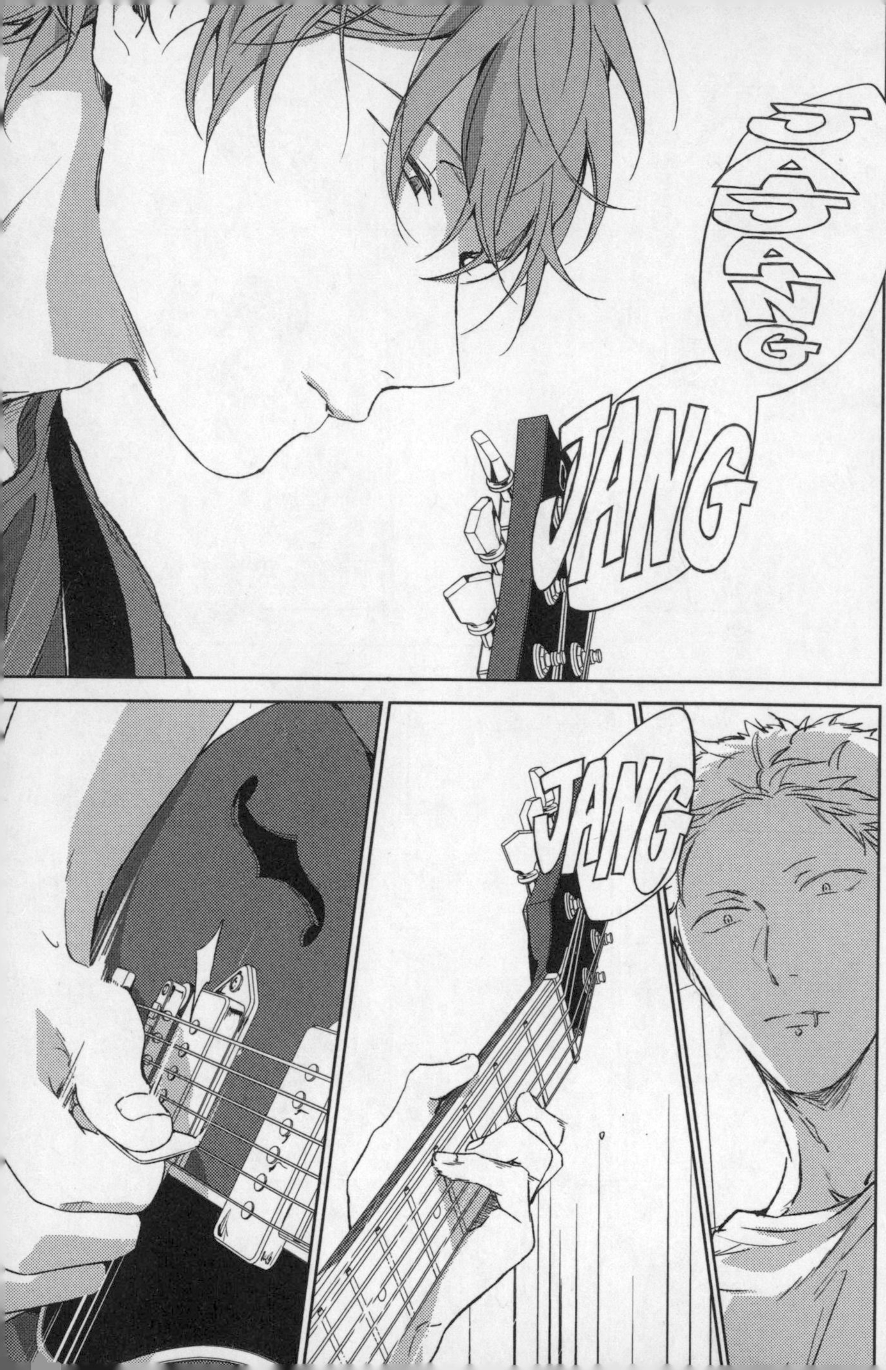
JAJANG
JANG
JANG

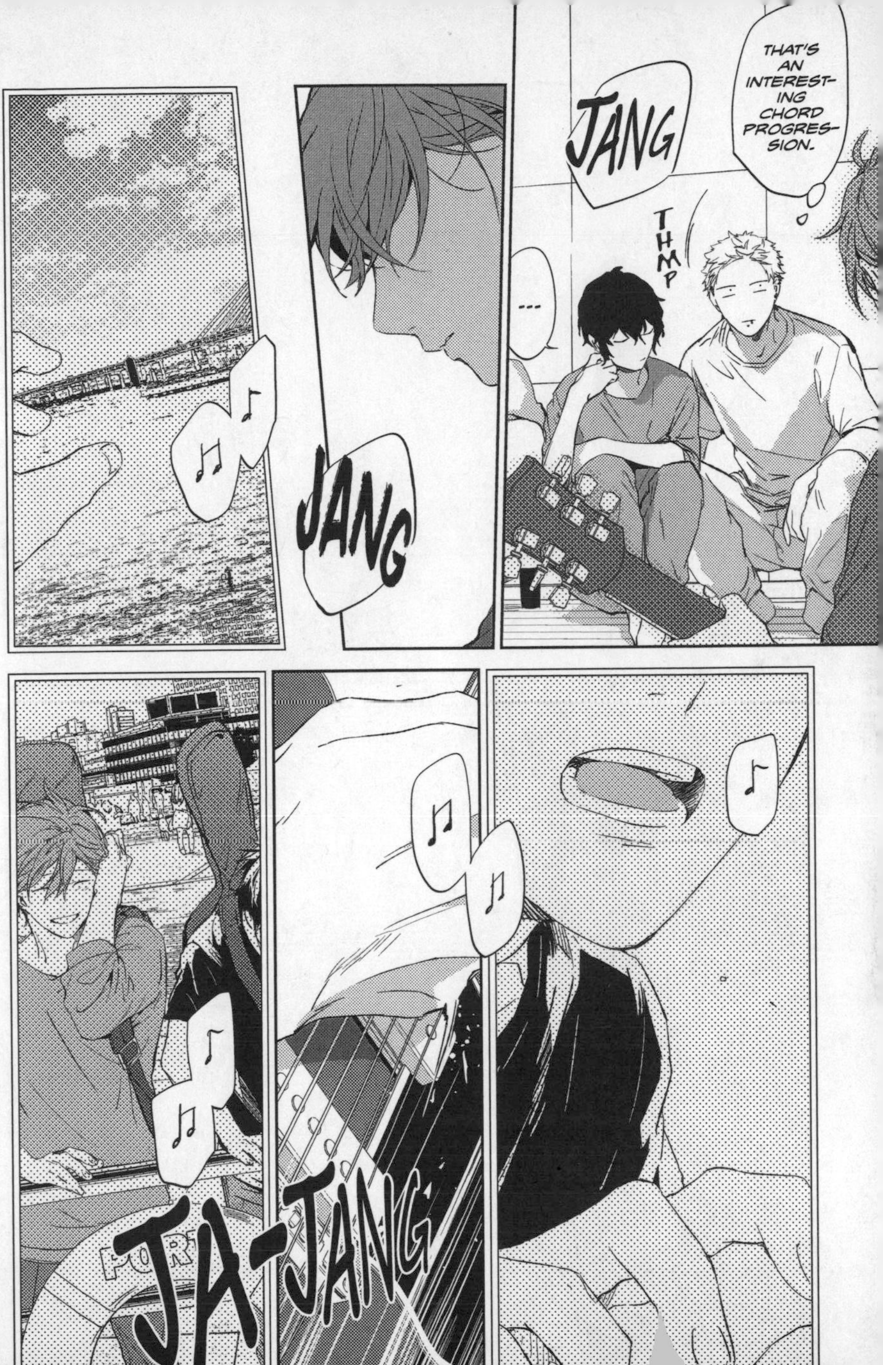
THAT'S AN INTEREST-ING CHORD PROGRES-SION.
JANG
THUMP
...
JANG
JA-JANG

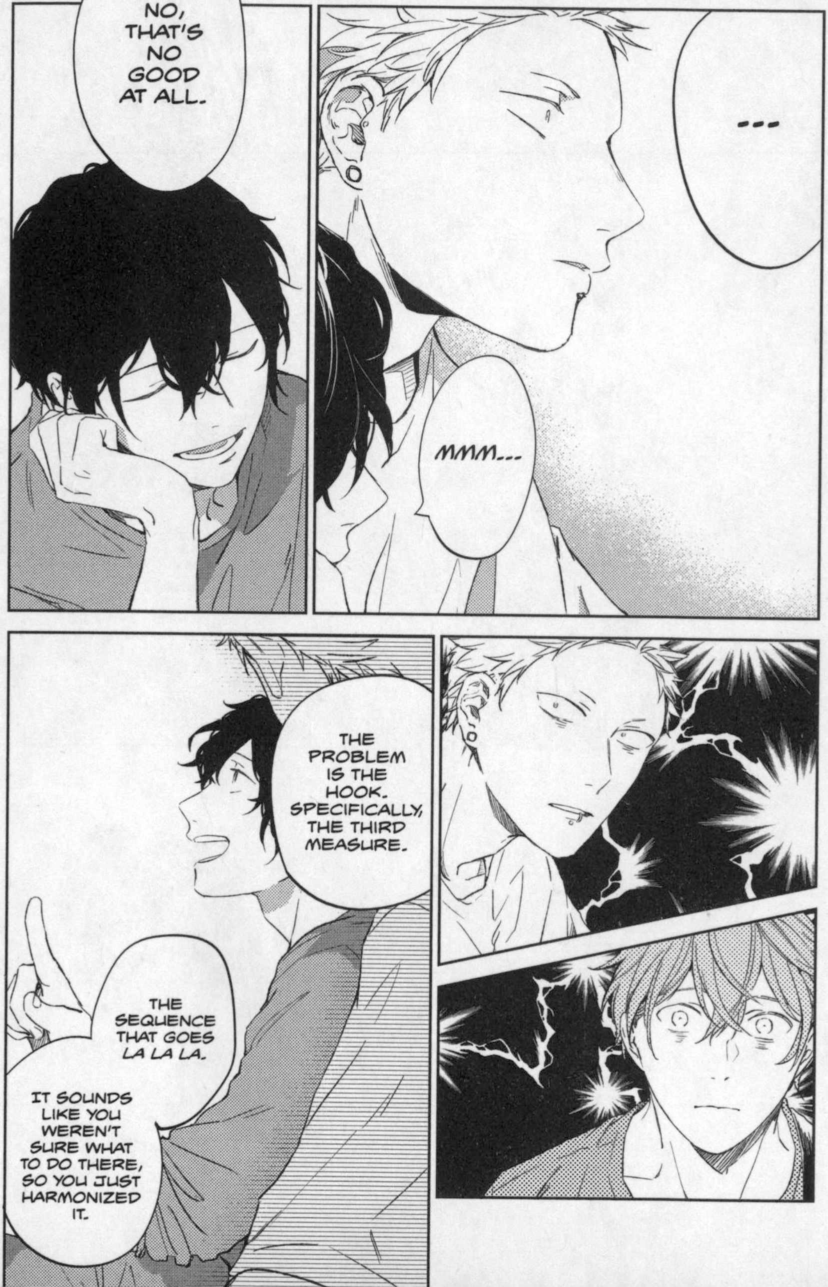
...
MMM...
NO, THAT'S NO GOOD AT ALL.
THE PROBLEM IS THE HOOK. SPECIFICALLY, THE THIRD MEASURE.
THE SEQUENCE THAT GOES LA LA LA.
IT SOUNDS LIKE YOU WEREN'T SURE WHAT TO DO THERE, SO YOU JUST HARMONIZED IT.

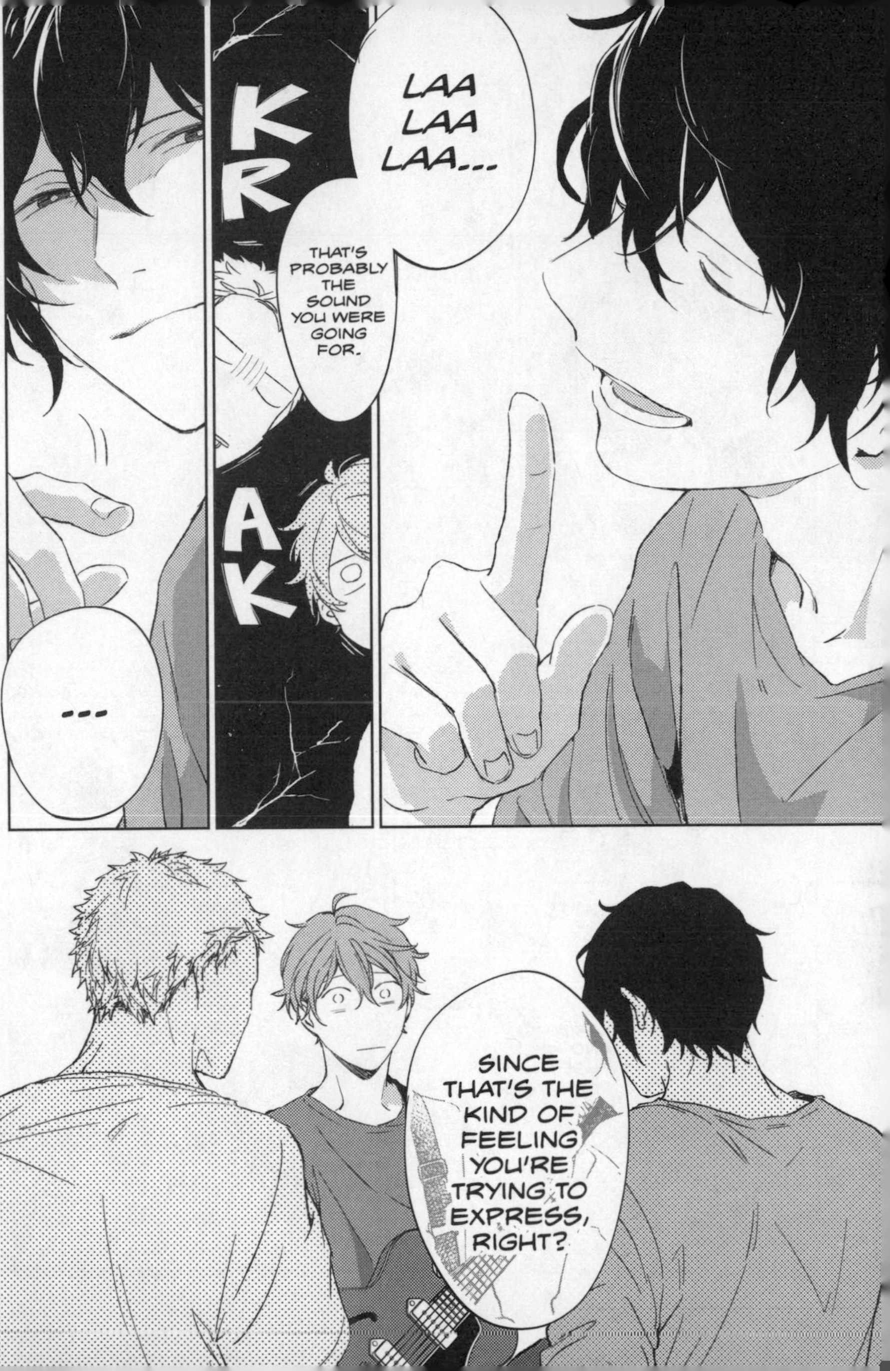
LAA LAA LAA...
THAT'S PROBABLY THE SOUND YOU WERE GOING FOR.
KRAK
...
SINCE THAT'S THE KIND OF FEELING YOU'RE TRYING TO EXPRESS, RIGHT?

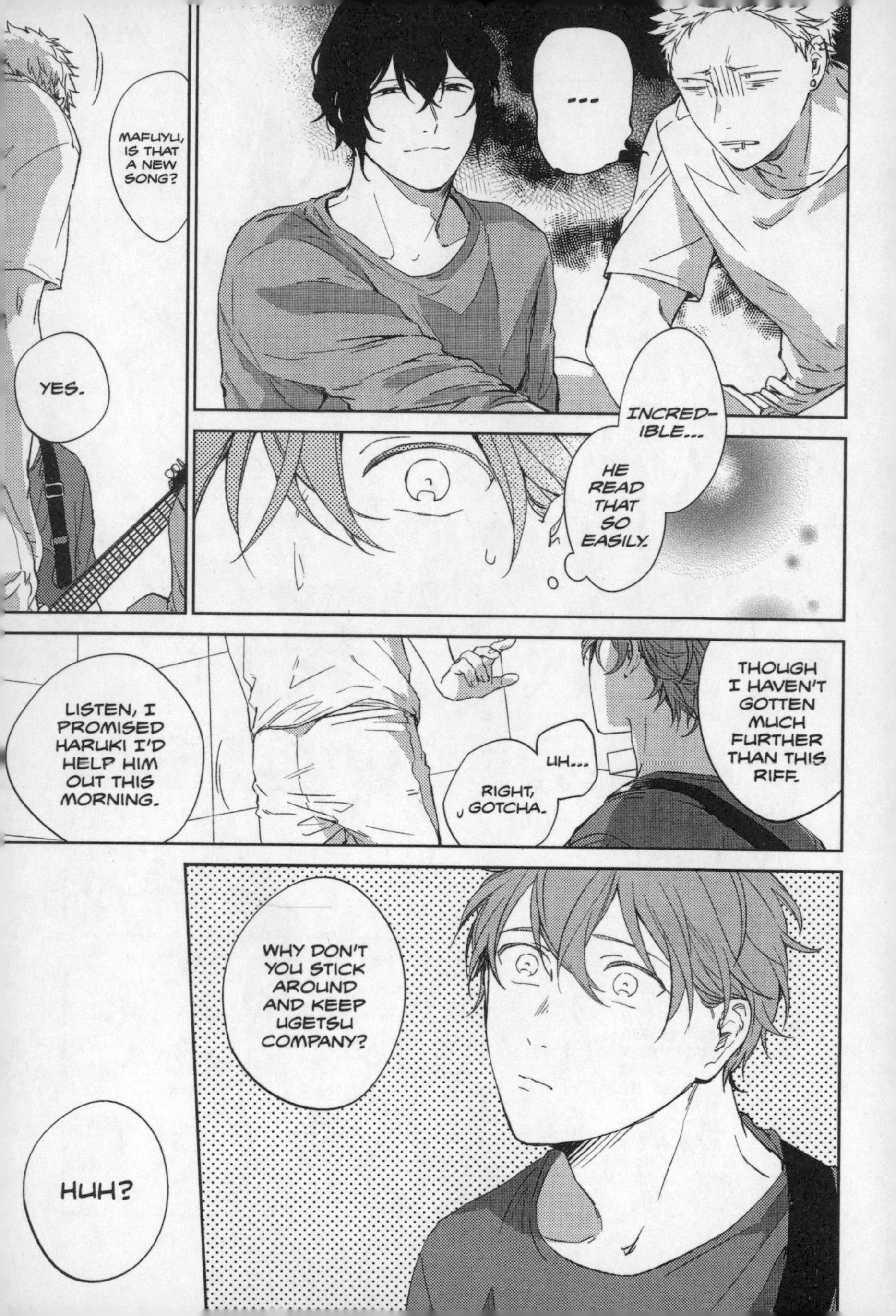
...
INCREDIBLE... HE READ THAT SO EASILY.
MAFUYU, IS THAT A NEW SONG?
YES.
THOUGH I HAVEN'T GOTTEN MUCH FURTHER THAN THIS RIFF.
UH...
RIGHT, GOTCHA.
LISTEN, I PROMISED HARUKI I'D HELP HIM OUT THIS MORNING.
WHY DON'T YOU STICK AROUND AND KEEP UGETSU COMPANY?
HUH?

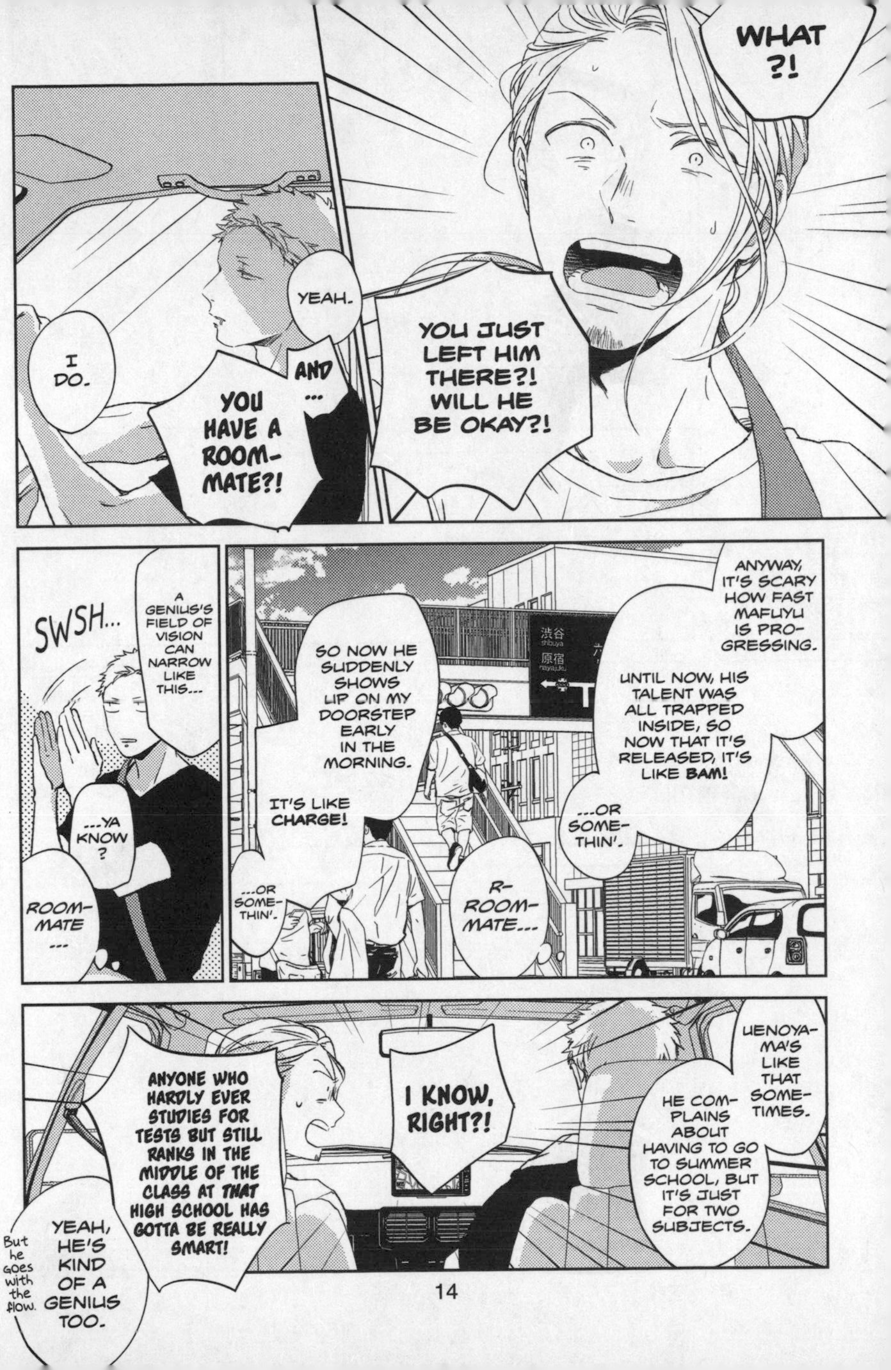
WHAT ?!
YOU JUST LEFT HIM THERE?! WILL HE BE OKAY?!
AND ... YOU HAVE A ROOM-MATE?!
YEAH.
I DO.
ANYWAY, IT'S SCARY HOW FAST MAFUYU IS PRO-GRESSING.
UNTIL NOW, HIS TALENT WAS ALL TRAPPED INSIDE, SO NOW THAT IT'S RELEASED, IT'S LIKE BAM!
...OR SOME-THIN'.
SO NOW HE SUDDENLY SHOWS UP ON MY DOORSTEP EARLY IN THE MORNING.
IT'S LIKE CHARGE!
R-ROOM-MATE...
...OR SOME-THIN'.
A GENIUS'S FIELD OF VISION CAN NARROW LIKE THIS...
SWSH...
...YA KNOW ?
ROOM-MATE ...
UENOYAMA'S LIKE THAT SOME-TIMES.
HE COM-PLAINS ABOUT HAVING TO GO TO SUMMER SCHOOL, BUT IT'S JUST FOR TWO SUBJECTS.
I KNOW, RIGHT?!
ANYONE WHO HARDLY EVER STUDIES FOR TESTS BUT STILL RANKS IN THE MIDDLE OF THE CLASS AT THAT HIGH SCHOOL HAS GOTTA BE REALLY SMART!
YEAH, HE'S KIND OF A GENIUS TOO.
But he goes with the flow.

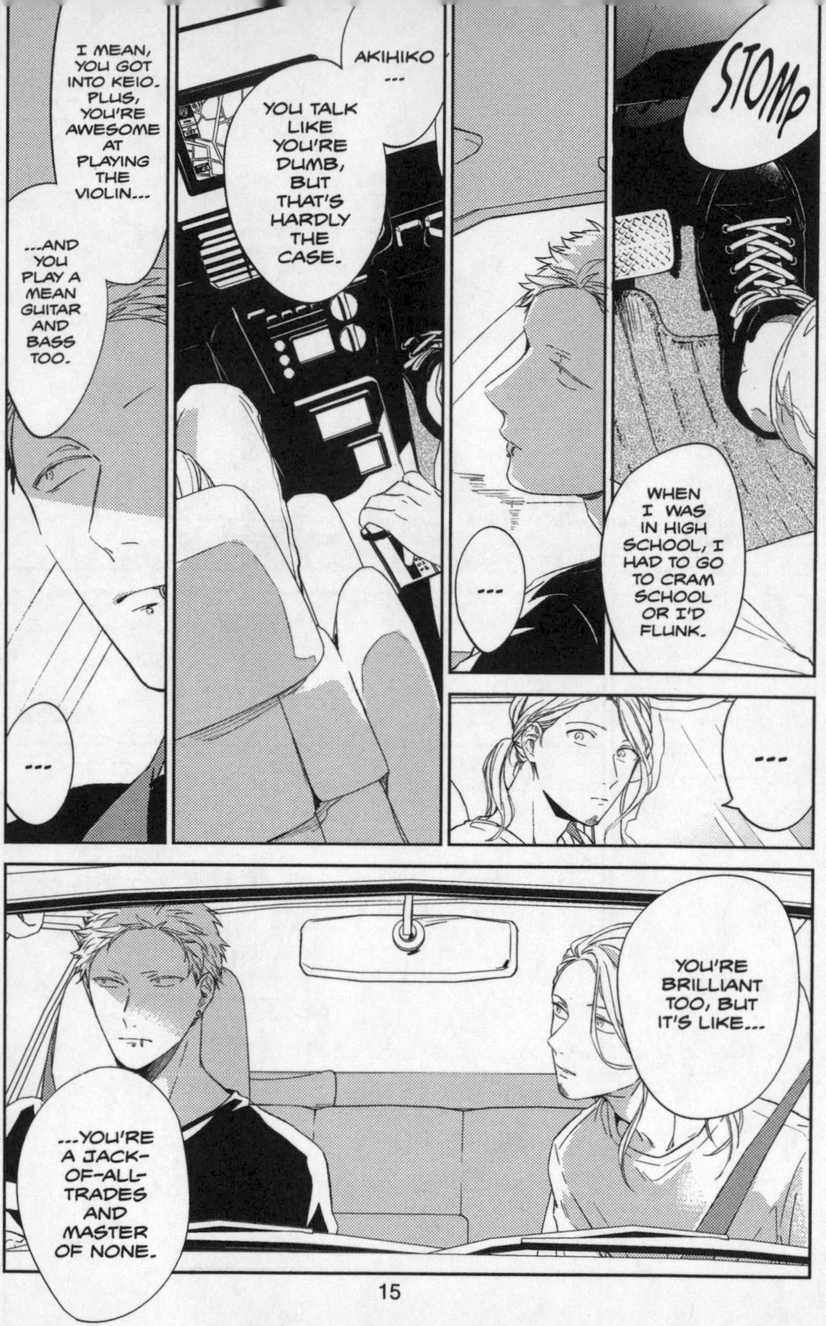
STOMP
WHEN I WAS IN HIGH SCHOOL, I HAD TO GO TO CRAM SCHOOL OR I'D FLUNK.
...
...
AKIHIKO...
YOU TALK LIKE YOU'RE DUMB, BUT THAT'S HARDLY THE CASE.
I MEAN, YOU GOT INTO KEIO. PLUS, YOU'RE AWESOME AT PLAYING THE VIOLIN...
...AND YOU PLAY A MEAN GUITAR AND BASS TOO.
...
YOU'RE BRILLIANT TOO, BUT IT'S LIKE...
...YOU'RE A JACK-OF-ALL-TRADES AND MASTER OF NONE.

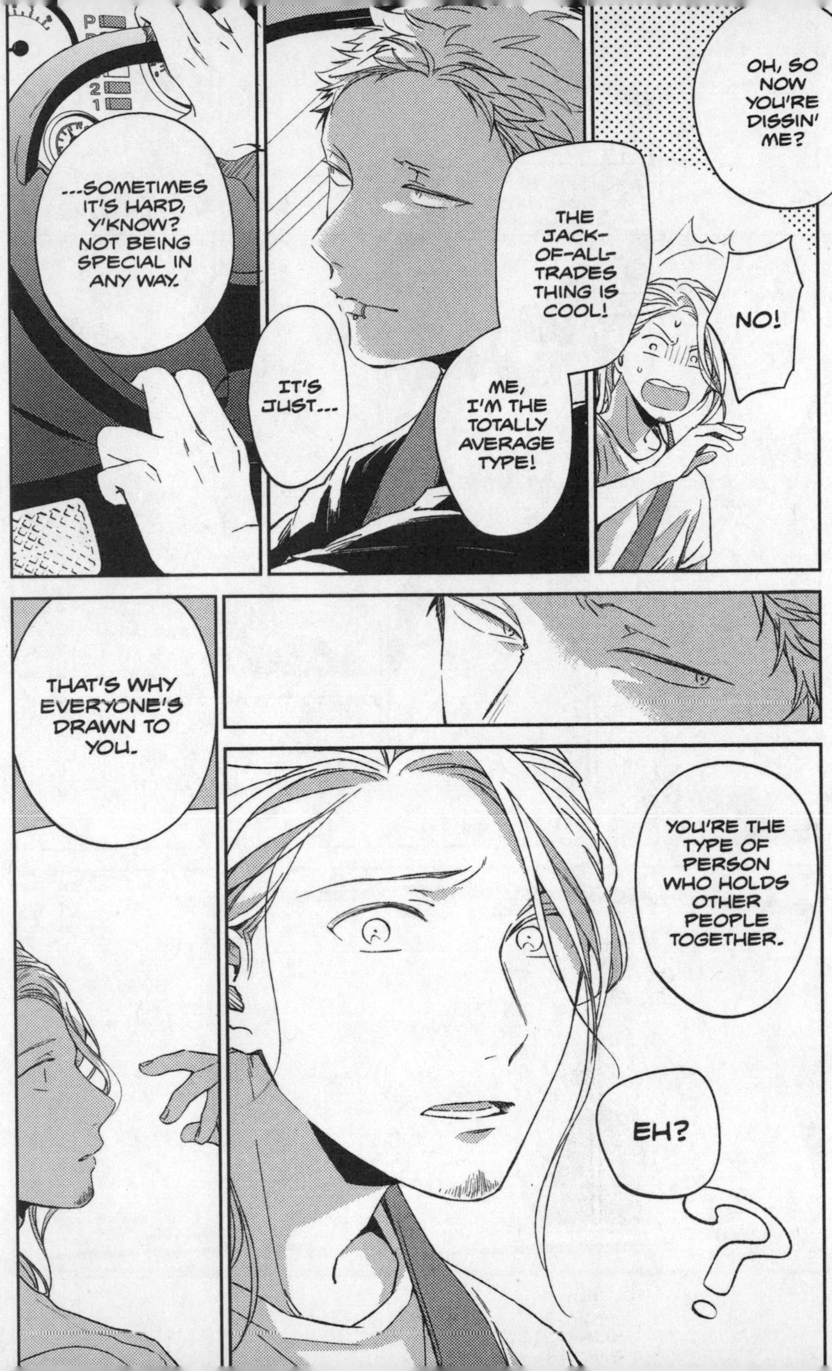
OH, SO NOW YOU'RE DISSIN' ME?
NO!
THE JACK-OF-ALL-TRADES THING IS COOL!
ME, I'M THE TOTALLY AVERAGE TYPE!
IT'S JUST...
...SOMETIMES IT'S HARD, Y'KNOW? NOT BEING SPECIAL IN ANY WAY.
YOU'RE THE TYPE OF PERSON WHO HOLDS OTHER PEOPLE TOGETHER.
EH?
THAT'S WHY EVERYONE'S DRAWN TO YOU.

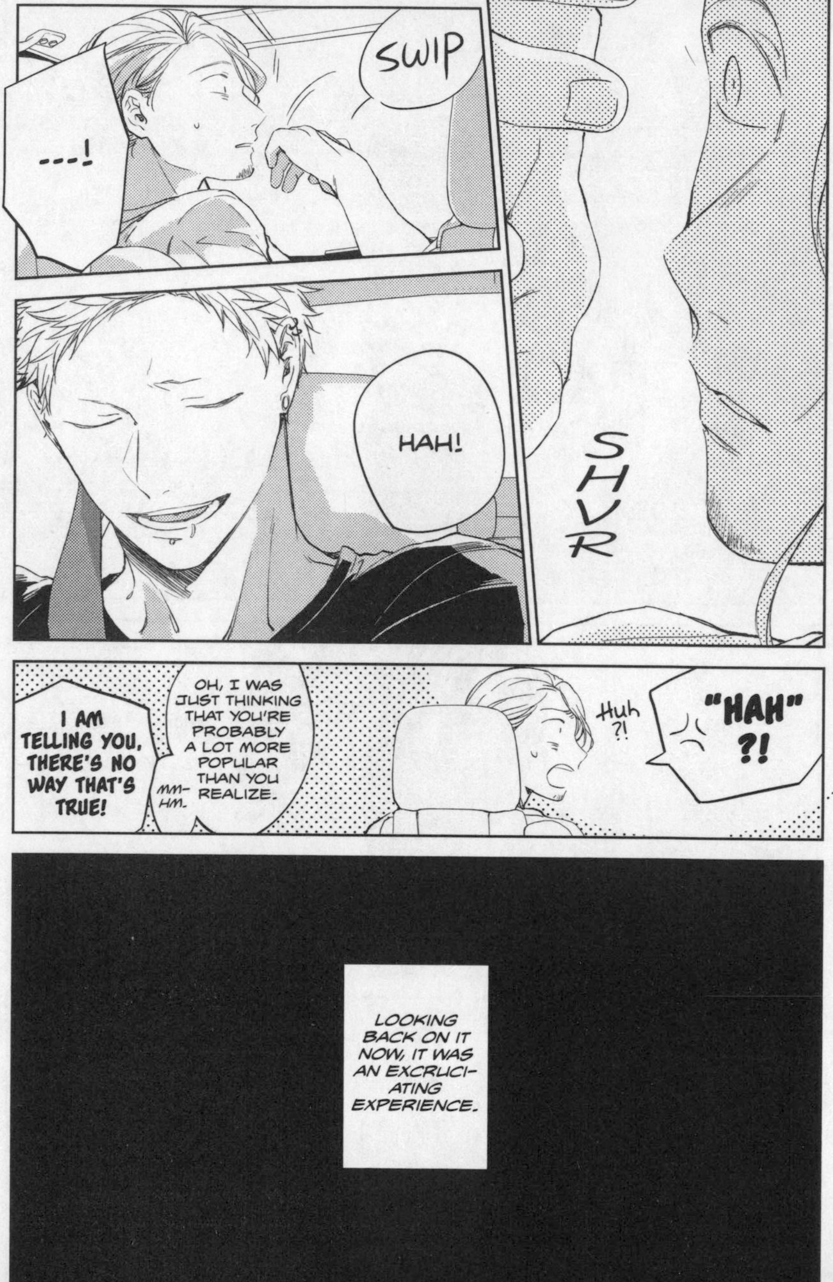
SHVR
SWIP
---!
HAH!
"HAH" ?!
Huh ?!
OH, I WAS JUST THINKING THAT YOU'RE PROBABLY A LOT MORE POPULAR THAN YOU REALIZE.
MM-HM.
I AM TELLING YOU, THERE'S NO WAY THAT'S TRUE!
LOOKING BACK ON IT NOW, IT WAS AN EXCRUCI-ATING EXPERIENCE.

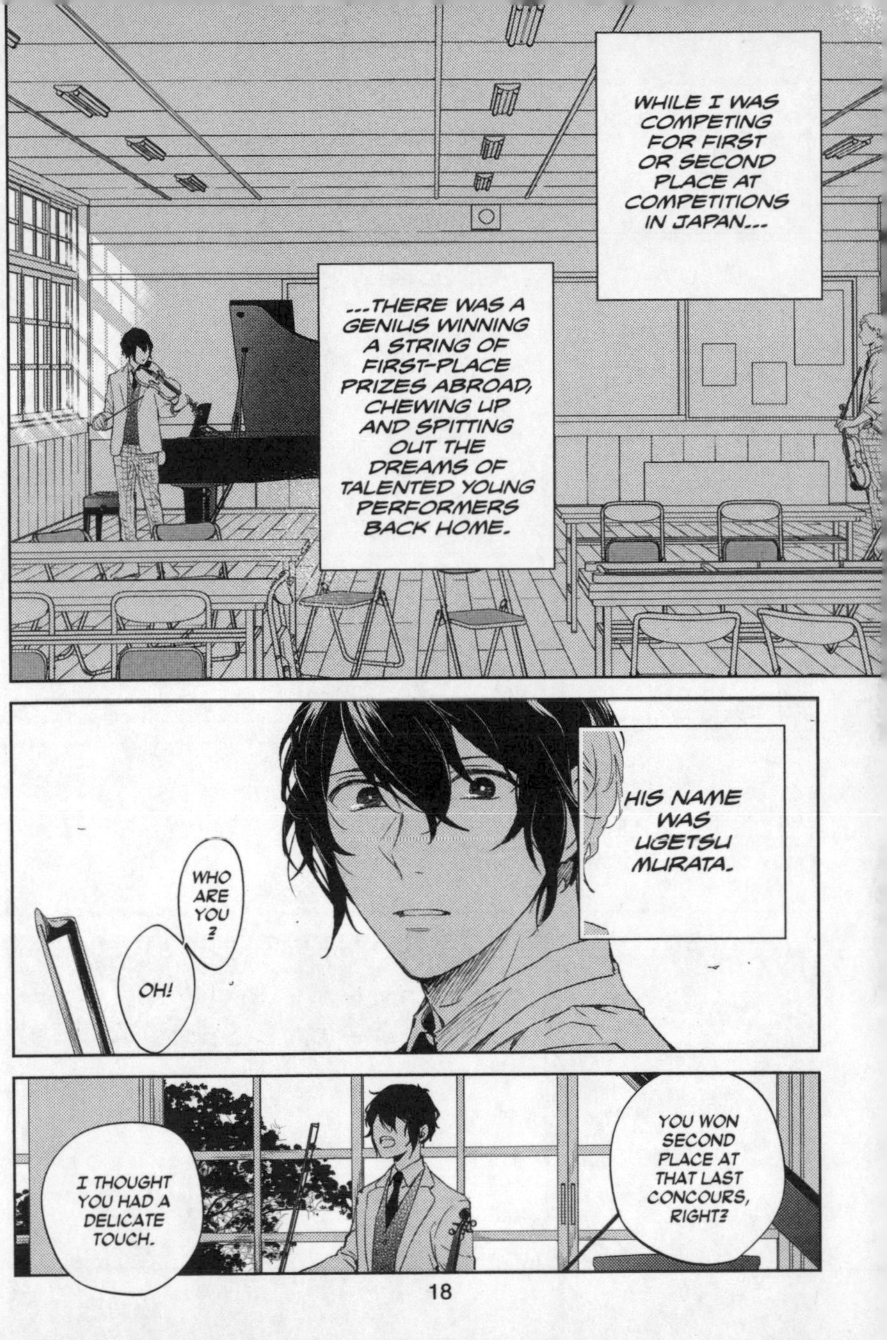
WHILE I WAS COMPETING FOR FIRST OR SECOND PLACE AT COMPETITIONS IN JAPAN...
...THERE WAS A GENIUS WINNING A STRING OF FIRST-PLACE PRIZES ABROAD, CHEWING UP AND SPITTING OUT THE DREAMS OF TALENTED YOUNG PERFORMERS BACK HOME.
HIS NAME WAS UGETSU MURATA.
WHO ARE YOU?
OH!
YOU WON SECOND PLACE AT THAT LAST CONCOURS, RIGHT?
I THOUGHT YOU HAD A DELICATE TOUCH.

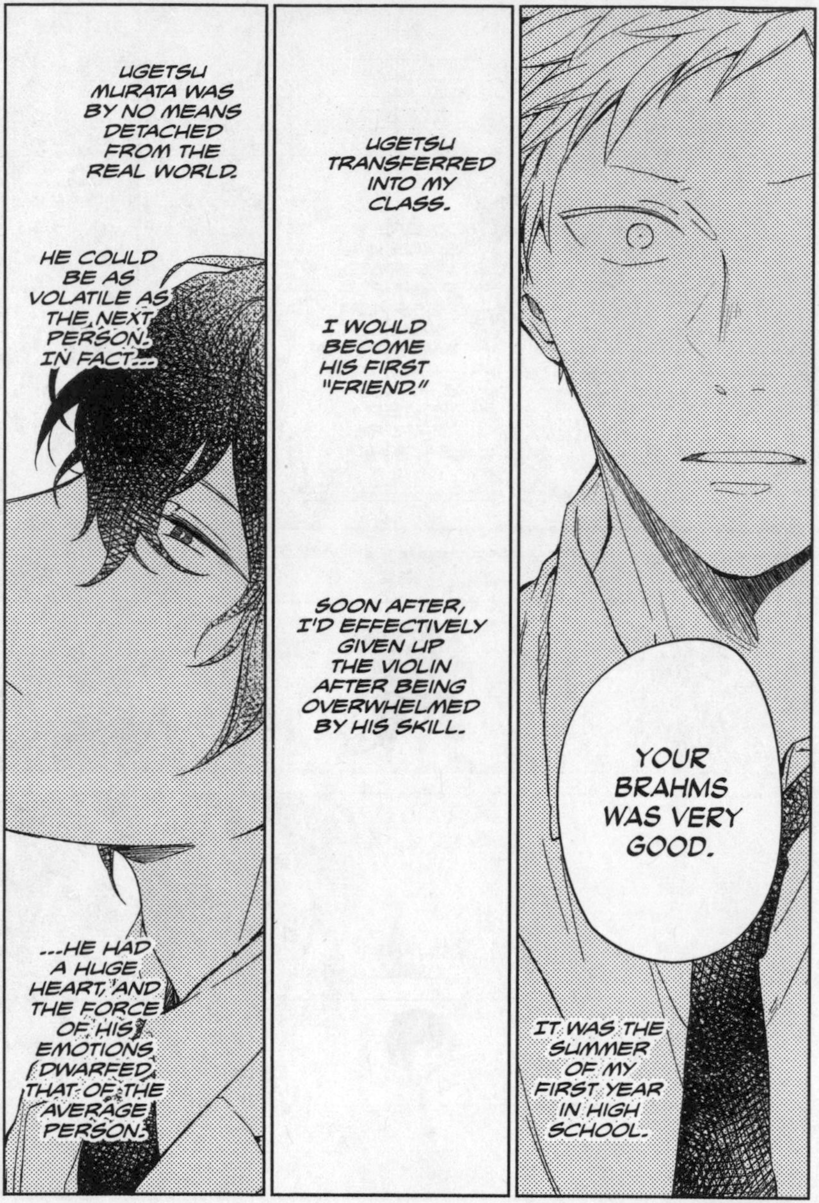
YOUR BRAHMS WAS VERY GOOD.
IT WAS THE SUMMER OF MY FIRST YEAR IN HIGH SCHOOL.
UGETSU TRANSFERRED INTO MY CLASS.
I WOULD BECOME HIS FIRST "FRIEND."
SOON AFTER, I'D EFFECTIVELY GIVEN UP THE VIOLIN AFTER BEING OVERWHELMED BY HIS SKILL.
UGETSU MURATA WAS BY NO MEANS DETACHED FROM THE REAL WORLD.
HE COULD BE AS VOLATILE AS THE NEXT PERSON. IN FACT...
...HE HAD A HUGE HEART, AND THE FORCE OF HIS EMOTIONS DWARFED THAT OF THE AVERAGE PERSON.

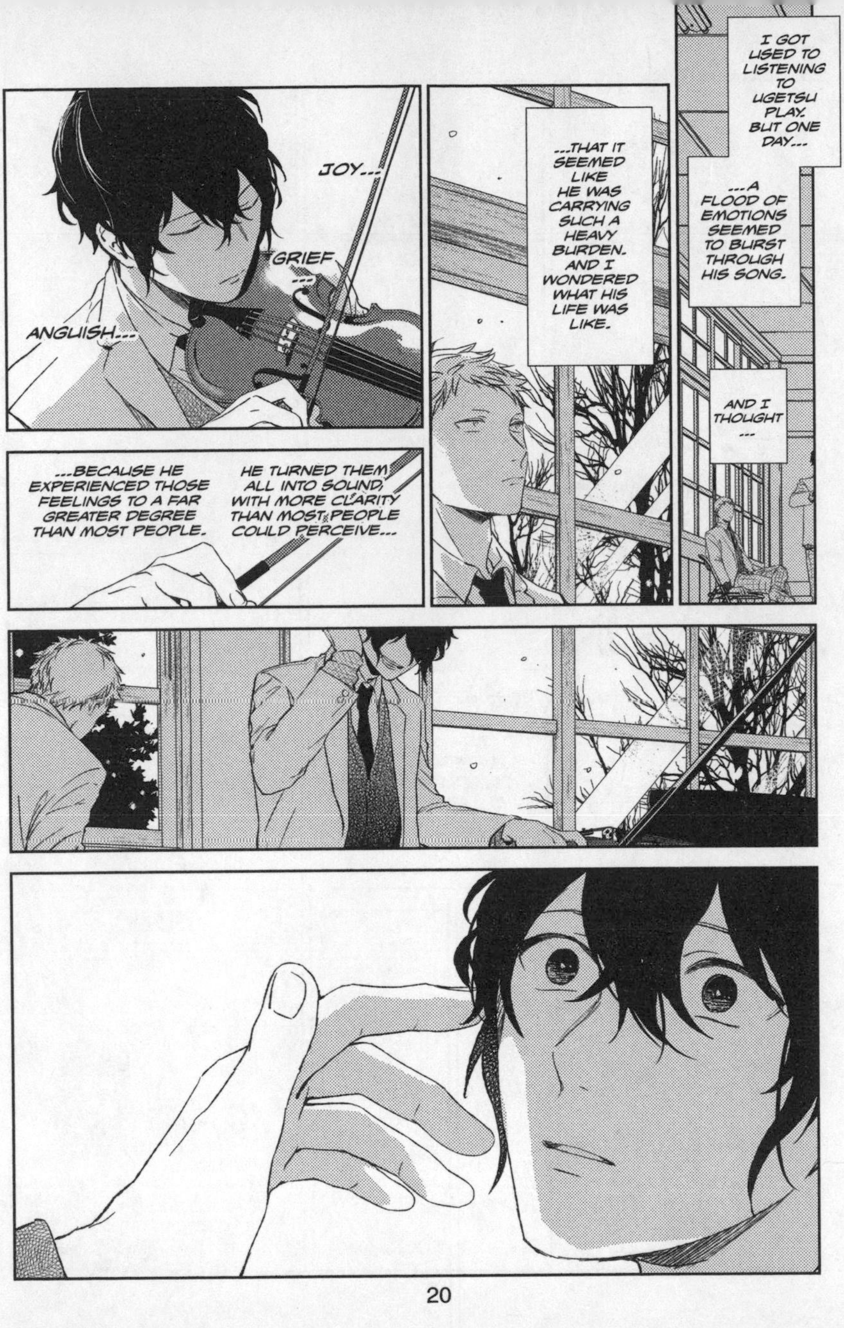
I GOT USED TO LISTENING TO UGETSU PLAY. BUT ONE DAY...
...A FLOOD OF EMOTIONS SEEMED TO BURST THROUGH HIS SONG.
AND I THOUGHT ...
...THAT IT SEEMED LIKE HE WAS CARRYING SUCH A HEAVY BURDEN. AND I WONDERED WHAT HIS LIFE WAS LIKE.
JOY...
GRIEF ...
ANGUISH...
HE TURNED THEM ALL INTO SOUND, WITH MORE CLARITY THAN MOST PEOPLE COULD PERCEIVE...
...BECAUSE HE EXPERIENCED THOSE FEELINGS TO A FAR GREATER DEGREE THAN MOST PEOPLE.

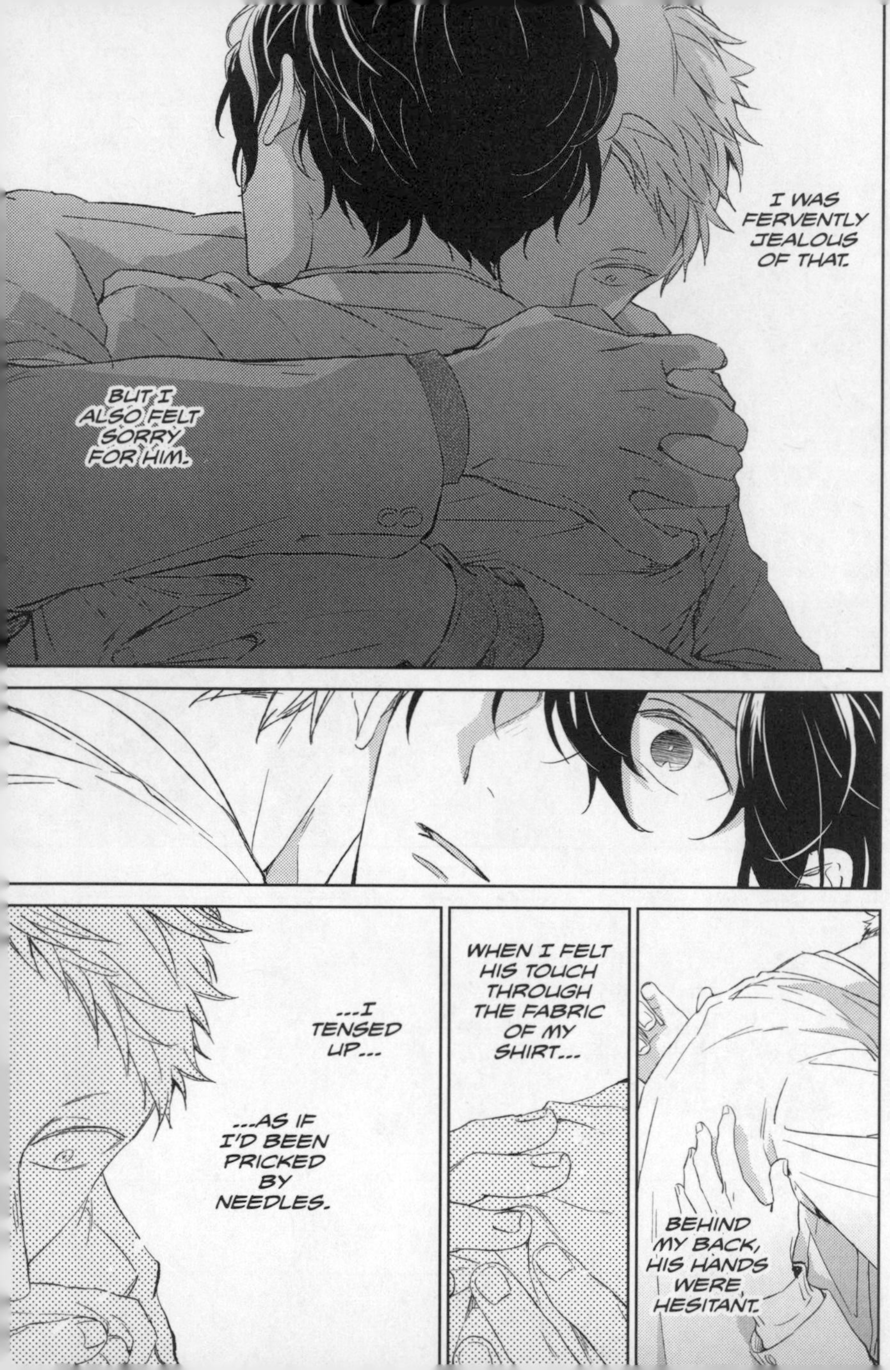
I WAS FERVENTLY JEALOUS OF THAT.
BUT I ALSO FELT SORRY FOR HIM.
BEHIND MY BACK, HIS HANDS WERE HESITANT.
WHEN I FELT HIS TOUCH THROUGH THE FABRIC OF MY SHIRT...
...I TENSED UP...
...AS IF I'D BEEN PRICKED BY NEEDLES.

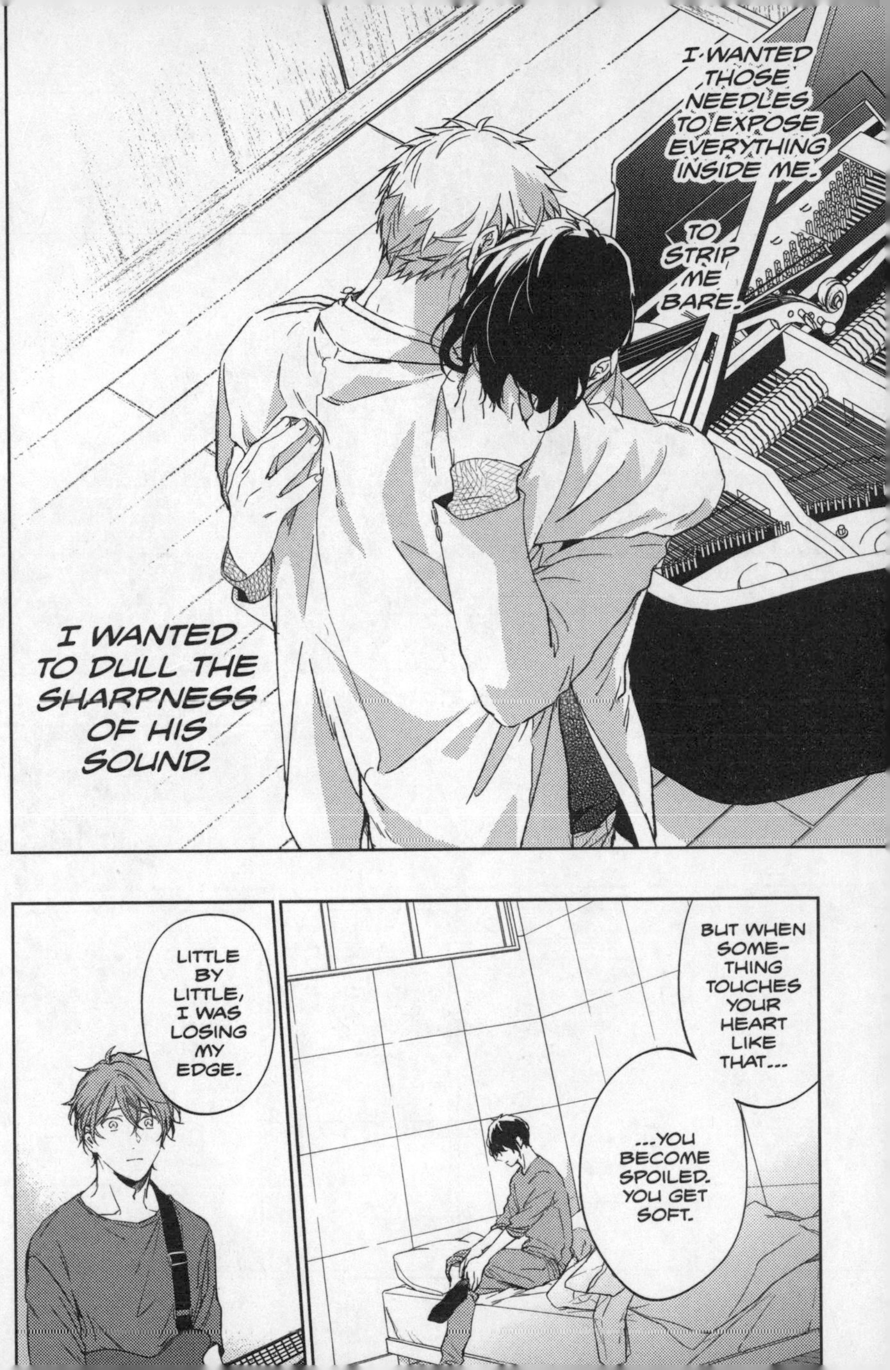
I WANTED THOSE NEEDLES TO EXPOSE EVERYTHING INSIDE ME.
TO STRIP ME BARE.
I WANTED TO DULL THE SHARPNESS OF HIS SOUND.
BUT WHEN SOMETHING TOUCHES YOUR HEART LIKE THAT...
...YOU BECOME SPOILED. YOU GET SOFT.
LITTLE BY LITTLE, I WAS LOSING MY EDGE.

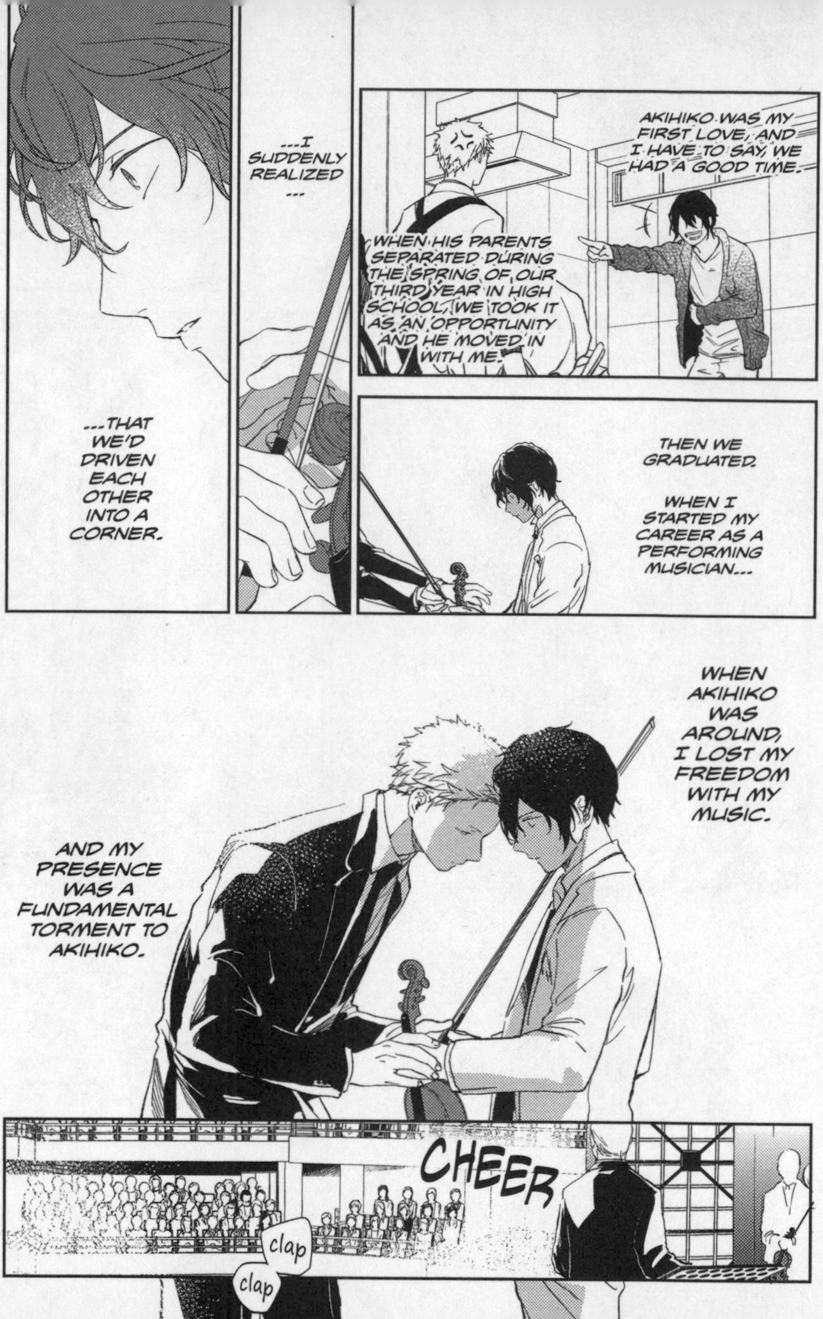
AKIHIKO WAS MY FIRST LOVE, AND I HAVE TO SAY, WE HAD A GOOD TIME.
WHEN HIS PARENTS SEPARATED DURING THE SPRING OF OUR THIRD YEAR IN HIGH SCHOOL, WE TOOK IT AS AN OPPORTUNITY AND HE MOVED IN WITH ME.
THEN WE GRADUATED.
WHEN I STARTED MY CAREER AS A PERFORMING MUSICIAN...
...I SUDDENLY REALIZED ...
...THAT WE'D DRIVEN EACH OTHER INTO A CORNER.
WHEN AKIHIKO WAS AROUND, I LOST MY FREEDOM WITH MY MUSIC.
AND MY PRESENCE WAS A FUNDAMENTAL TORMENT TO AKIHIKO.
CHEER
clap
clap

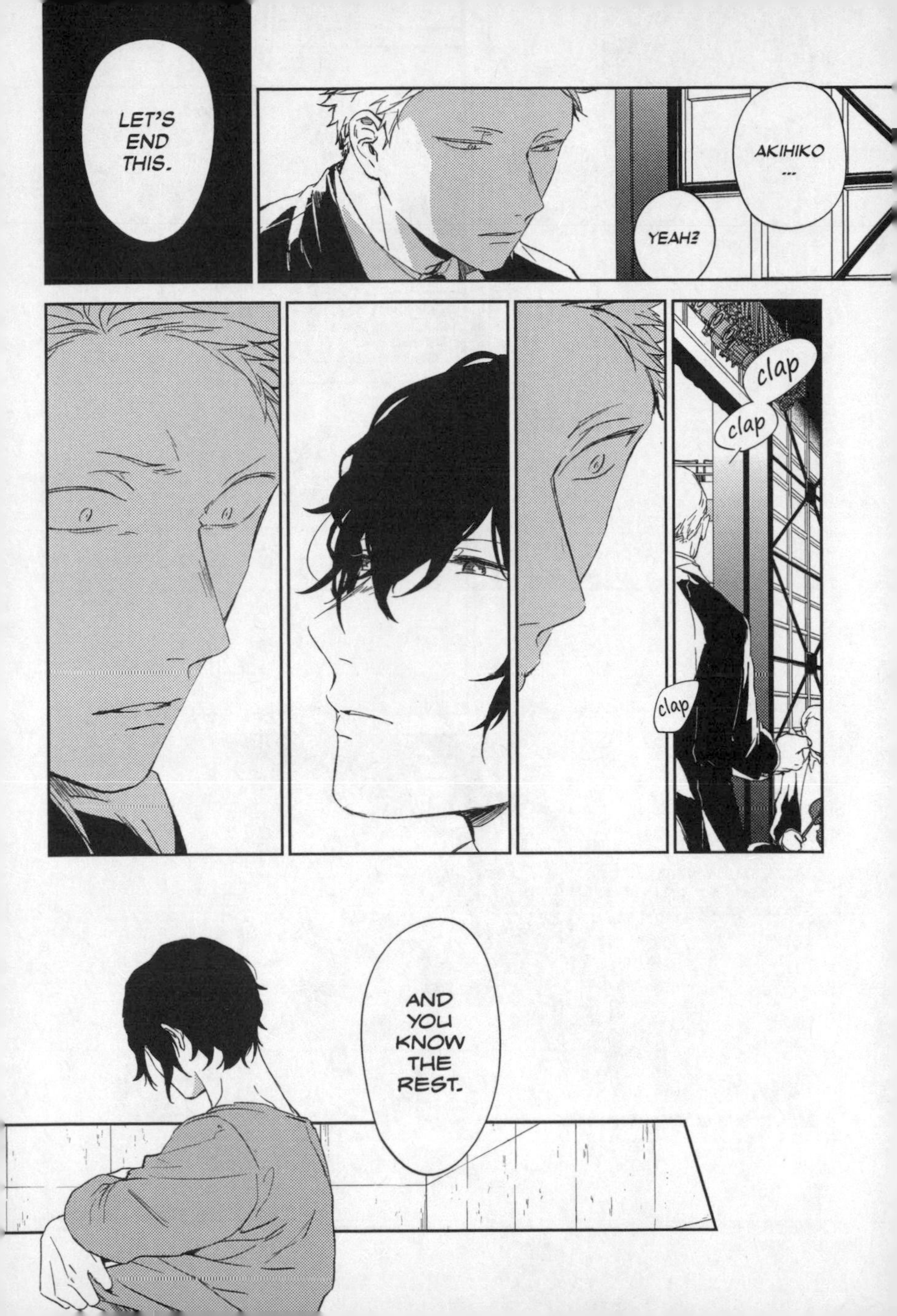
AKIHIKO ...
YEAH?
LET'S END THIS.
clap
clap
clap
AND YOU KNOW THE REST.

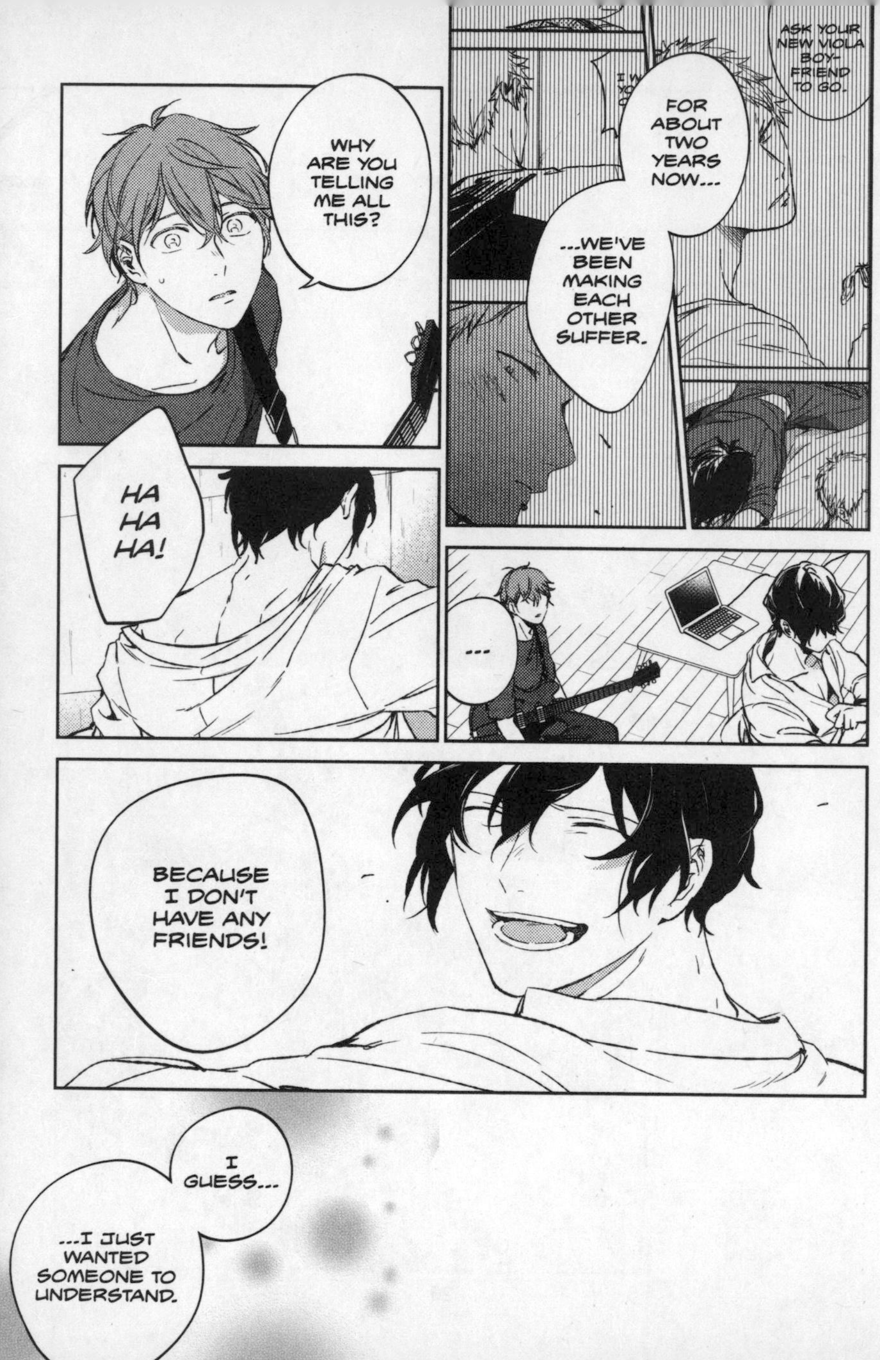
ASK YOUR NEW VIOLA BOY-FRIEND TO GO.
FOR ABOUT TWO YEARS NOW...
...WE'VE BEEN MAKING EACH OTHER SUFFER.
WHY ARE YOU TELLING ME ALL THIS?
...
HA HA HA!
BECAUSE I DON'T HAVE ANY FRIENDS!
I GUESS...
...I JUST WANTED SOMEONE TO UNDERSTAND.

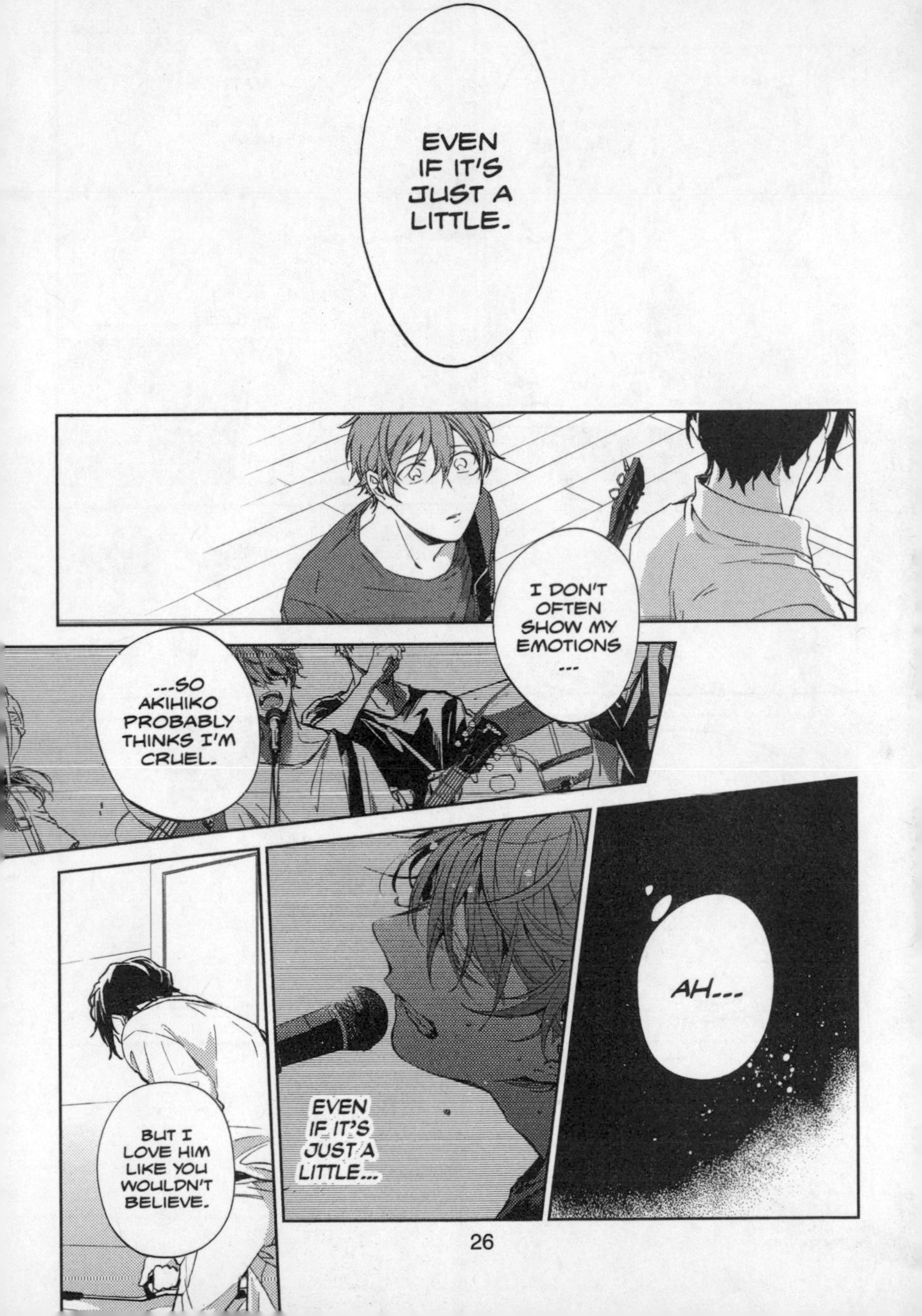
EVEN IF IT'S JUST A LITTLE.
I DON'T OFTEN SHOW MY EMOTIONS ...
...SO AKIHIKO PROBABLY THINKS I'M CRUEL.
AH...
EVEN IF IT'S JUST A LITTLE...
BUT I LOVE HIM LIKE YOU WOULDN'T BELIEVE.

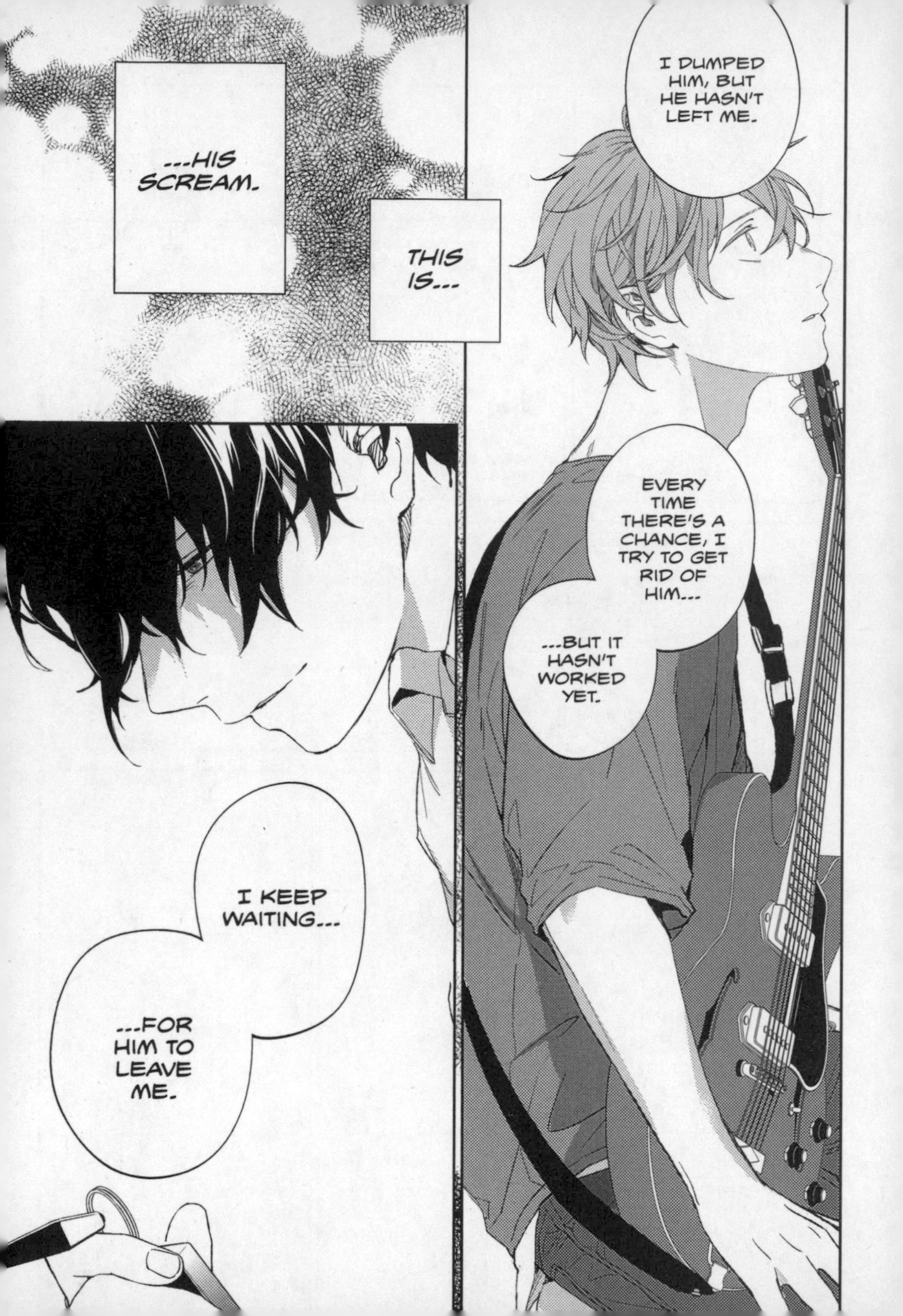
I DUMPED HIM, BUT HE HASN'T LEFT ME.
EVERY TIME THERE'S A CHANCE, I TRY TO GET RID OF HIM...
...BUT IT HASN'T WORKED YET.
THIS IS...
...HIS SCREAM.
I KEEP WAITING...
...FOR HIM TO LEAVE ME.

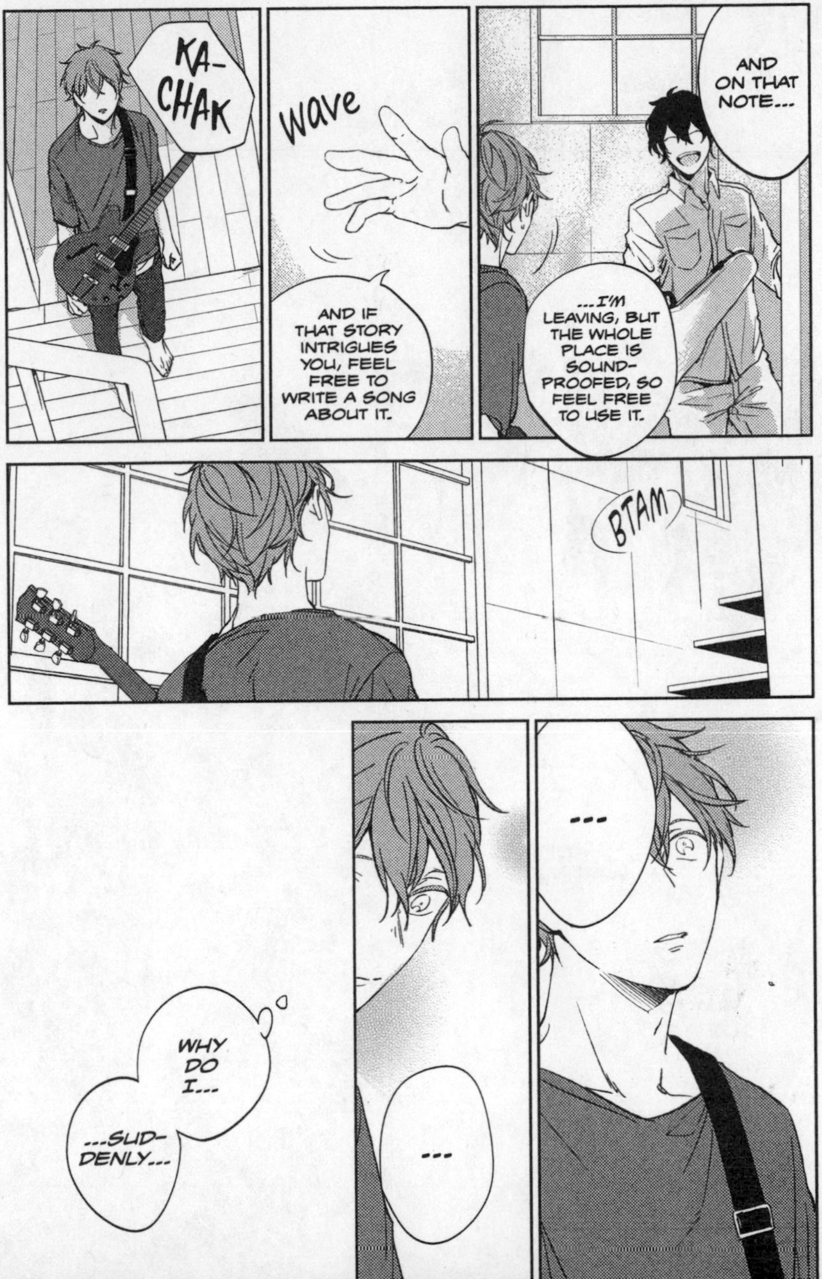
AND ON THAT NOTE...
...I'M LEAVING, BUT THE WHOLE PLACE IS SOUND-PROOFED, SO FEEL FREE TO USE IT.
wave
AND IF THAT STORY INTRIGUES YOU, FEEL FREE TO WRITE A SONG ABOUT IT.
KA-CHAK
BTAM
...
...
WHY DO I...
...SUD-DENLY...

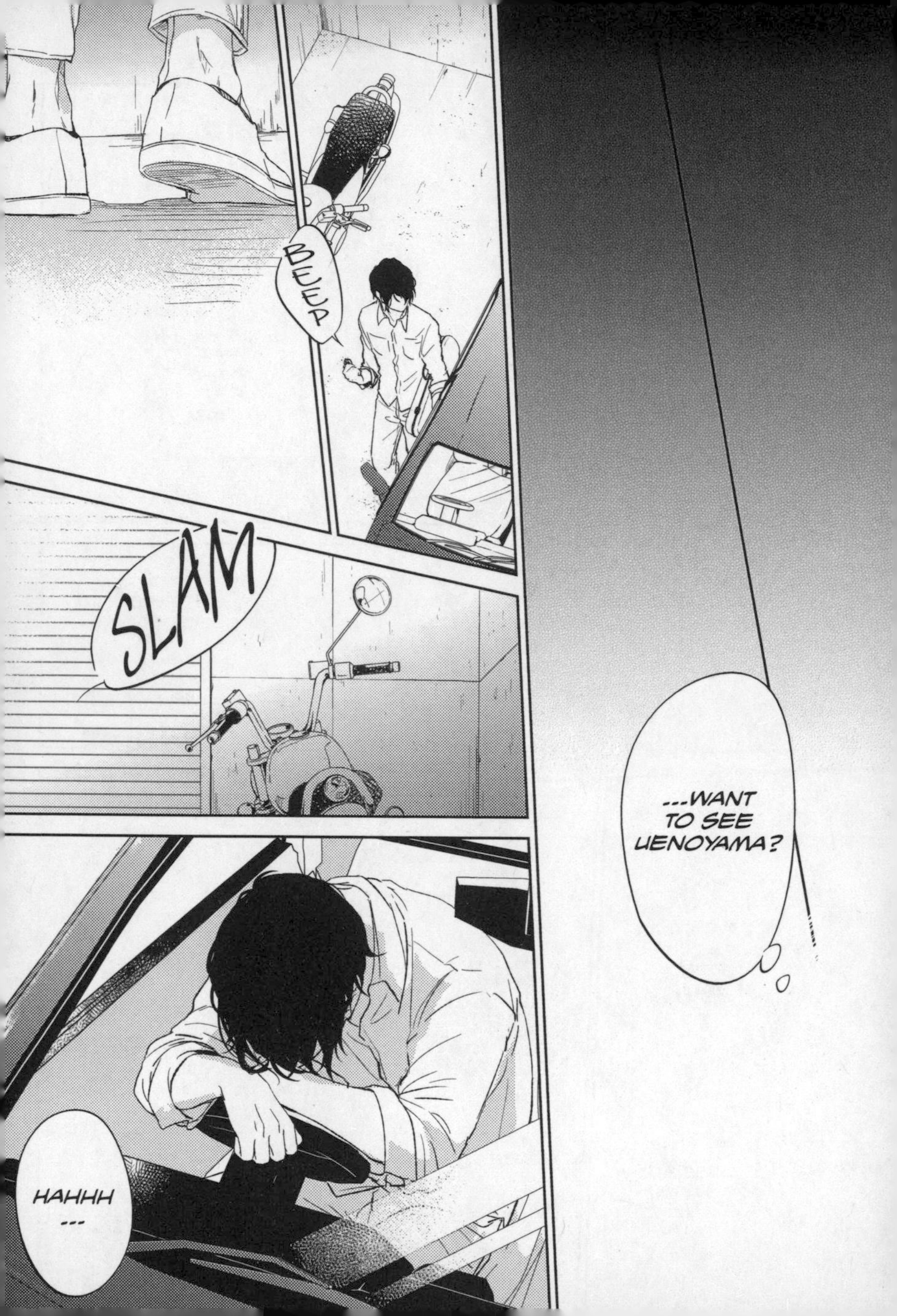
...WANT TO SEE UENOYAMA?
BEEP
SLAM
HAHHH ---

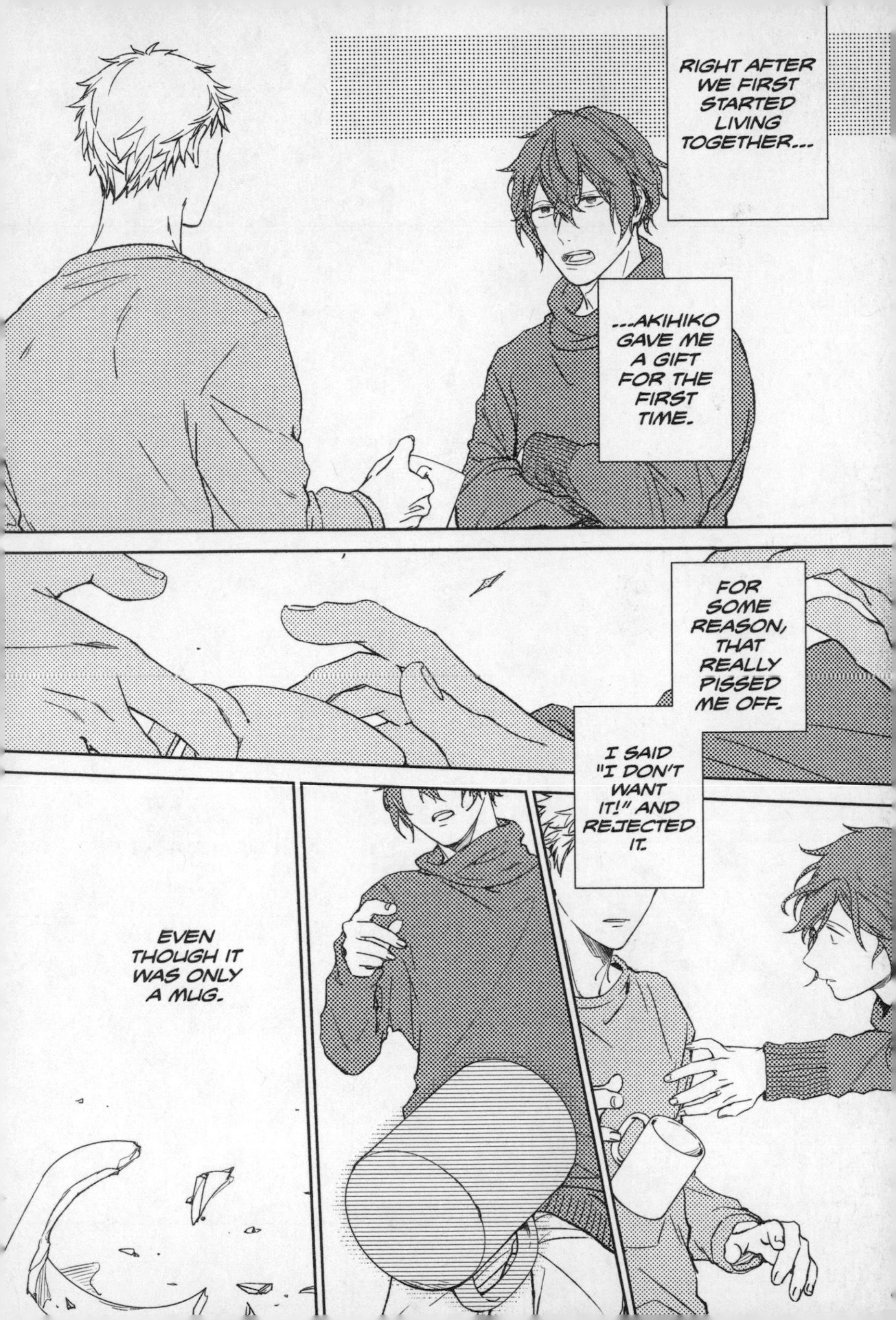
RIGHT AFTER WE FIRST STARTED LIVING TOGETHER...
...AKIHIKO GAVE ME A GIFT FOR THE FIRST TIME.
FOR SOME REASON, THAT REALLY PISSED ME OFF.
I SAID "I DON'T WANT IT!" AND REJECTED IT.
EVEN THOUGH IT WAS ONLY A MUG.

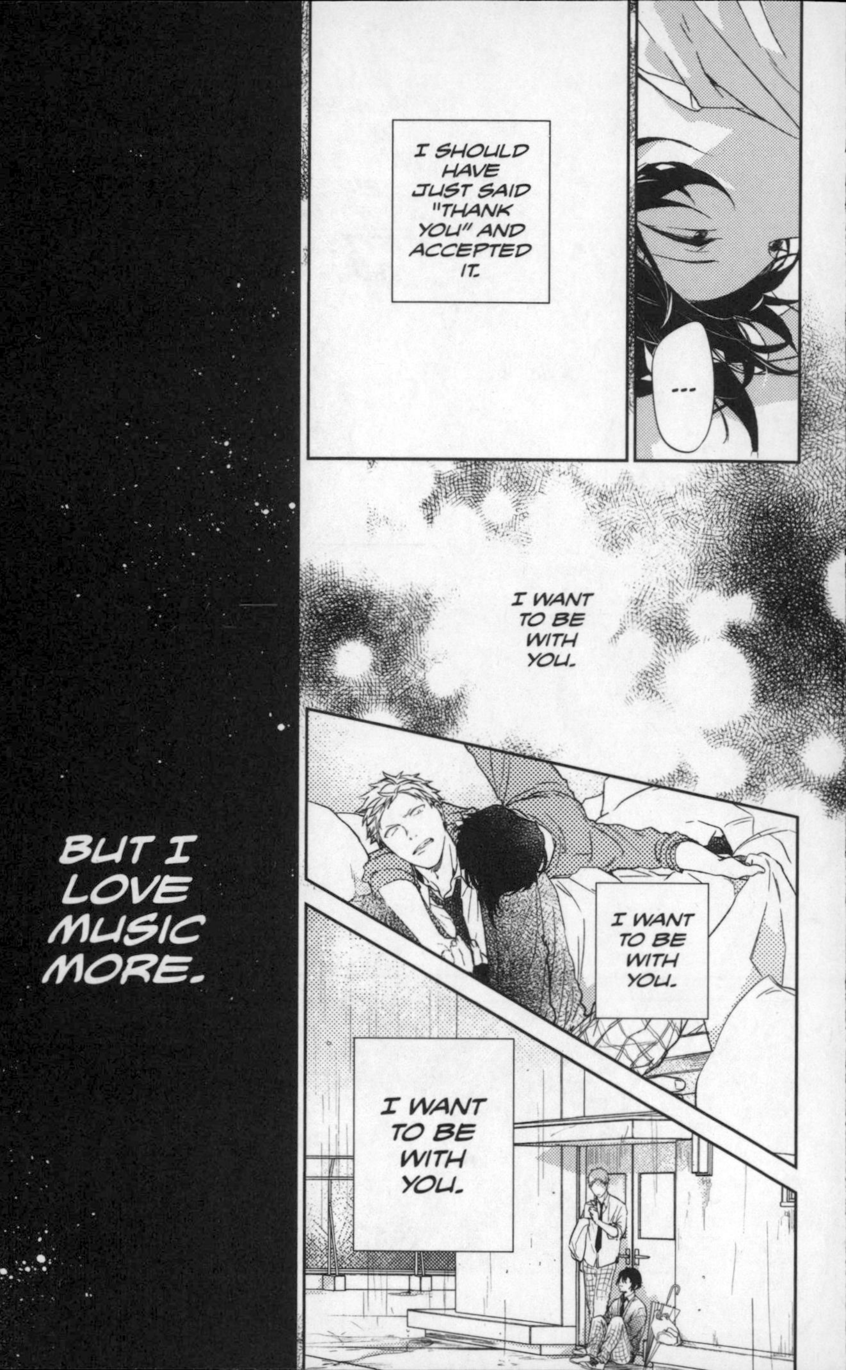
...
I SHOULD HAVE JUST SAID "THANK YOU" AND ACCEPTED IT.
I WANT TO BE WITH YOU.
I WANT TO BE WITH YOU.
I WANT TO BE WITH YOU.
BUT I LOVE MUSIC MORE.

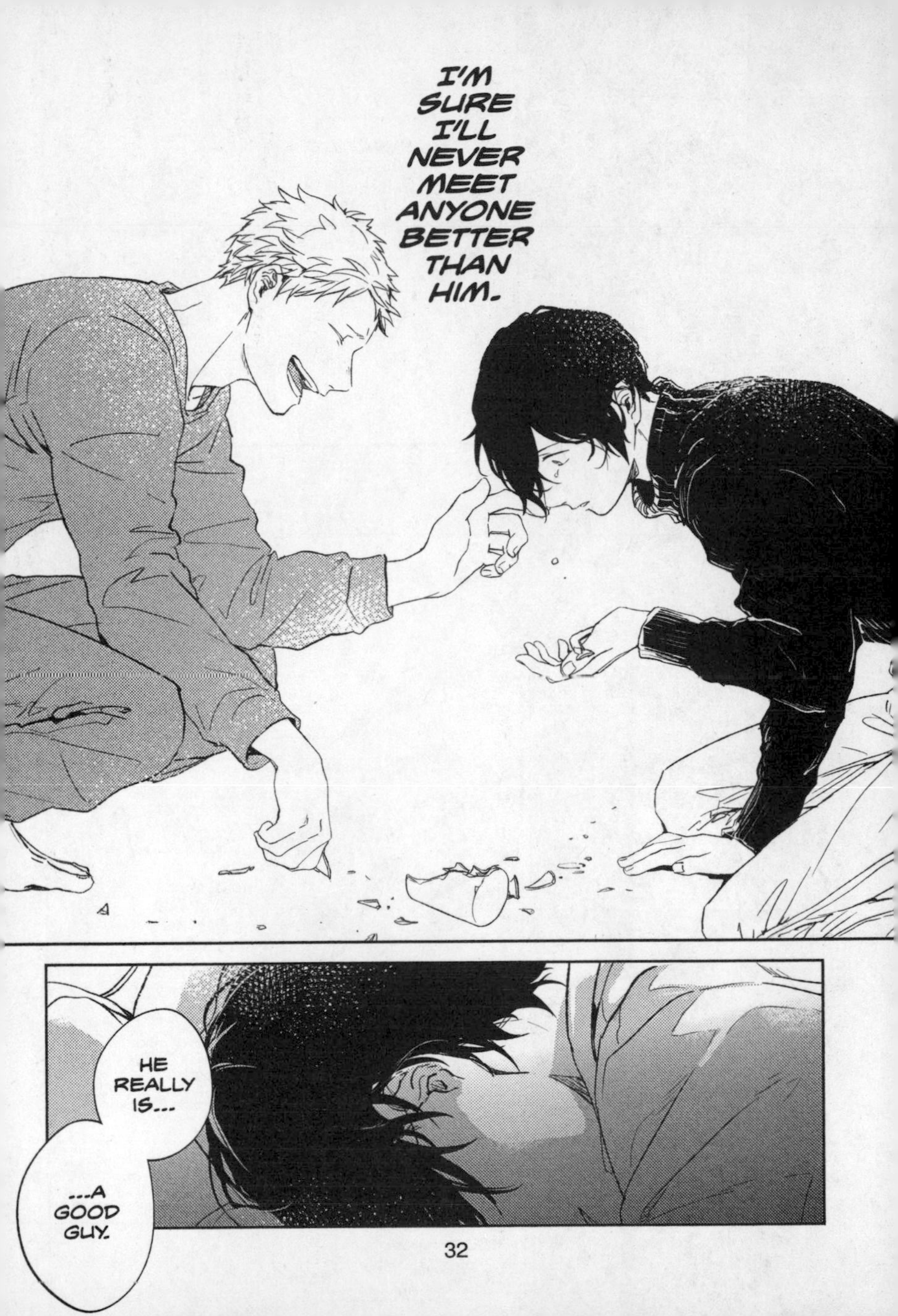
I'M SURE I'LL NEVER MEET ANYONE BETTER THAN HIM.
HE REALLY IS...
...A GOOD GUY.

ugetsumurataofficial ...

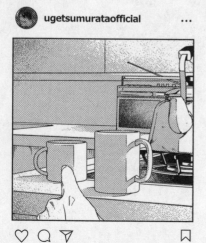

I got a new mug but I hate this one.

given

by Natsuki Kizu

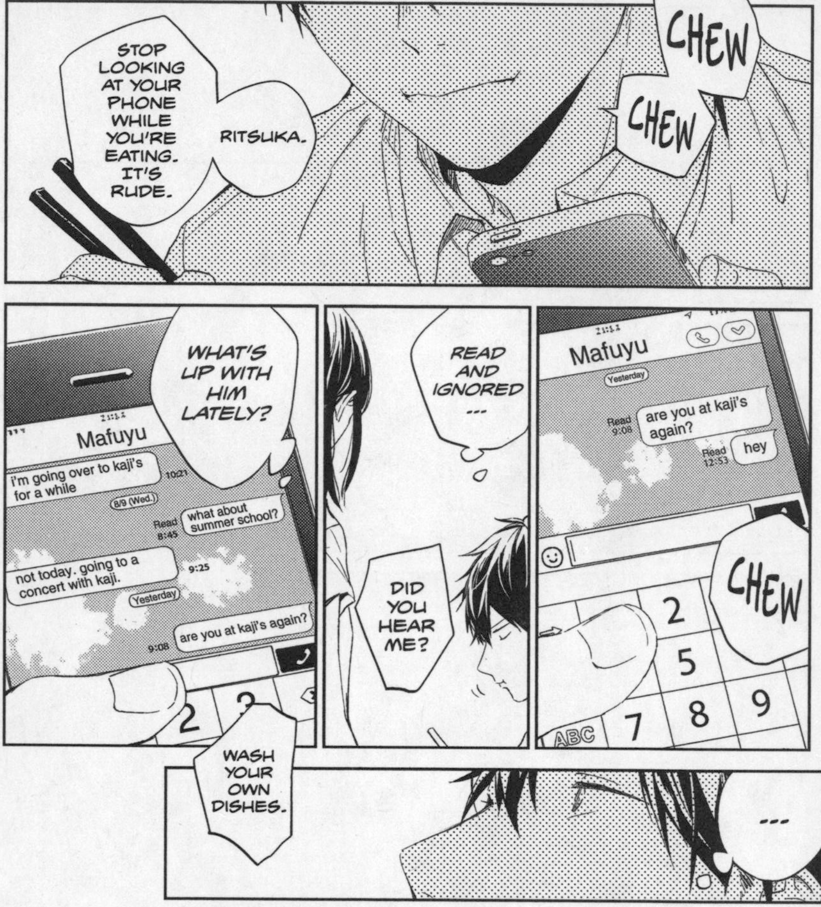
CHEW
CHEW
RITSUKA.
STOP LOOKING AT YOUR PHONE WHILE YOU'RE EATING. IT'S RUDE.
Mafuyu
Yesterday
Read 9:08 are you at kaji's again?
Read 12:53 hey
CHEW
2
5
7 8 9
ABC
READ AND IGNORED ---
DID YOU HEAR ME?
WHAT'S UP WITH HIM LATELY?
Mafuyu
i'm going over to kaji's for a while 10:21
8/9 (Wed.)
Read 8:45 what about summer school?
not today. going to a concert with kaji. 9:25
Yesterday
9:08 are you at kaji's again?

WASH YOUR OWN DISHES.

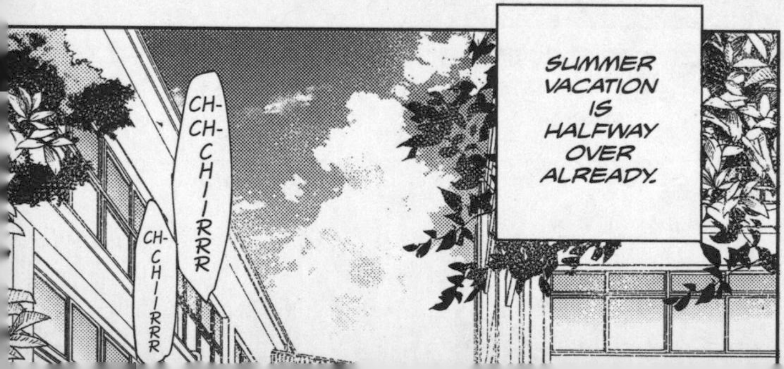
SUMMER VACATION IS HALFWAY OVER ALREADY.
CH-CH-CHIRRR
CH-CHIRRR

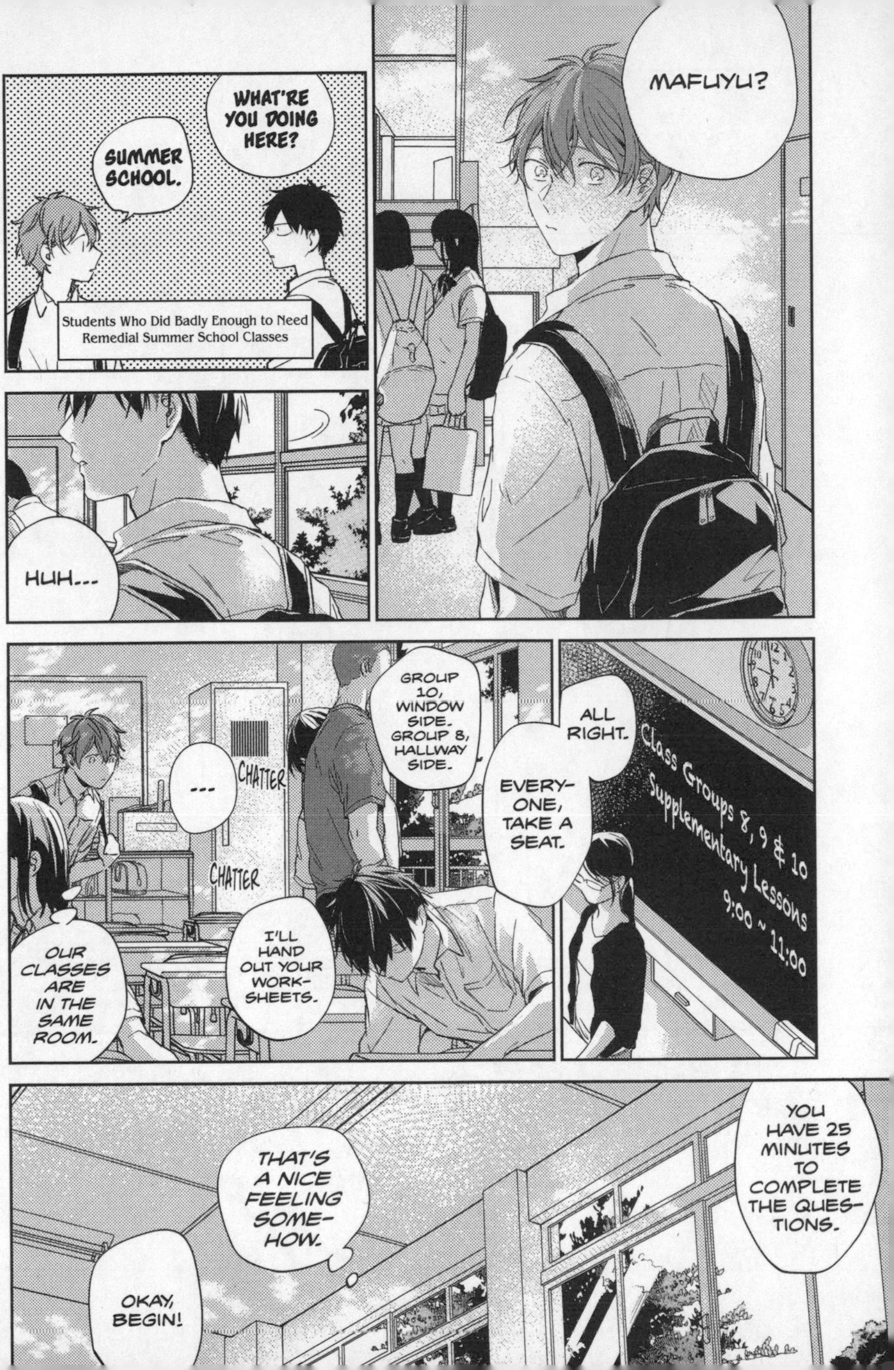
MAFUYU?
WHAT'RE YOU DOING HERE?
SUMMER SCHOOL.
Students Who Did Badly Enough to Need Remedial Summer School Classes
HUH...
ALL RIGHT.
EVERY-ONE, TAKE A SEAT.
Class Groups 8, 9 & 10 Supplementary Lessons 9:00 ~ 11:00
GROUP 10, WINDOW SIDE. GROUP 8, HALLWAY SIDE.
...
CHATTER
CHATTER
I'LL HAND OUT YOUR WORK-SHEETS.
OUR CLASSES ARE IN THE SAME ROOM.
YOU HAVE 25 MINUTES TO COMPLETE THE QUES-TIONS.
THAT'S A NICE FEELING SOME-HOW.
OKAY, BEGIN!

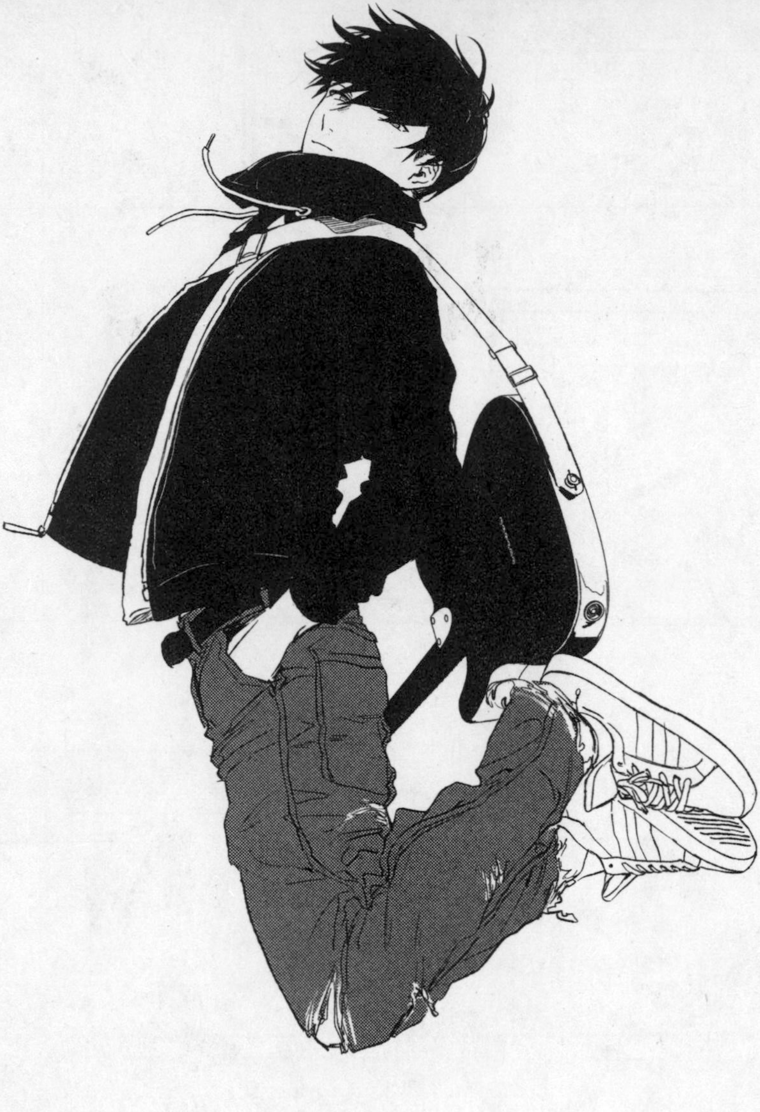

chapter 18

given

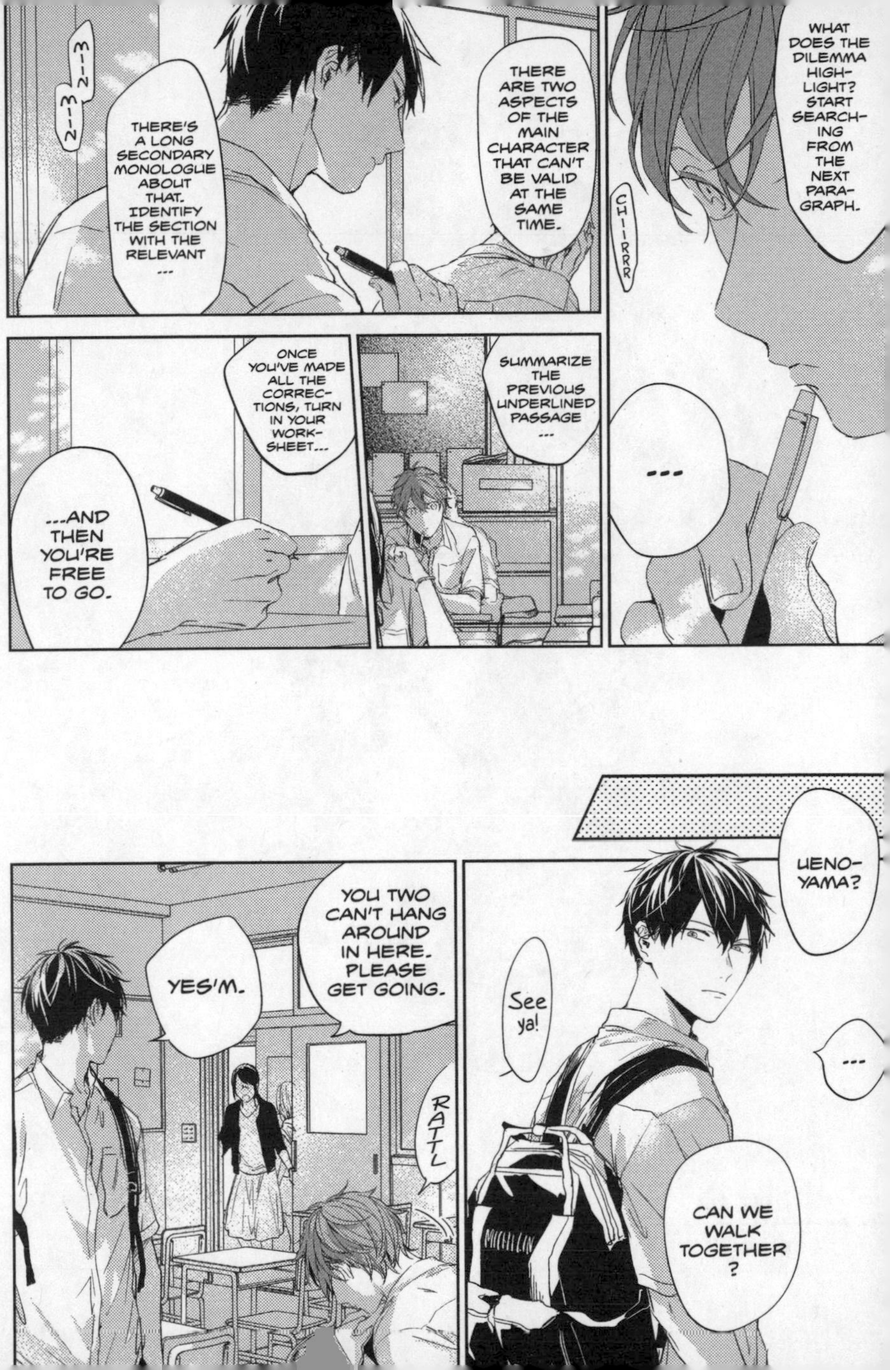
WHAT DOES THE DILEMMA HIGHLIGHT? START SEARCHING FROM THE NEXT PARAGRAPH.
CHIRRR
...
THERE ARE TWO ASPECTS OF THE MAIN CHARACTER THAT CAN'T BE VALID AT THE SAME TIME.
THERE'S A LONG SECONDARY MONOLOGUE ABOUT THAT. IDENTIFY THE SECTION WITH THE RELEVANT ...
MIIN MIIN
SUMMARIZE THE PREVIOUS UNDERLINED PASSAGE ...
ONCE YOU'VE MADE ALL THE CORRECTIONS, TURN IN YOUR WORKSHEET...
...AND THEN YOU'RE FREE TO GO.
UENO-YAMA?
...
See ya!
CAN WE WALK TOGETHER?
YOU TWO CAN'T HANG AROUND IN HERE. PLEASE GET GOING.
YES'M.
RATTL

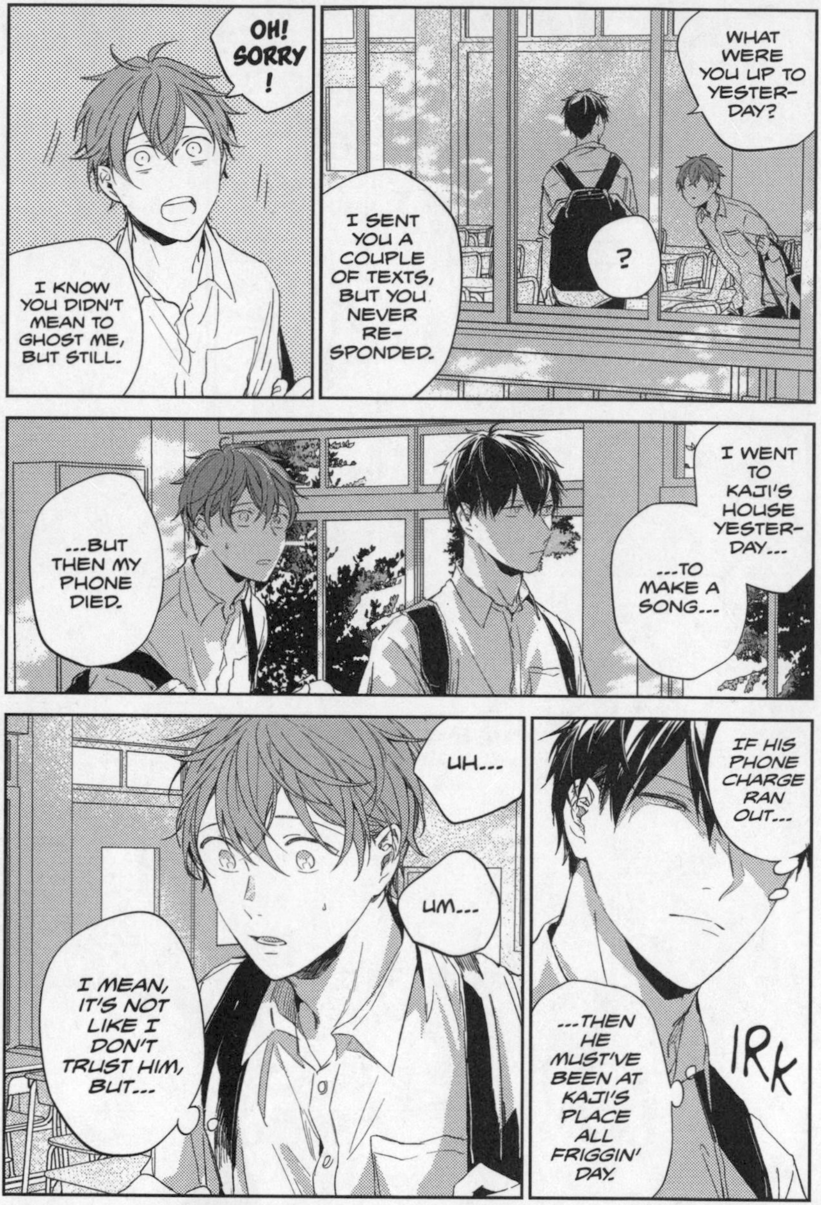
WHAT WERE YOU UP TO YESTER-DAY?
?
I SENT YOU A COUPLE OF TEXTS, BUT YOU NEVER RE-SPONDED.
OH! SORRY!
I KNOW YOU DIDN'T MEAN TO GHOST ME, BUT STILL.
I WENT TO KAJI'S HOUSE YESTER-DAY...
...TO MAKE A SONG...
...BUT THEN MY PHONE DIED.
IF HIS PHONE CHARGE RAN OUT...
...THEN HE MUST'VE BEEN AT KAJI'S PLACE ALL FRIGGIN' DAY.
IRK
UH...
UM...
I MEAN, IT'S NOT LIKE I DON'T TRUST HIM, BUT...

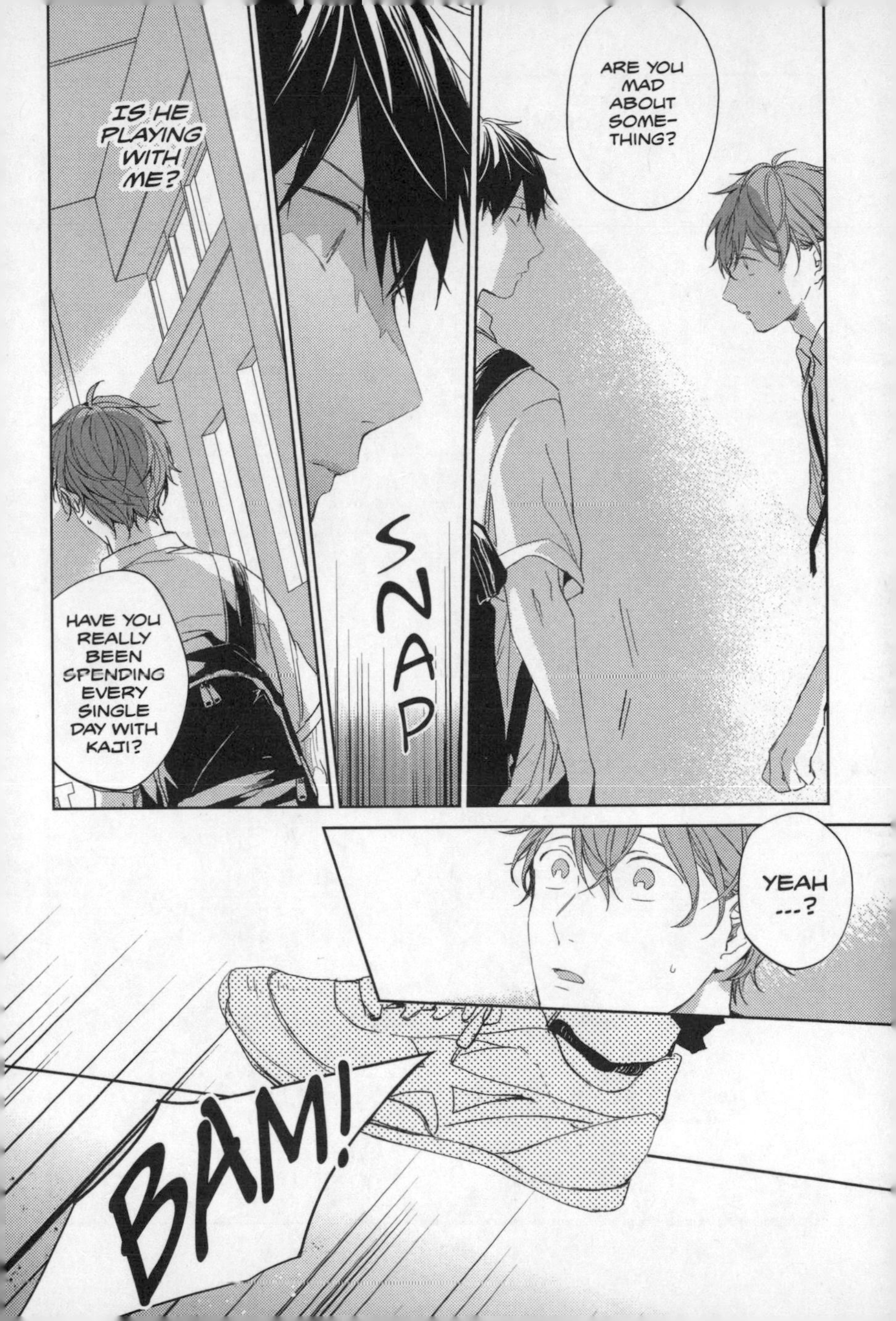
ARE YOU MAD ABOUT SOME-THING?
SNAP
IS HE PLAYING WITH ME?
HAVE YOU REALLY BEEN SPENDING EVERY SINGLE DAY WITH KAJI?
YEAH ---?
BAM!

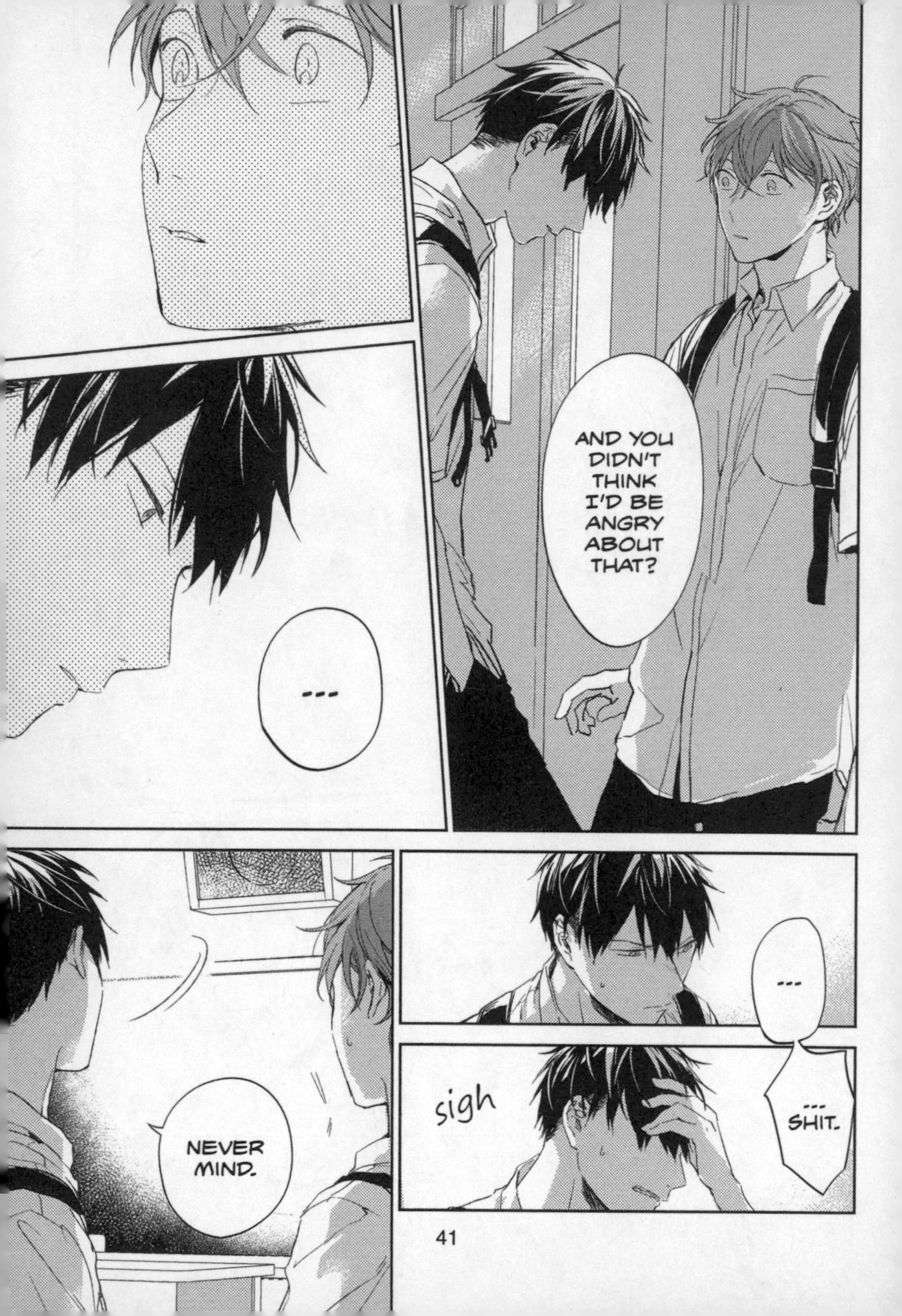
AND YOU DIDN'T THINK I'D BE ANGRY ABOUT THAT?

--- SHIT.
sigh
NEVER MIND.

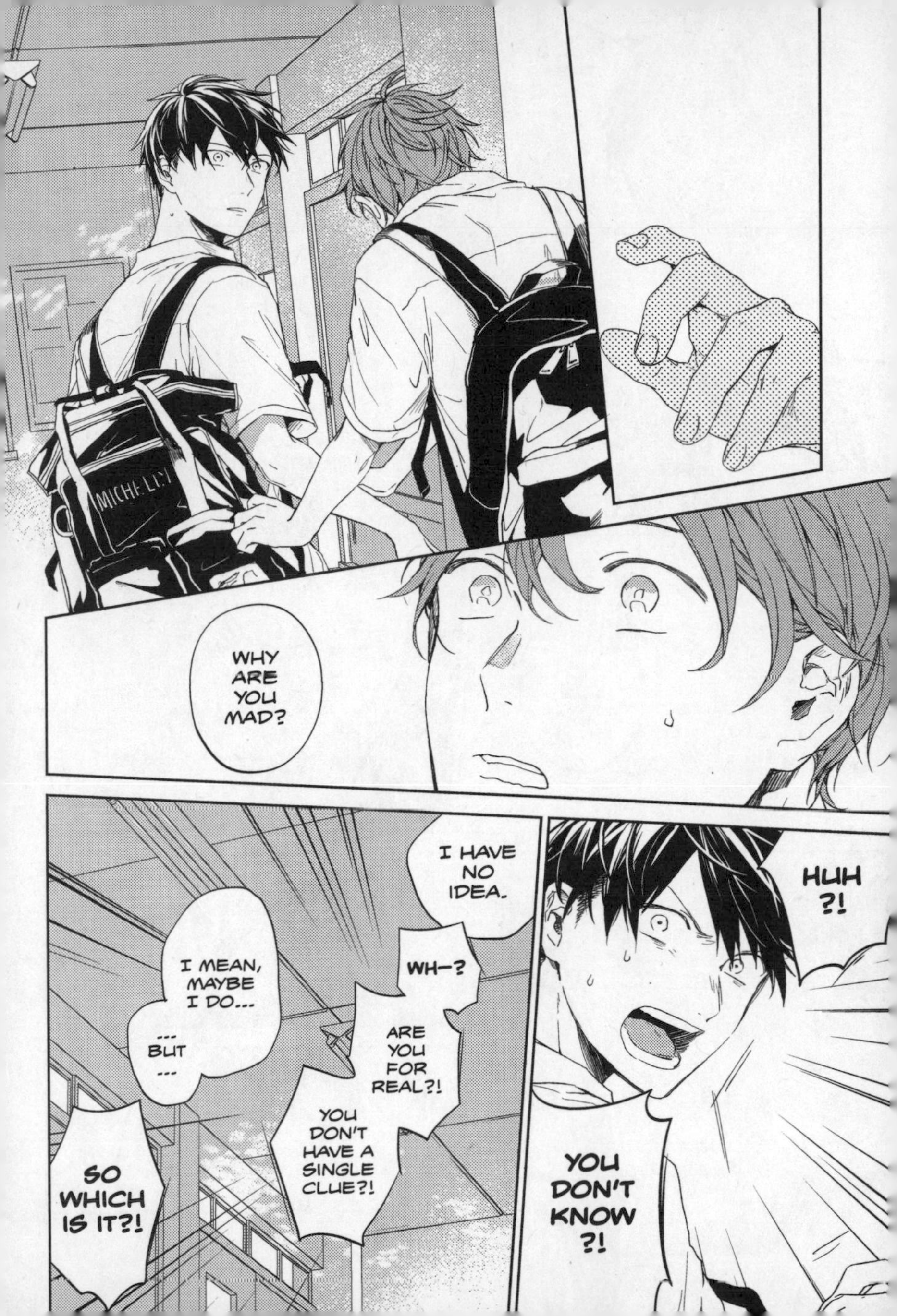
WHY ARE YOU MAD?
I HAVE NO IDEA.
HUH?!
YOU DON'T KNOW?!
WH-?
I MEAN, MAYBE I DO...
ARE YOU FOR REAL?!
...BUT...
YOU DON'T HAVE A SINGLE CLUE?!
SO WHICH IS IT?!

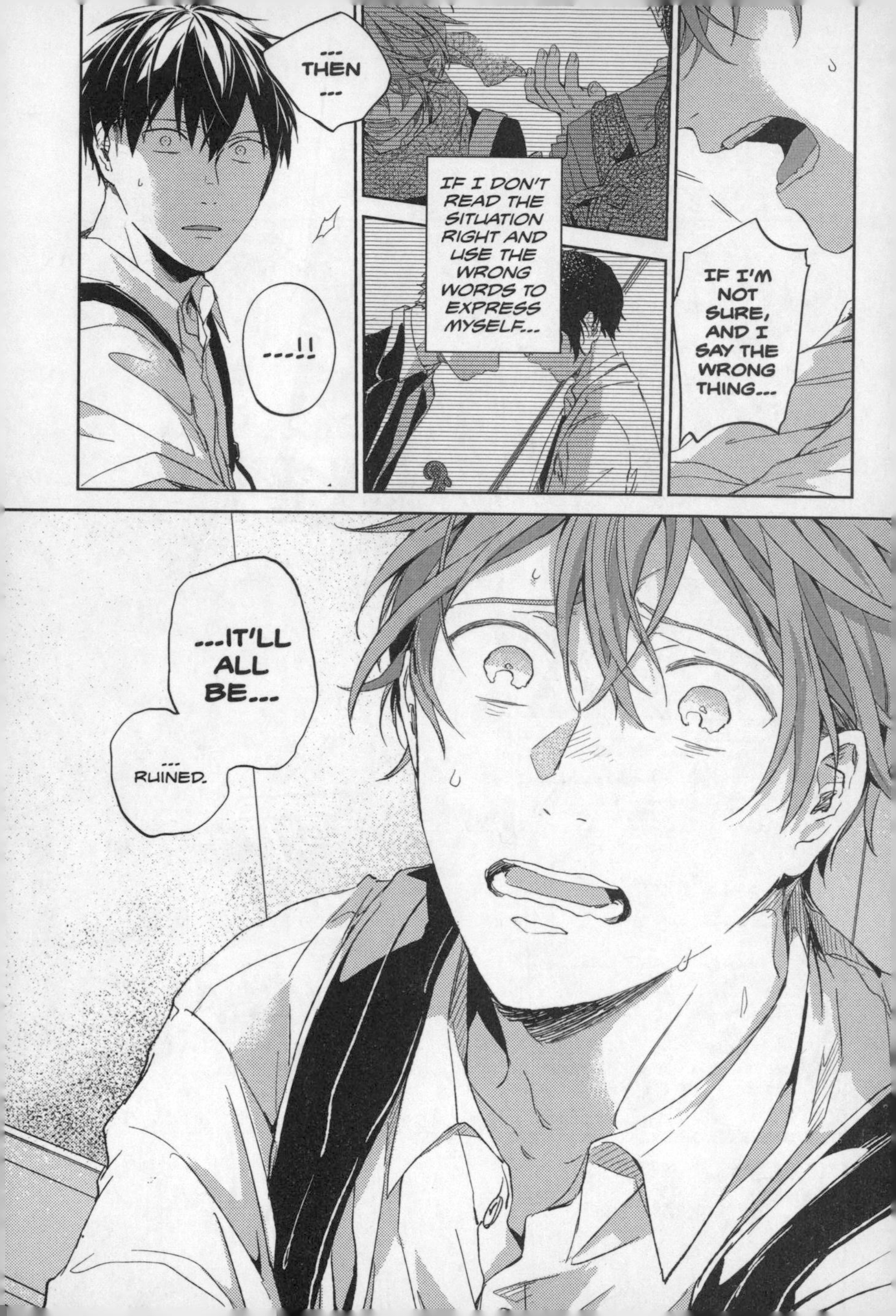
IF I'M NOT SURE, AND I SAY THE WRONG THING...
IF I DON'T READ THE SITUATION RIGHT AND USE THE WRONG WORDS TO EXPRESS MYSELF...
...THEN...
...!!
...IT'LL ALL BE...
...RUINED.

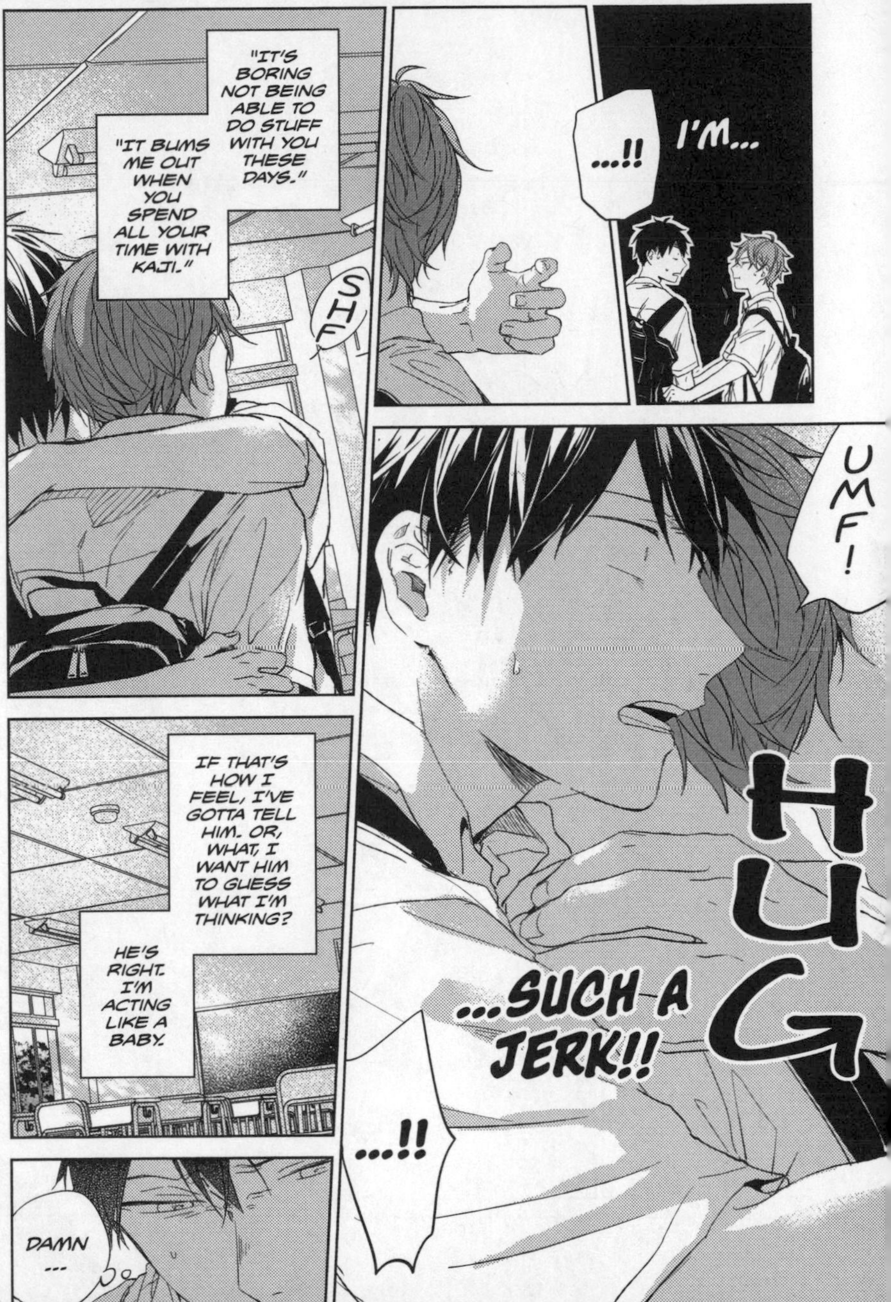
I'M...
...!!
"IT'S BORING NOT BEING ABLE TO DO STUFF WITH YOU THESE DAYS."
"IT BUMS ME OUT WHEN YOU SPEND ALL YOUR TIME WITH KAJI."
SHF
UMF!
HUG
...SUCH A JERK!!
...!!
IF THAT'S HOW I FEEL, I'VE GOTTA TELL HIM. OR, WHAT, I WANT HIM TO GUESS WHAT I'M THINKING?
HE'S RIGHT. I'M ACTING LIKE A BABY.
DAMN ...

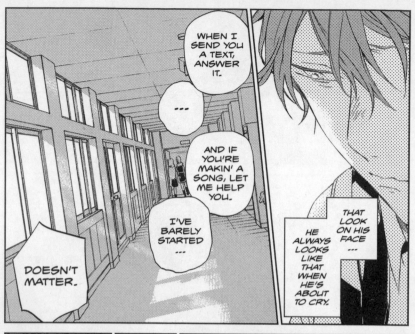

THAT LOOK ON HIS FACE ...
HE ALWAYS LOOKS LIKE THAT WHEN HE'S ABOUT TO CRY.
WHEN I SEND YOU A TEXT, ANSWER IT.
...
AND IF YOU'RE MAKIN' A SONG, LET ME HELP YOU.
I'VE BARELY STARTED ...
DOESN'T MATTER.
KAJI ISN'T ...
MURMR
...INTO ME LIKE THAT.
PINCH
I...
... KNOW ...
... THAT !!
TUG
ba-thmp
ba-thmp
...

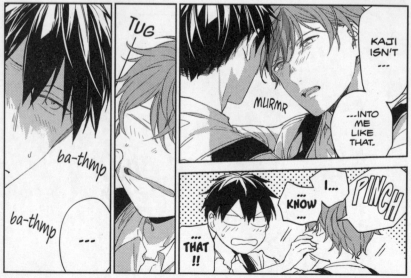

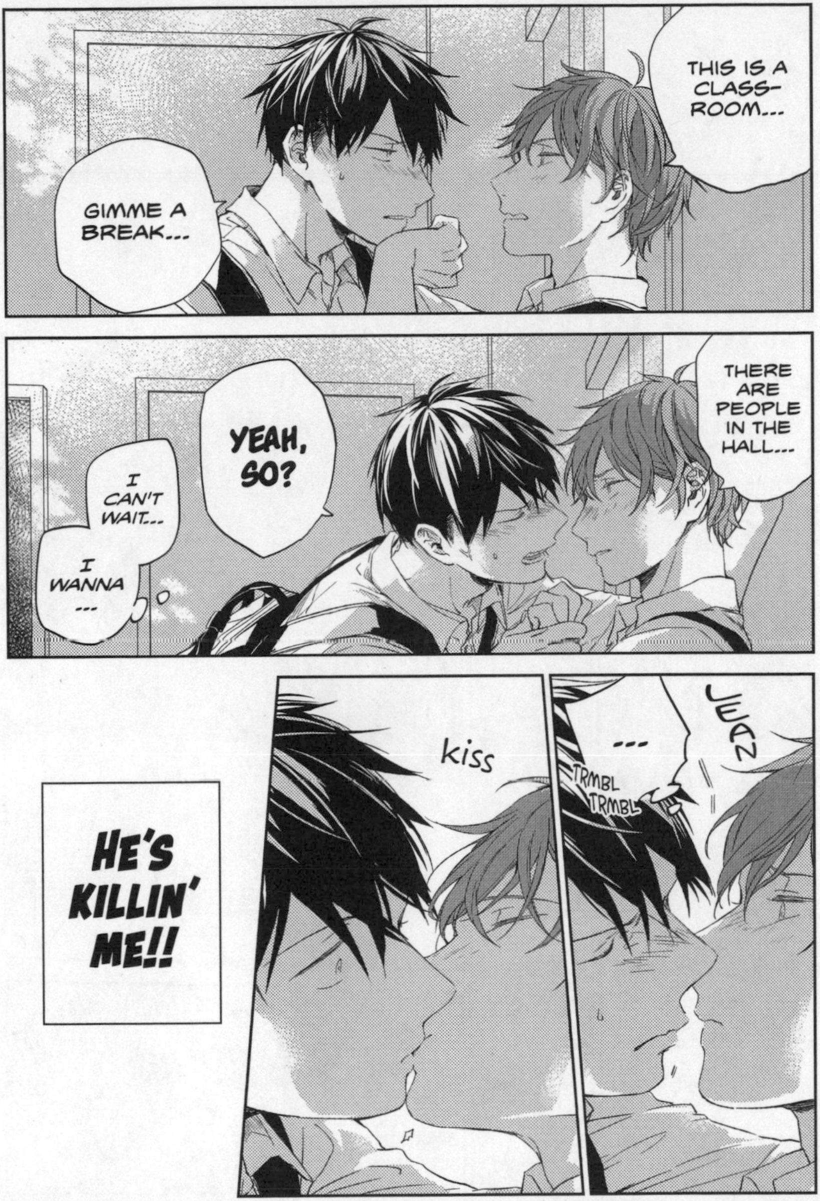
THIS IS A CLASS-ROOM...
GIMME A BREAK...
THERE ARE PEOPLE IN THE HALL...
YEAH, SO?
I CAN'T WAIT...
I WANNA ---
JEAN

TRMBL TRMBL
kiss
HE'S KILLIN' ME!!

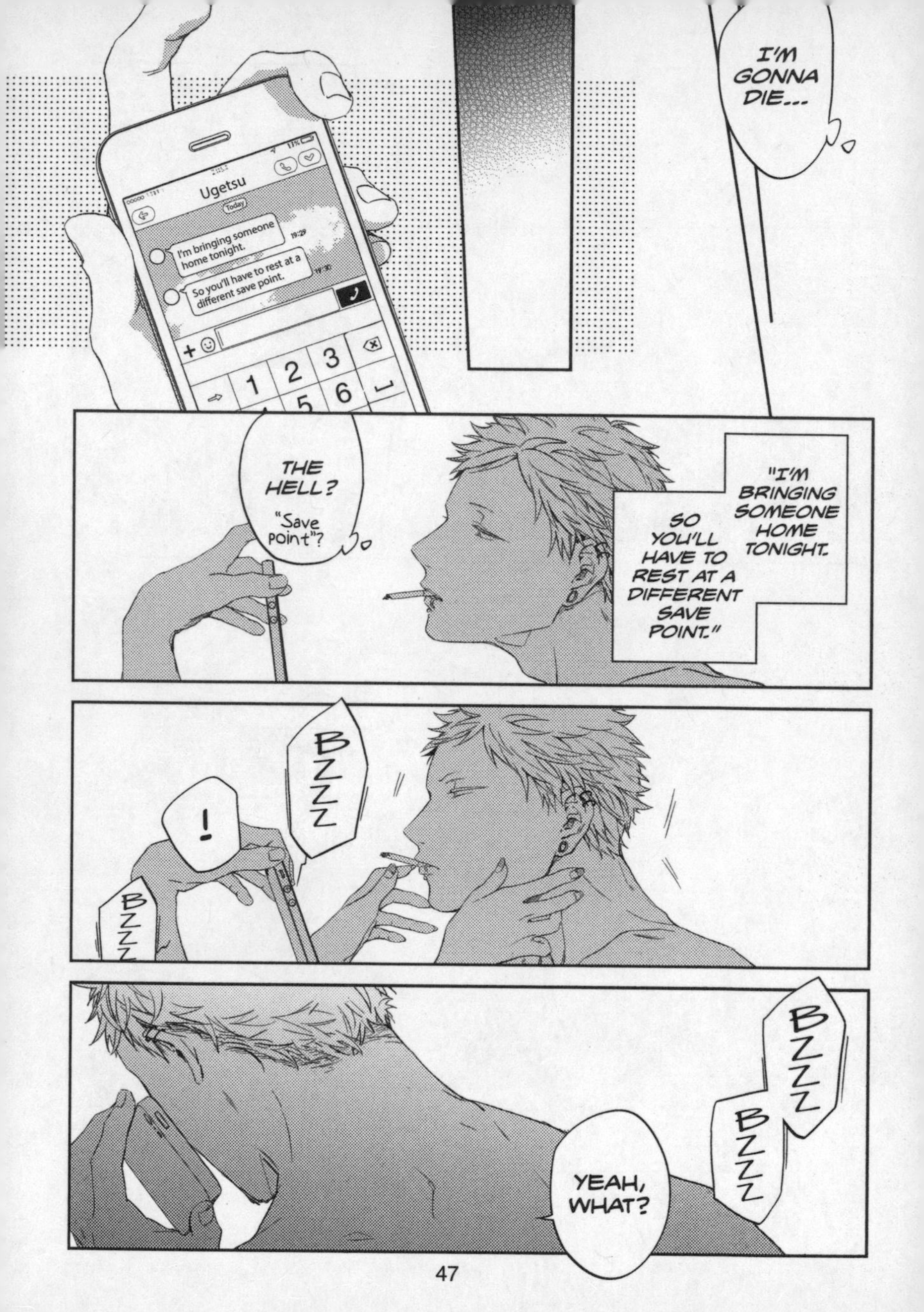
I'M GONNA DIE...
Ugetsu
Today
I'm bringing someone home tonight.
19:29
So you'll have to rest at a different save point.
19:30
"I'M BRINGING SOMEONE HOME TONIGHT. SO YOU'LL HAVE TO REST AT A DIFFERENT SAVE POINT."
THE HELL? "Save point"?
BZZZ
!
BZZZ
BZZZ
BZZZ
YEAH, WHAT?

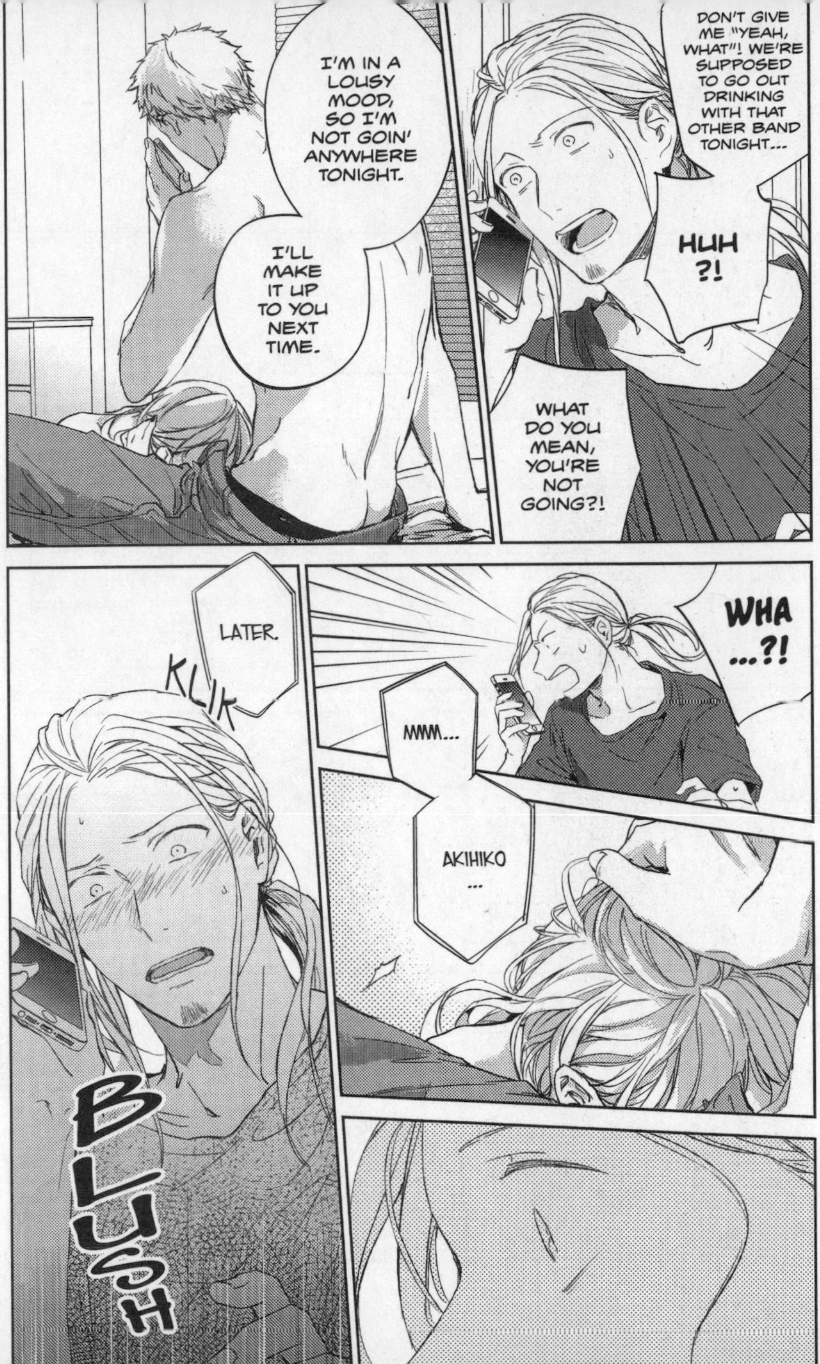
DON'T GIVE ME "YEAH, WHAT"! WE'RE SUPPOSED TO GO OUT DRINKING WITH THAT OTHER BAND TONIGHT...
HUH ?!
WHAT DO YOU MEAN, YOU'RE NOT GOING?!
I'M IN A LOUSY MOOD, SO I'M NOT GOIN' ANYWHERE TONIGHT.
I'LL MAKE IT UP TO YOU NEXT TIME.
WHA ...?!
MMM...
AKIHIKO ...
LATER.
KLIK
BLUSH

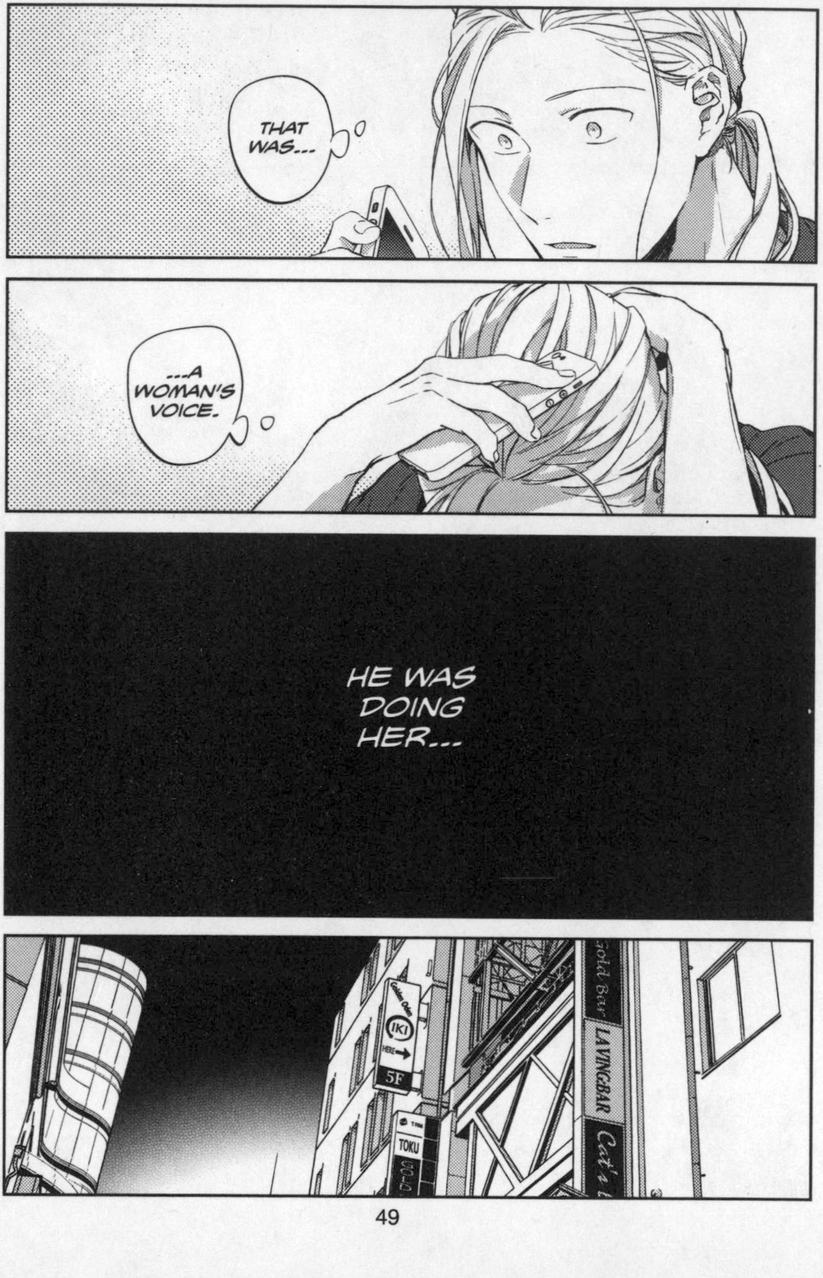
THAT WAS...
...A WOMAN'S VOICE.
HE WAS DOING HER...
IKI
HERE
5F
TOKU
Gold Bar
LAVINGBAR

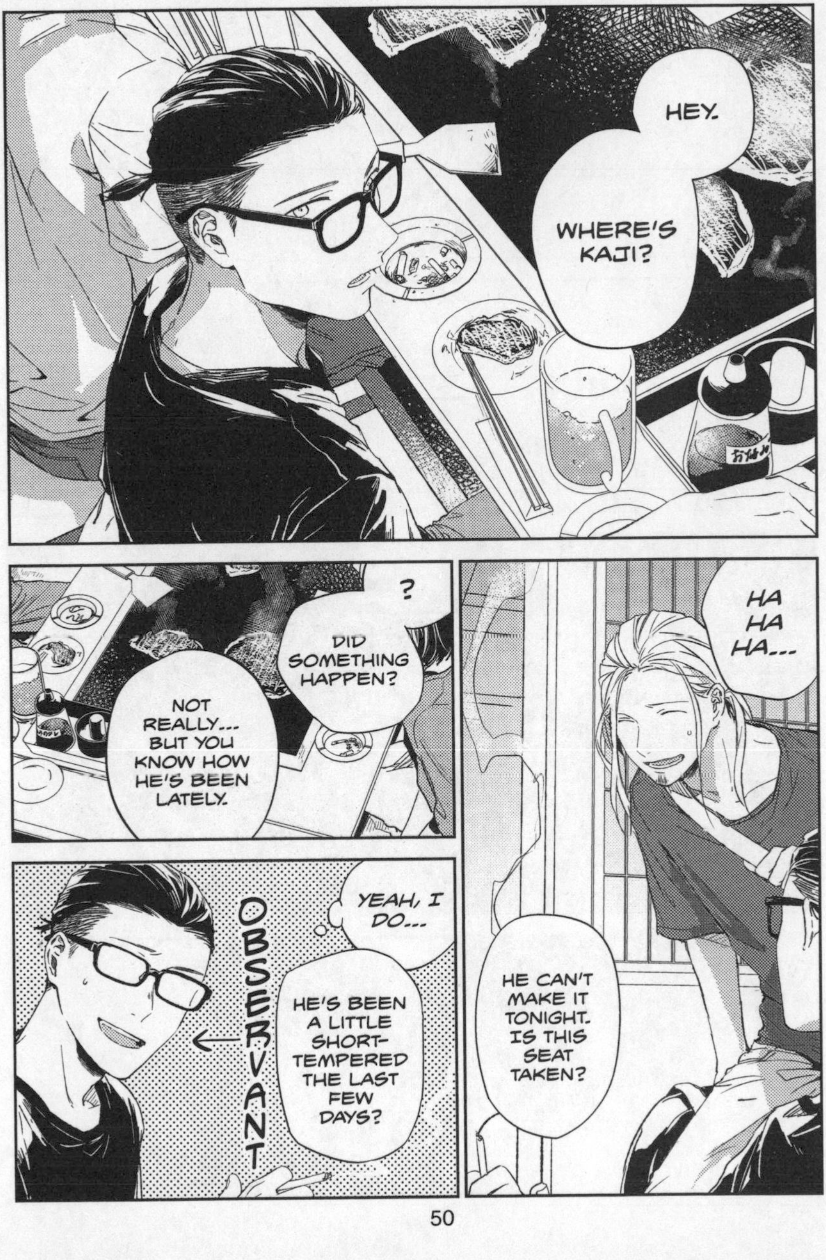
HEY.
WHERE'S KAJI?
HA HA HA...
HE CAN'T MAKE IT TONIGHT. IS THIS SEAT TAKEN?
?
DID SOMETHING HAPPEN?
NOT REALLY... BUT YOU KNOW HOW HE'S BEEN LATELY.
YEAH, I DO...
HE'S BEEN A LITTLE SHORT-TEMPERED THE LAST FEW DAYS?
OBSERVANT

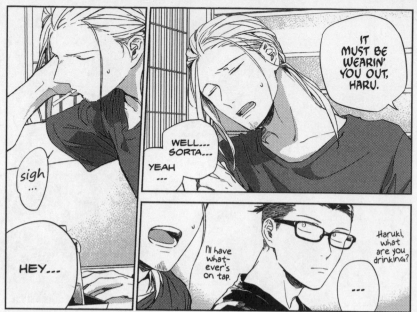

IT MUST BE WEARIN' YOU OUT, HARU.
WELL... SORTA...
YEAH ...
Haruki, what are you drinking?
...
I'll have what-ever's on tap.
sigh ...
HEY...
HM?
WHAT?
I WASN'T GONNA BRING THIS UP, BUT...
...SEEING HOW THINGS ARE GOING RIGHT NOW...

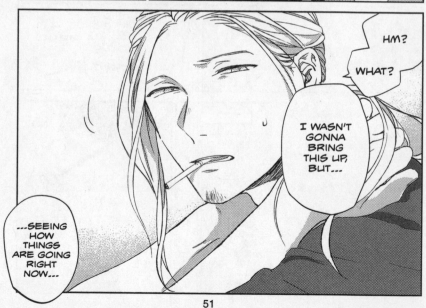

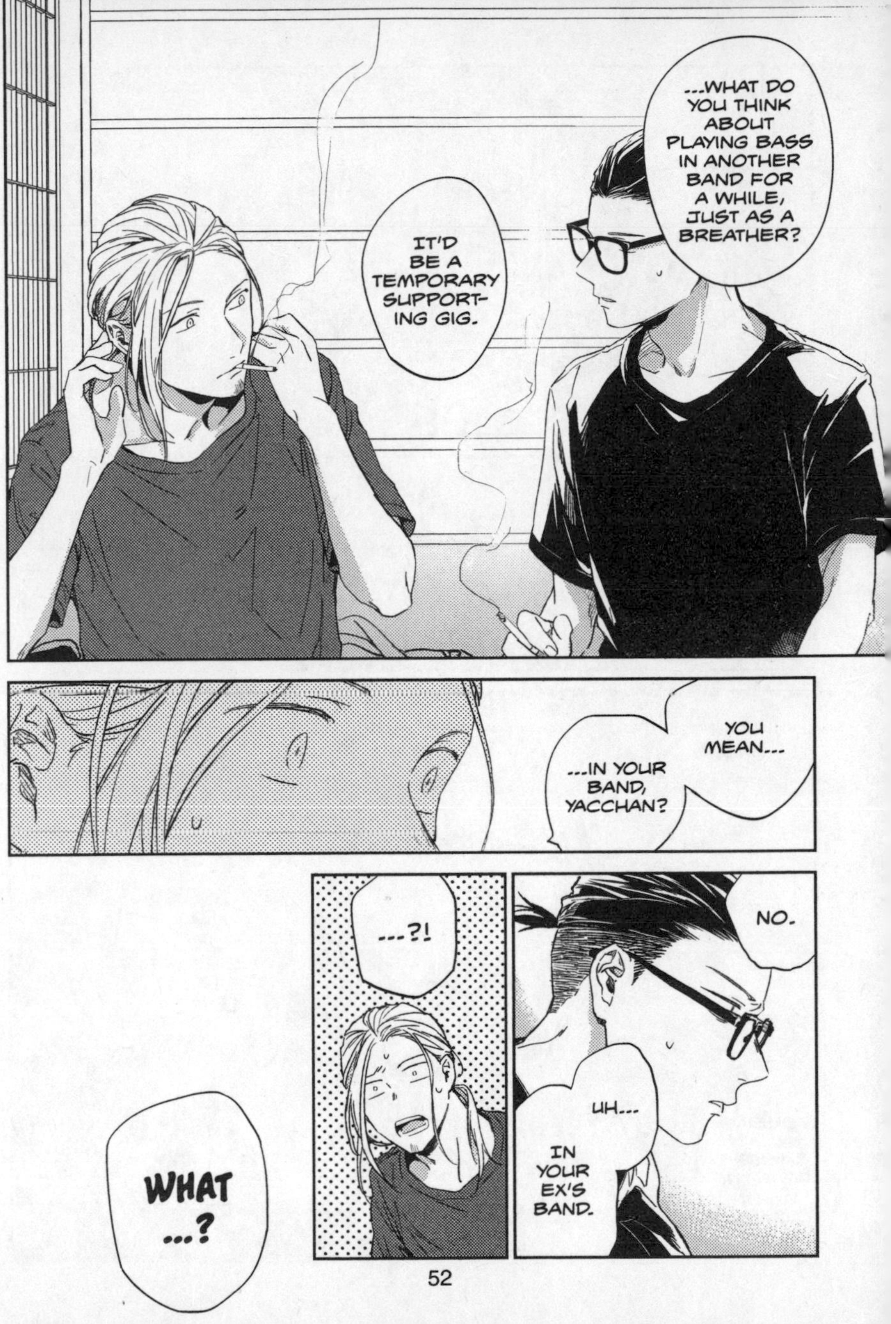
...WHAT DO YOU THINK ABOUT PLAYING BASS IN ANOTHER BAND FOR A WHILE, JUST AS A BREATHER?
IT'D BE A TEMPORARY SUPPORT-ING GIG.
YOU MEAN...
...IN YOUR BAND, YACCHAN?
NO.
UH...
IN YOUR EX'S BAND.
...?!
WHAT ...?

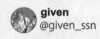
given
@given_ssn

Happy birthday to our guitarist, Ritsuka

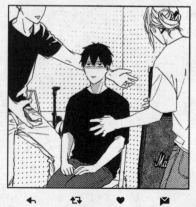

given

by Natsuki Kizu

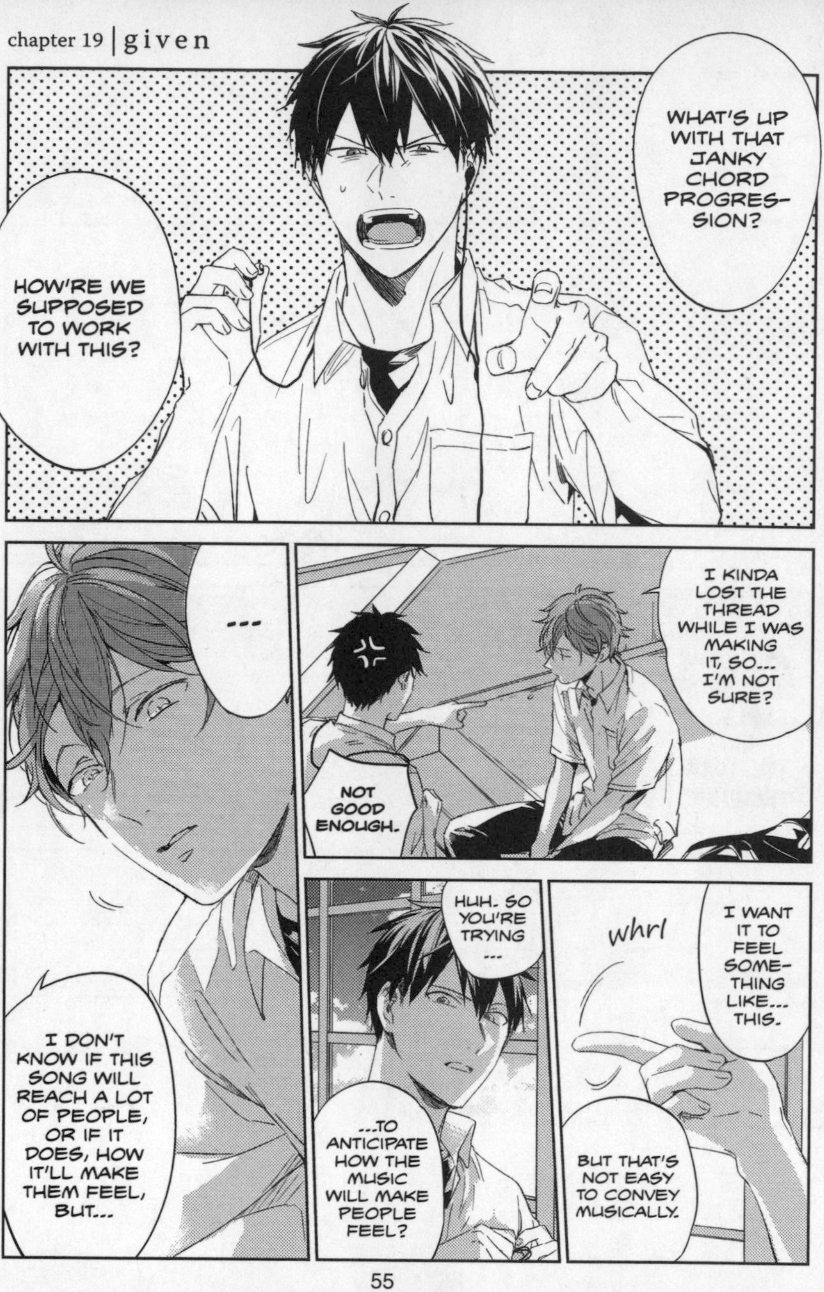
WHAT'S UP WITH THAT JANKY CHORD PROGRESSION?
HOW'RE WE SUPPOSED TO WORK WITH THIS?
I KINDA LOST THE THREAD WHILE I WAS MAKING IT, SO... I'M NOT SURE?
NOT GOOD ENOUGH.
whrl
I WANT IT TO FEEL SOMETHING LIKE... THIS.
BUT THAT'S NOT EASY TO CONVEY MUSICALLY.
HUH. SO YOU'RE TRYING...
...TO ANTICIPATE HOW THE MUSIC WILL MAKE PEOPLE FEEL?
...
I DON'T KNOW IF THIS SONG WILL REACH A LOT OF PEOPLE, OR IF IT DOES, HOW IT'LL MAKE THEM FEEL, BUT...

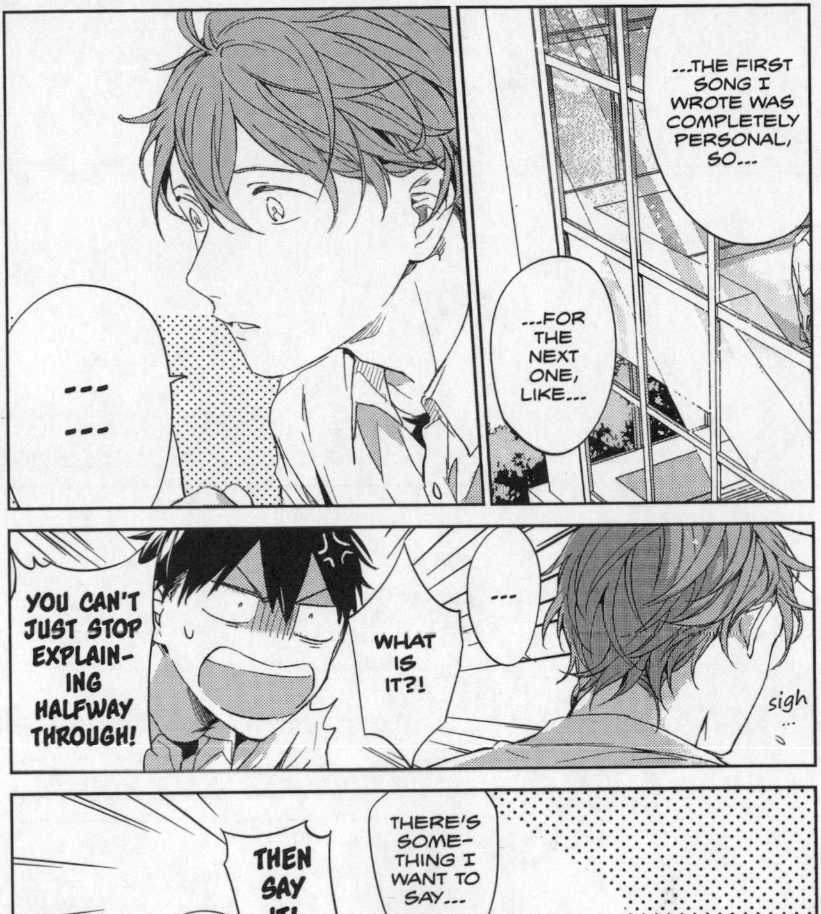
...THE FIRST SONG I WROTE WAS COMPLETELY PERSONAL, SO...
...FOR THE NEXT ONE, LIKE...
...
...
...
sigh...
WHAT IS IT?!
YOU CAN'T JUST STOP EXPLAINING HALFWAY THROUGH!
THERE'S SOMETHING I WANT TO SAY...
THEN SAY IT!
Next time.
HUH?!

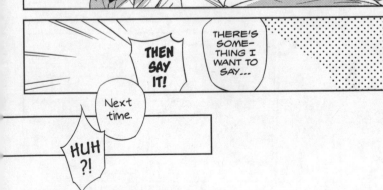

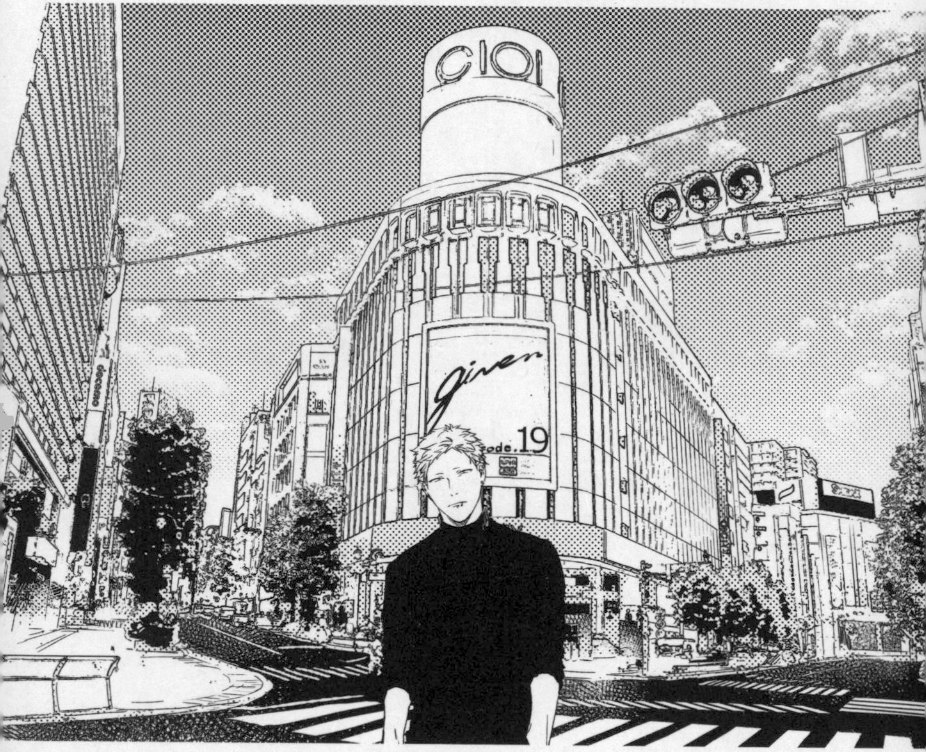
given
19

chapter 19

given

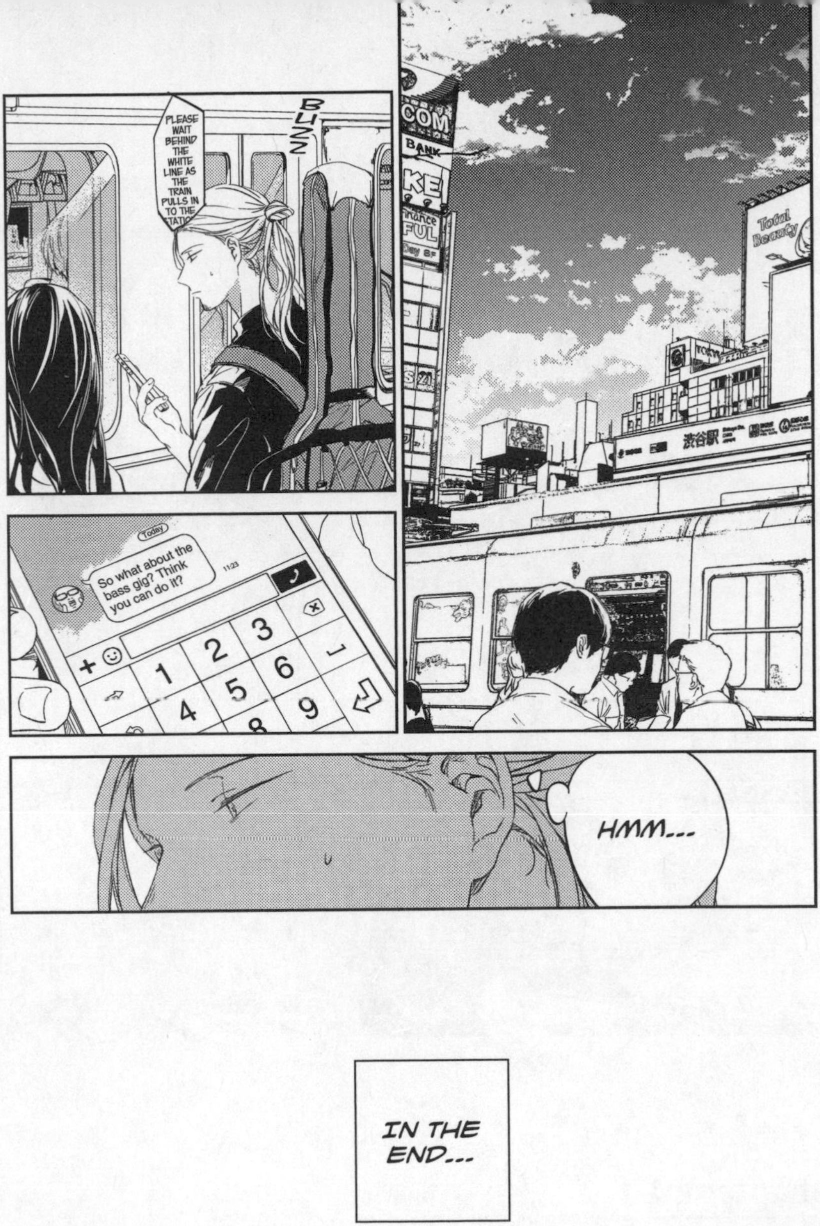
COM
BANK
KE
FUL
Total Beauty
渋谷駅
PLEASE WAIT BEHIND THE WHITE LINE AS THE TRAIN PULLS IN TO THE STATION
BUZZ
Today
So what about the bass gig? Think you can do it?
11:23
HMM...
IN THE END...

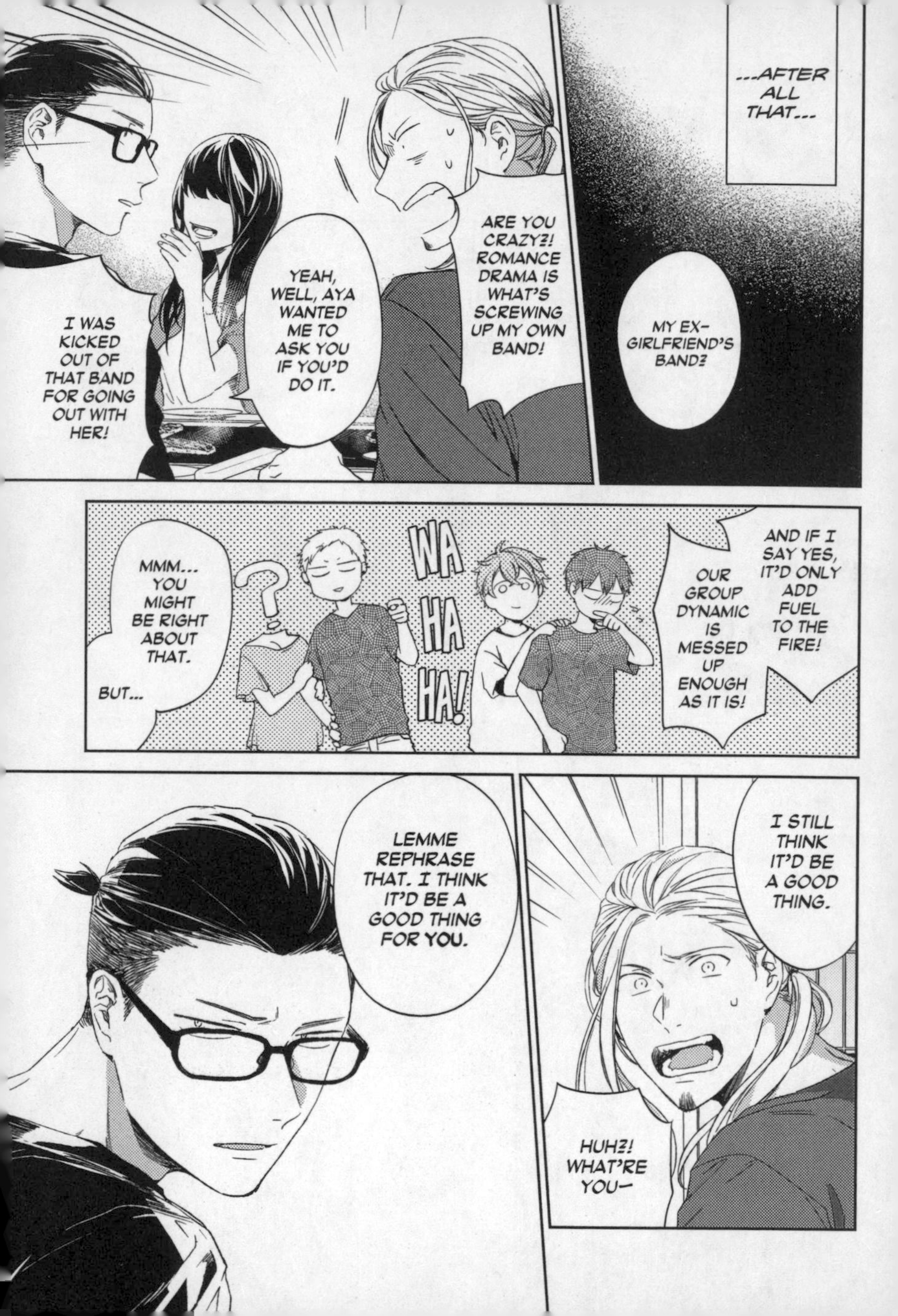
...AFTER ALL THAT...
MY EX-GIRLFRIEND'S BAND?
ARE YOU CRAZY?! ROMANCE DRAMA IS WHAT'S SCREWING UP MY OWN BAND!
YEAH, WELL, AYA WANTED ME TO ASK YOU IF YOU'D DO IT.
I WAS KICKED OUT OF THAT BAND FOR GOING OUT WITH HER!
AND IF I SAY YES, IT'D ONLY ADD FUEL TO THE FIRE!
OUR GROUP DYNAMIC IS MESSED UP ENOUGH AS IT IS!
WA HA HA!
MMM... YOU MIGHT BE RIGHT ABOUT THAT.
BUT...
I STILL THINK IT'D BE A GOOD THING.
HUH?! WHAT'RE YOU—
LEMME REPHRASE THAT. I THINK IT'D BE A GOOD THING FOR YOU.

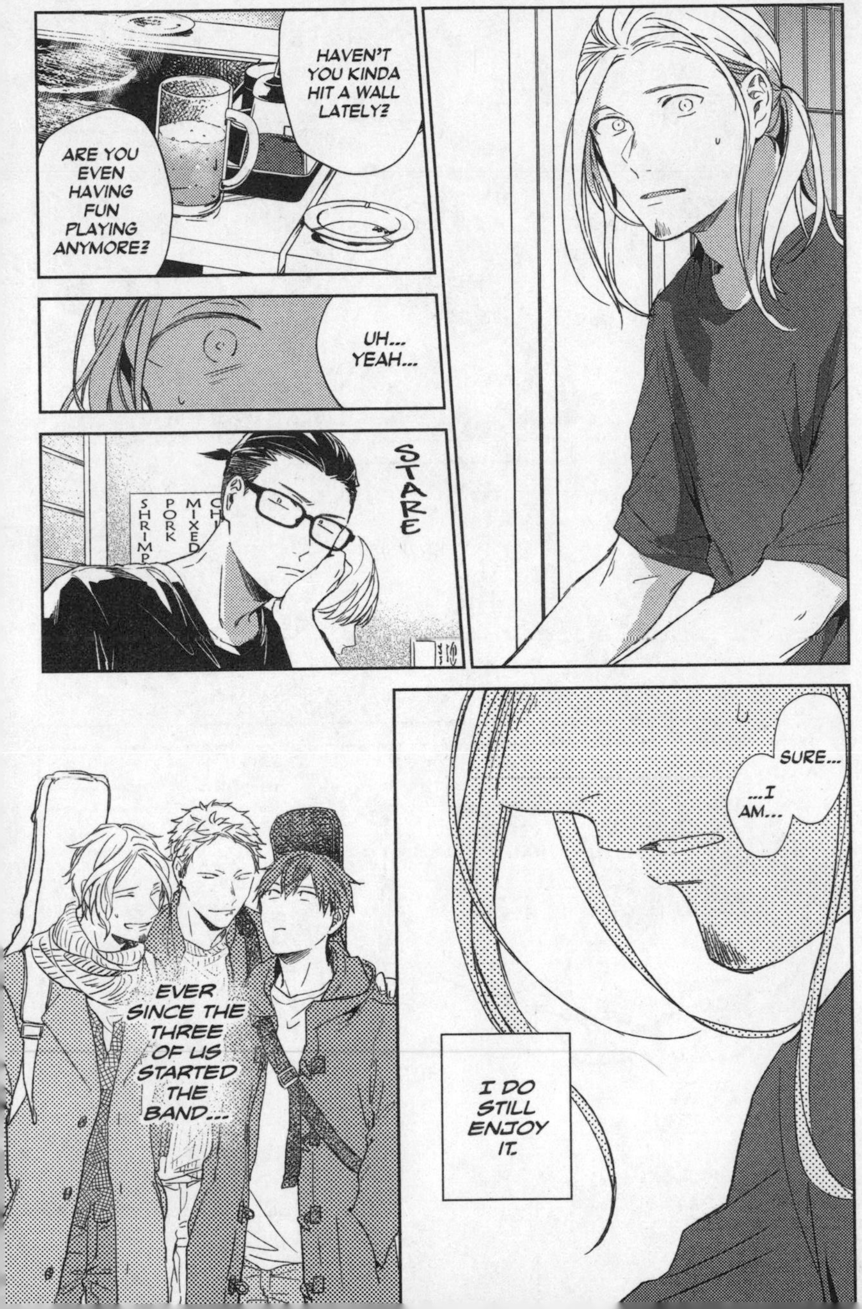
HAVEN'T YOU KINDA HIT A WALL LATELY?
ARE YOU EVEN HAVING FUN PLAYING ANYMORE?
UH... YEAH...
STARE
MIXED
PORK
SHRIMP
SURE...
...I AM...
I DO STILL ENJOY IT.
EVER SINCE THE THREE OF US STARTED THE BAND...

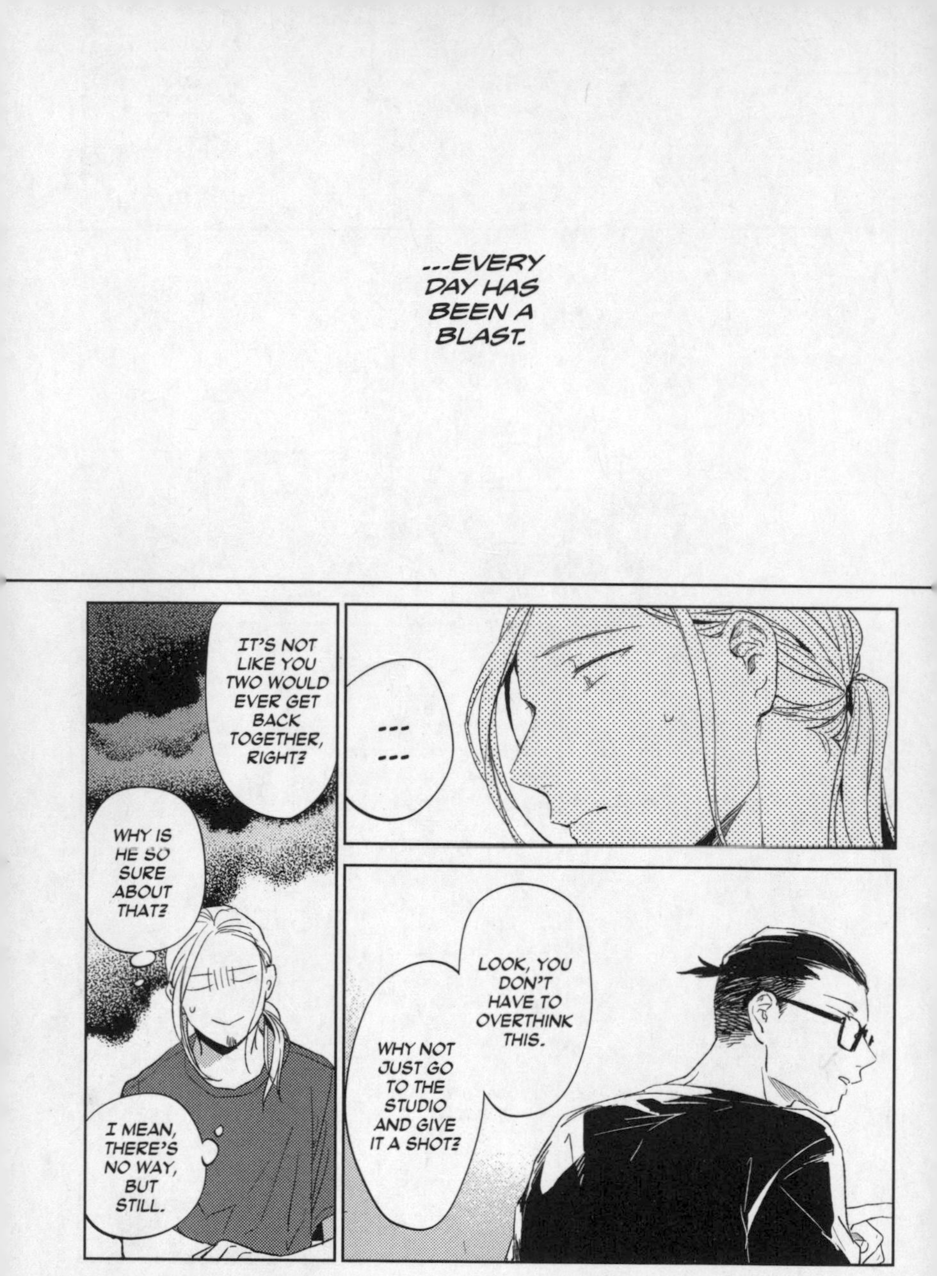
...EVERY DAY HAS BEEN A BLAST.
... ...
LOOK, YOU DON'T HAVE TO OVERTHINK THIS.
WHY NOT JUST GO TO THE STUDIO AND GIVE IT A SHOT?
IT'S NOT LIKE YOU TWO WOULD EVER GET BACK TOGETHER, RIGHT?
WHY IS HE SO SURE ABOUT THAT?
I MEAN, THERE'S NO WAY, BUT STILL.

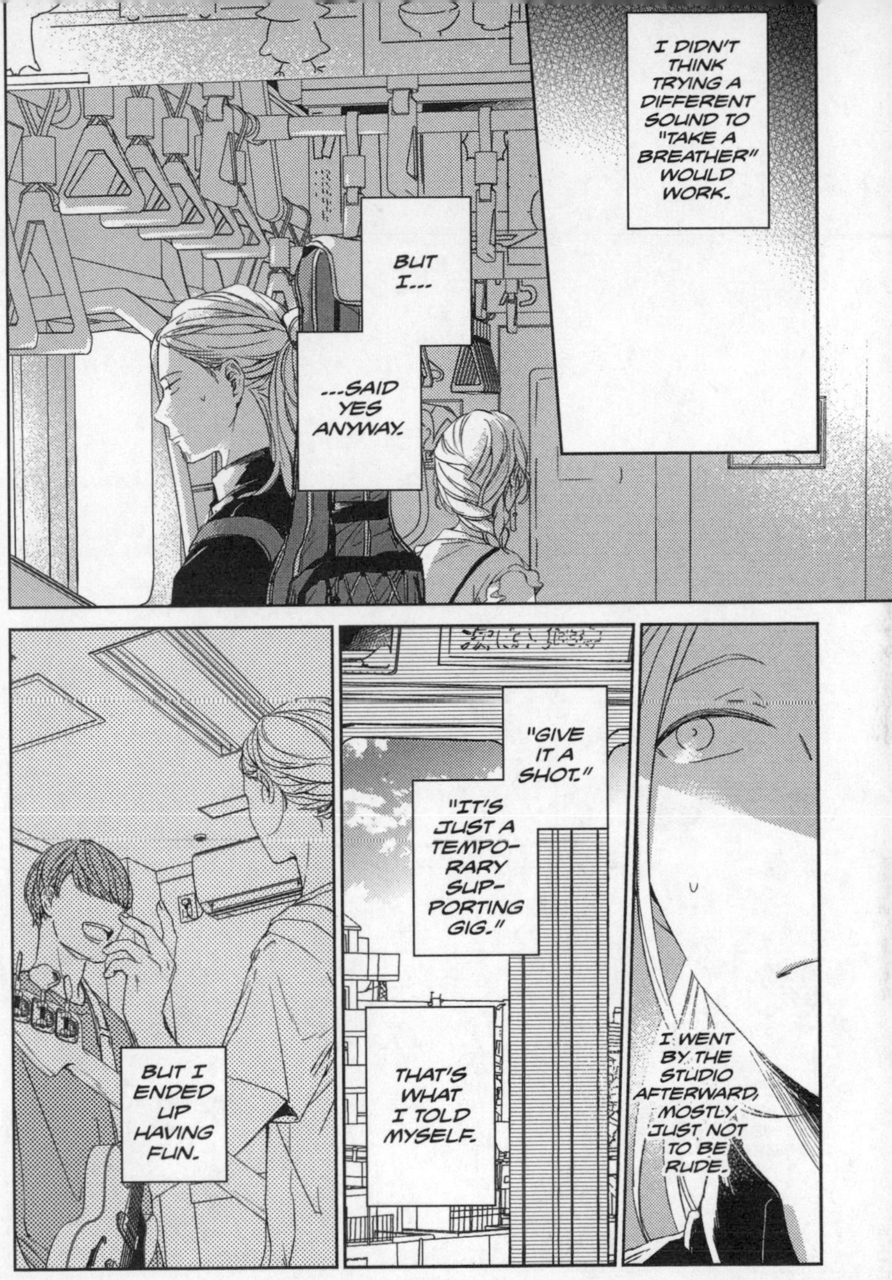
I DIDN'T THINK TRYING A DIFFERENT SOUND TO "TAKE A BREATHER" WOULD WORK.
BUT I...
...SAID YES ANYWAY.
I WENT BY THE STUDIO AFTERWARD, MOSTLY JUST NOT TO BE RUDE.
"GIVE IT A SHOT."
"IT'S JUST A TEMPORARY SUPPORTING GIG."
THAT'S WHAT I TOLD MYSELF.
BUT I ENDED UP HAVING FUN.

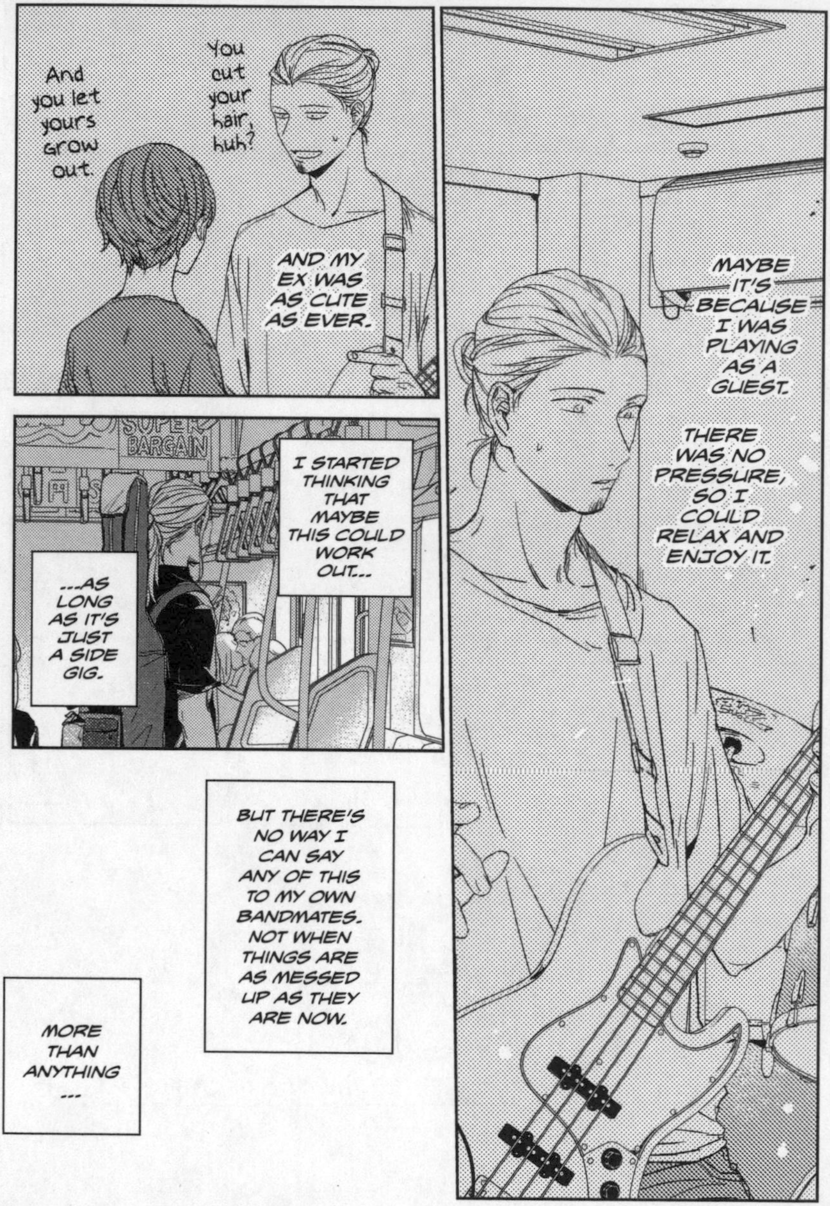
MAYBE IT'S BECAUSE I WAS PLAYING AS A GUEST.
THERE WAS NO PRESSURE, SO I COULD RELAX AND ENJOY IT.
You cut your hair, huh?
And you let yours grow out.
AND MY EX WAS AS CUTE AS EVER.
SUPER BARGAIN
I STARTED THINKING THAT MAYBE THIS COULD WORK OUT...
...AS LONG AS IT'S JUST A SIDE GIG.
BUT THERE'S NO WAY I CAN SAY ANY OF THIS TO MY OWN BANDMATES. NOT WHEN THINGS ARE AS MESSED UP AS THEY ARE NOW.
MORE THAN ANYTHING ---

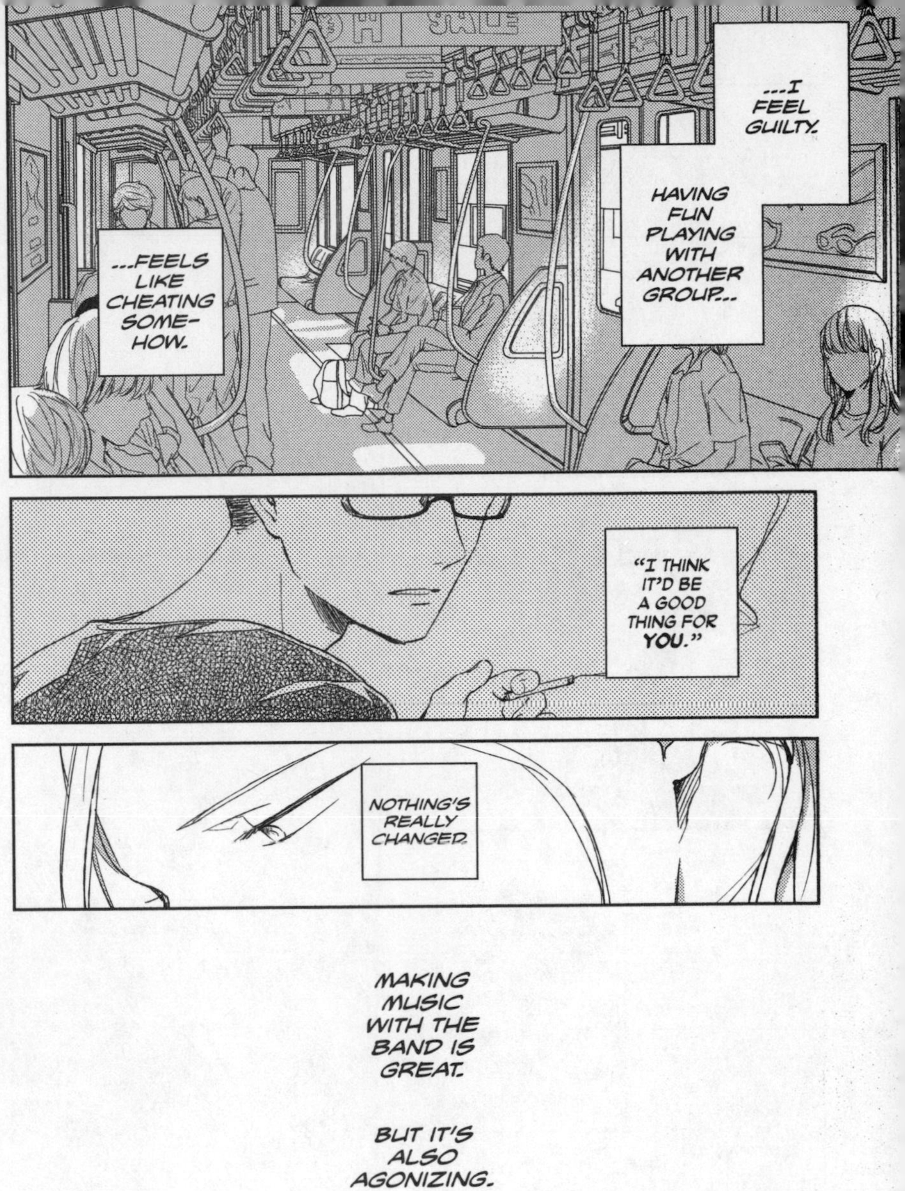
...I FEEL GUILTY.
HAVING FUN PLAYING WITH ANOTHER GROUP...
...FEELS LIKE CHEATING SOME-HOW.
"I THINK IT'D BE A GOOD THING FOR YOU."
NOTHING'S REALLY CHANGED.
MAKING MUSIC WITH THE BAND IS GREAT.
BUT IT'S ALSO AGONIZING.

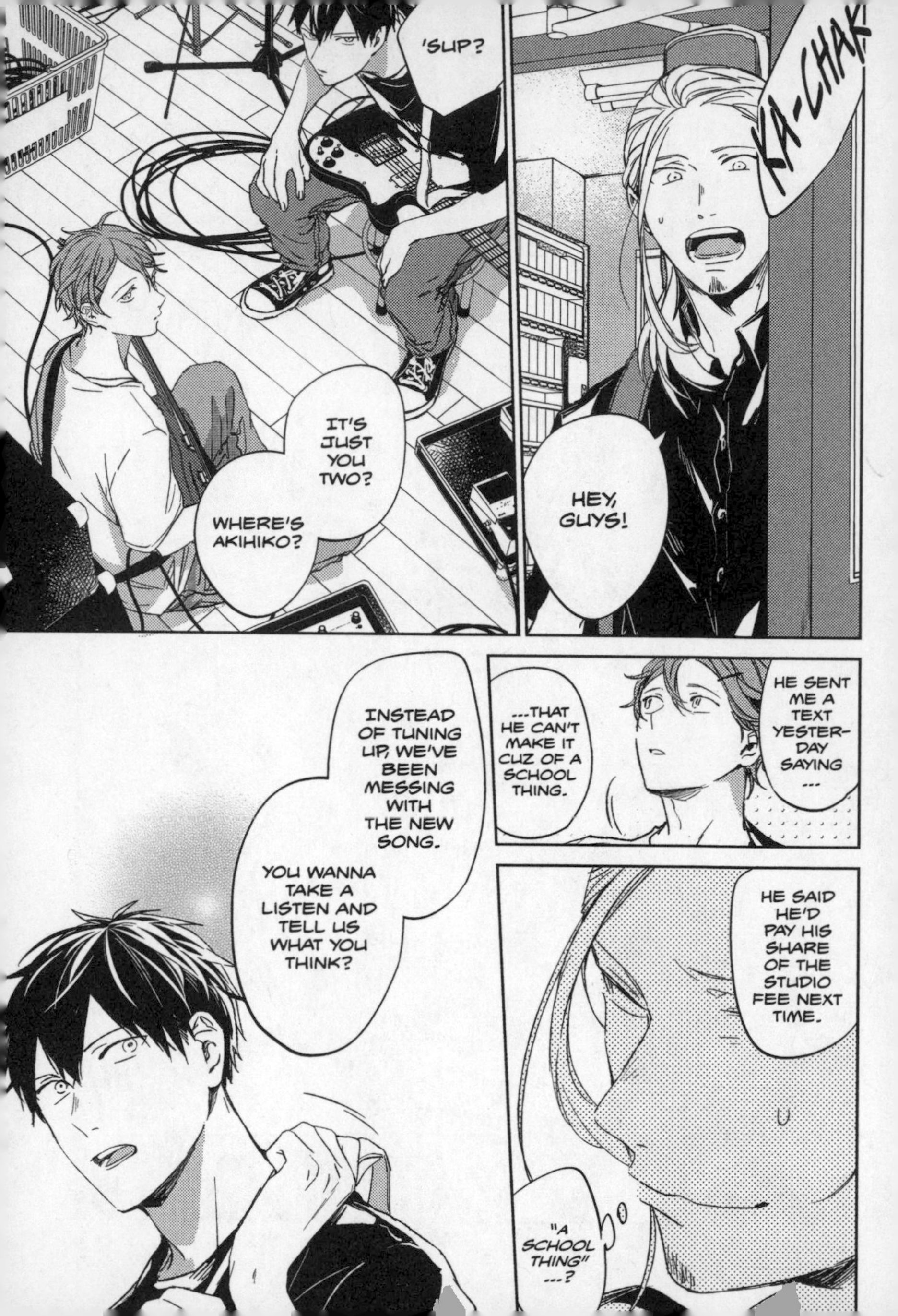
KA-CHAK
HEY, GUYS!
'SUP?
IT'S JUST YOU TWO?
WHERE'S AKIHIKO?
HE SENT ME A TEXT YESTER-DAY SAYING ...
...THAT HE CAN'T MAKE IT CUZ OF A SCHOOL THING.
HE SAID HE'D PAY HIS SHARE OF THE STUDIO FEE NEXT TIME.
"A SCHOOL THING" ...?
INSTEAD OF TUNING UP, WE'VE BEEN MESSING WITH THE NEW SONG.
YOU WANNA TAKE A LISTEN AND TELL US WHAT YOU THINK?

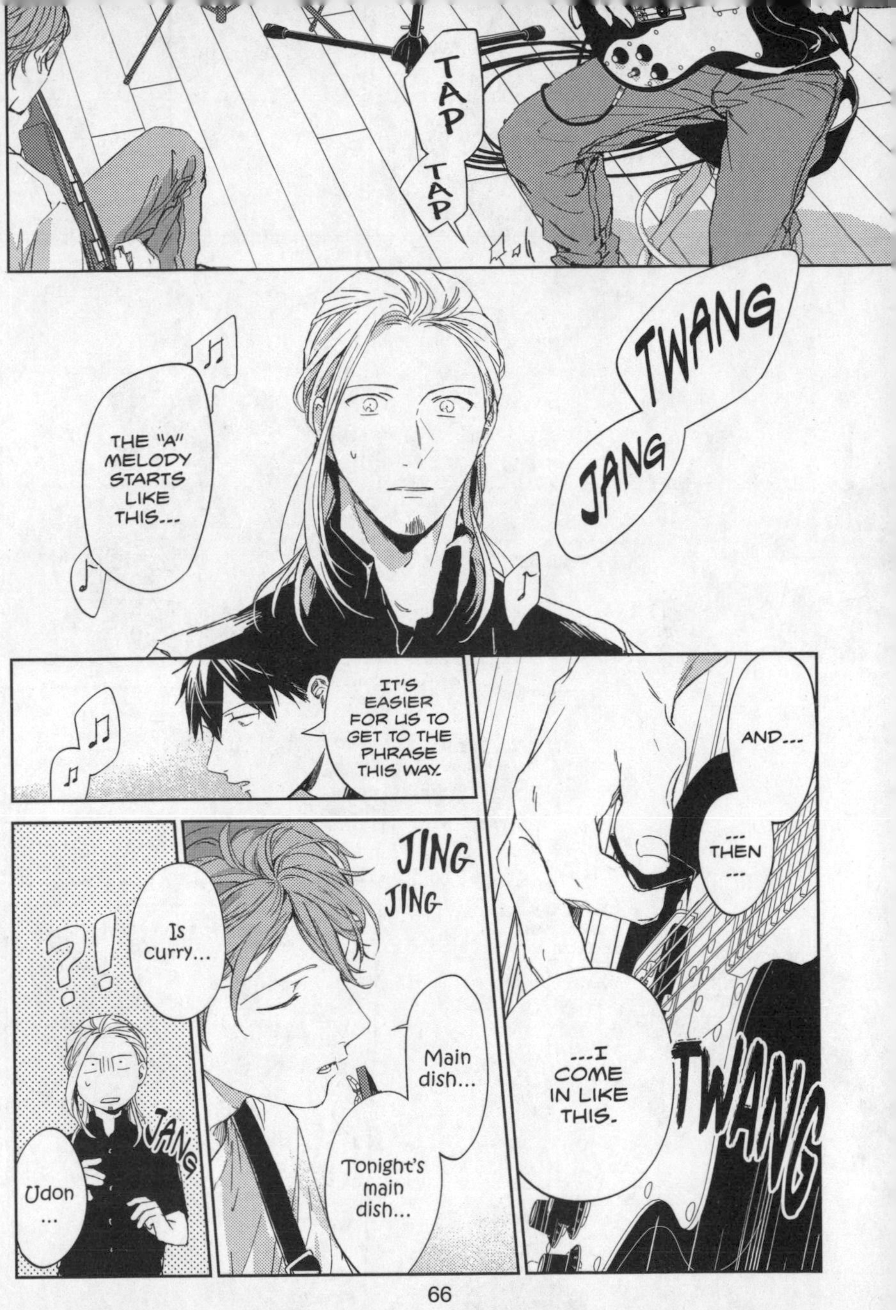
TAP
TAP
TAP
TAP
TWANG
JANG
THE "A" MELODY STARTS LIKE THIS...
AND...
...THEN...
...I COME IN LIKE THIS.
TWANG
IT'S EASIER FOR US TO GET TO THE PHRASE THIS WAY.
JING
JING
Main dish...
Tonight's main dish...
Is curry...
?!
Udon...
JANG

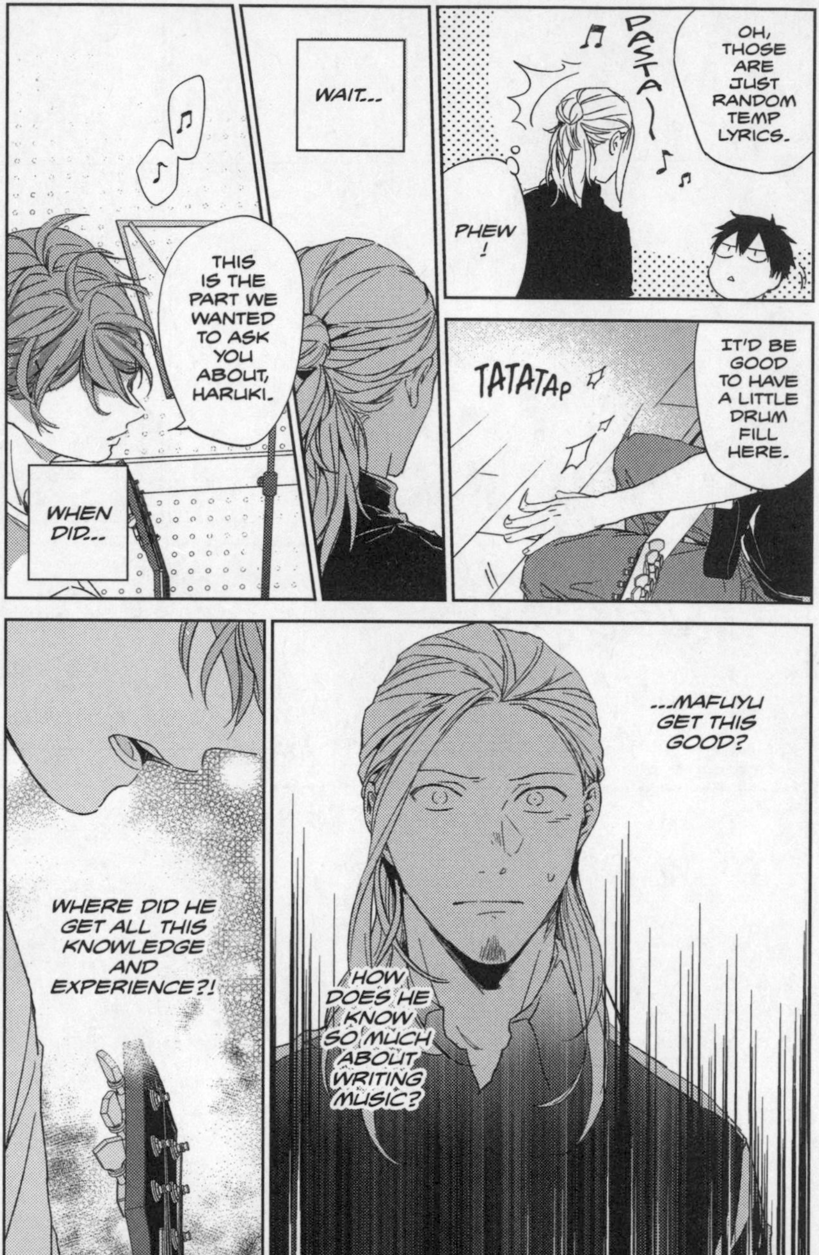
OH, THOSE ARE JUST RANDOM TEMP LYRICS.
PASTA~
PHEW!
IT'D BE GOOD TO HAVE A LITTLE DRUM FILL HERE.
TATATAP
WAIT...
THIS IS THE PART WE WANTED TO ASK YOU ABOUT, HARUKI.
WHEN DID...
...MAFUYU GET THIS GOOD?
HOW DOES HE KNOW SO MUCH ABOUT WRITING MUSIC?
WHERE DID HE GET ALL THIS KNOWLEDGE AND EXPERIENCE?!

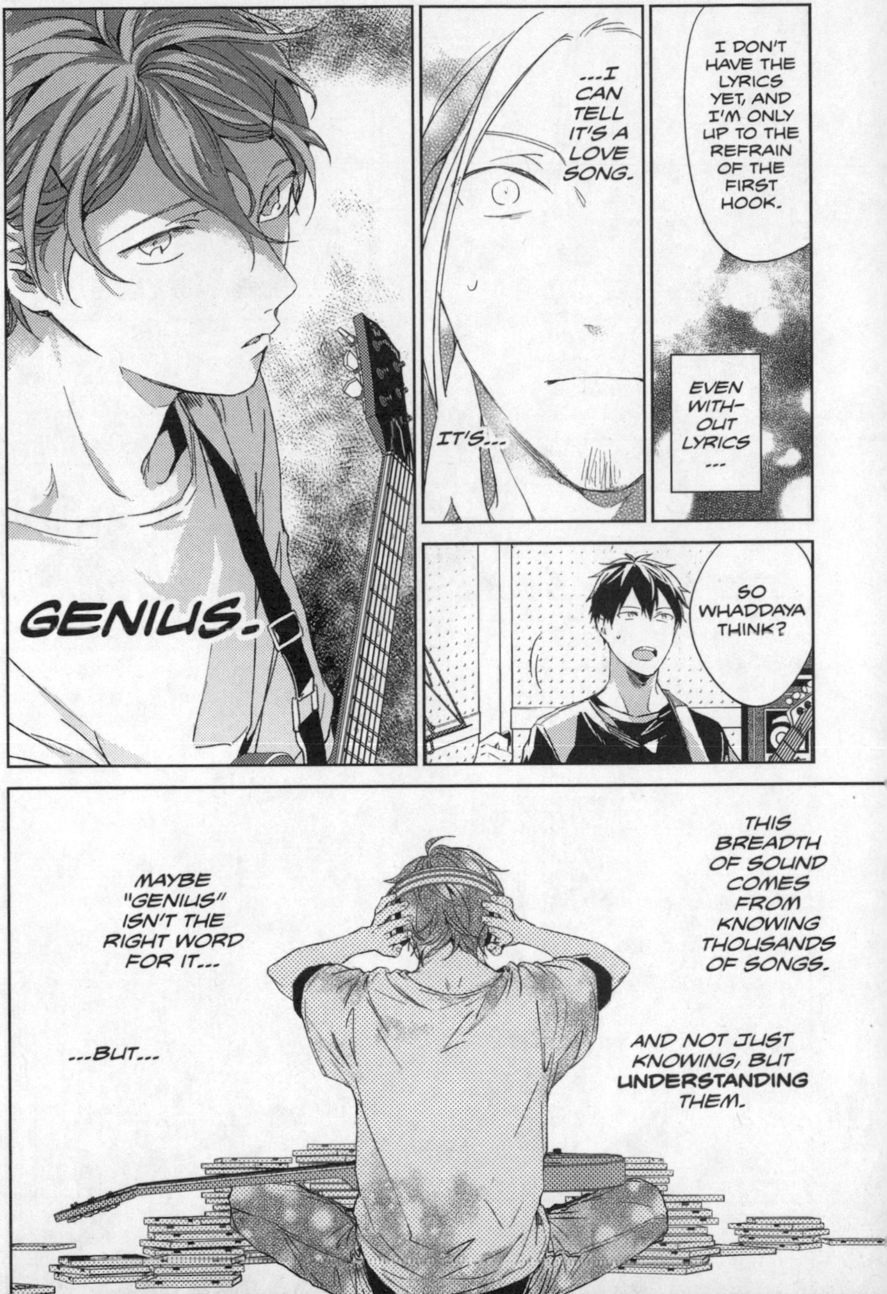
I DON'T HAVE THE LYRICS YET, AND I'M ONLY UP TO THE REFRAIN OF THE FIRST HOOK.
EVEN WITHOUT LYRICS ...
...I CAN TELL IT'S A LOVE SONG.
IT'S...
SO WHADDAYA THINK?
GENIUS.
THIS BREADTH OF SOUND COMES FROM KNOWING THOUSANDS OF SONGS.
MAYBE "GENIUS" ISN'T THE RIGHT WORD FOR IT...
AND NOT JUST KNOWING, BUT UNDERSTANDING THEM.
...BUT...

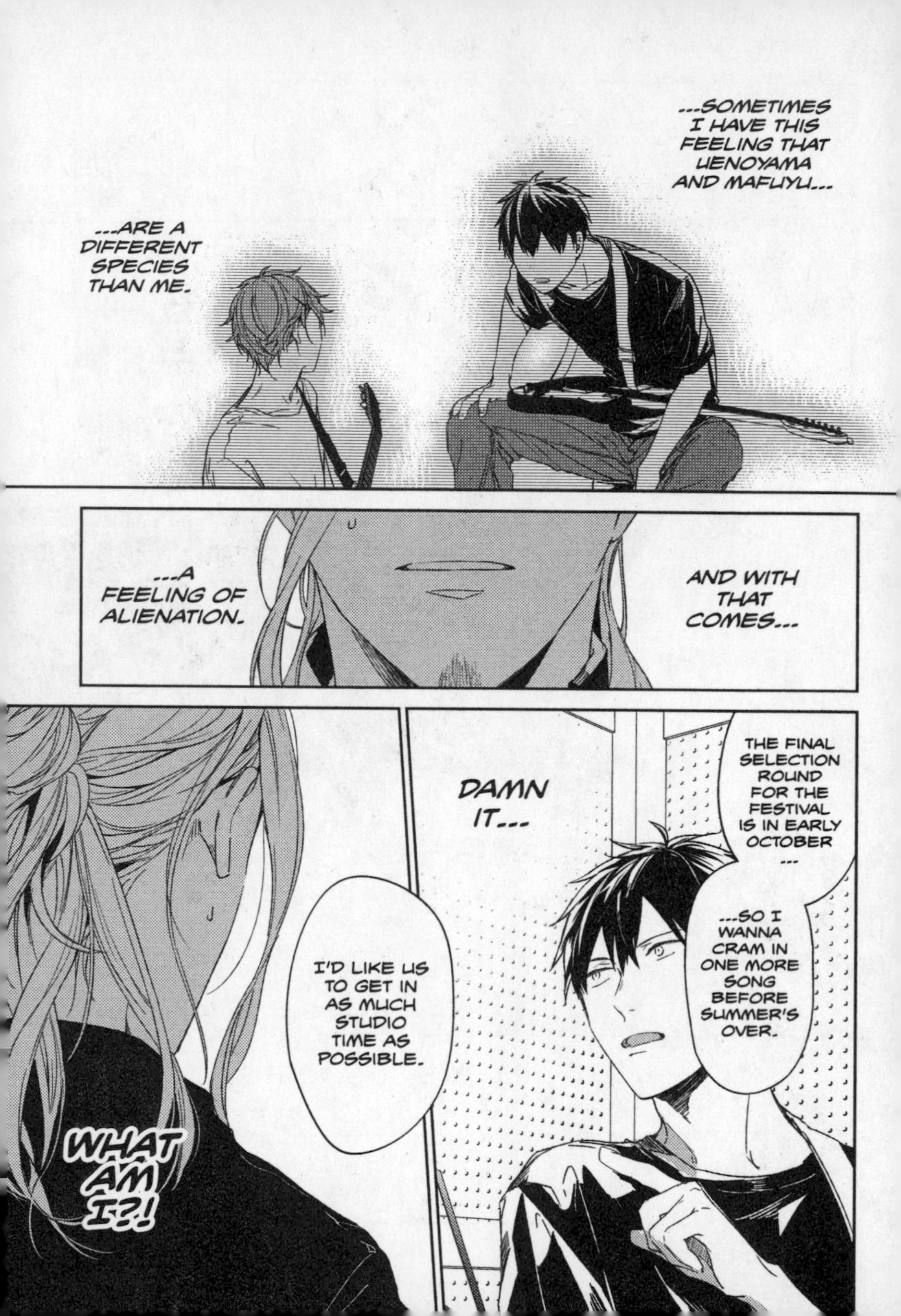
...SOMETIMES I HAVE THIS FEELING THAT UENOYAMA AND MAFUYU...
...ARE A DIFFERENT SPECIES THAN ME.
AND WITH THAT COMES...
...A FEELING OF ALIENATION.
THE FINAL SELECTION ROUND FOR THE FESTIVAL IS IN EARLY OCTOBER...
DAMN IT...
...SO I WANNA CRAM IN ONE MORE SONG BEFORE SUMMER'S OVER.
I'D LIKE US TO GET IN AS MUCH STUDIO TIME AS POSSIBLE.
WHAT AM I?!

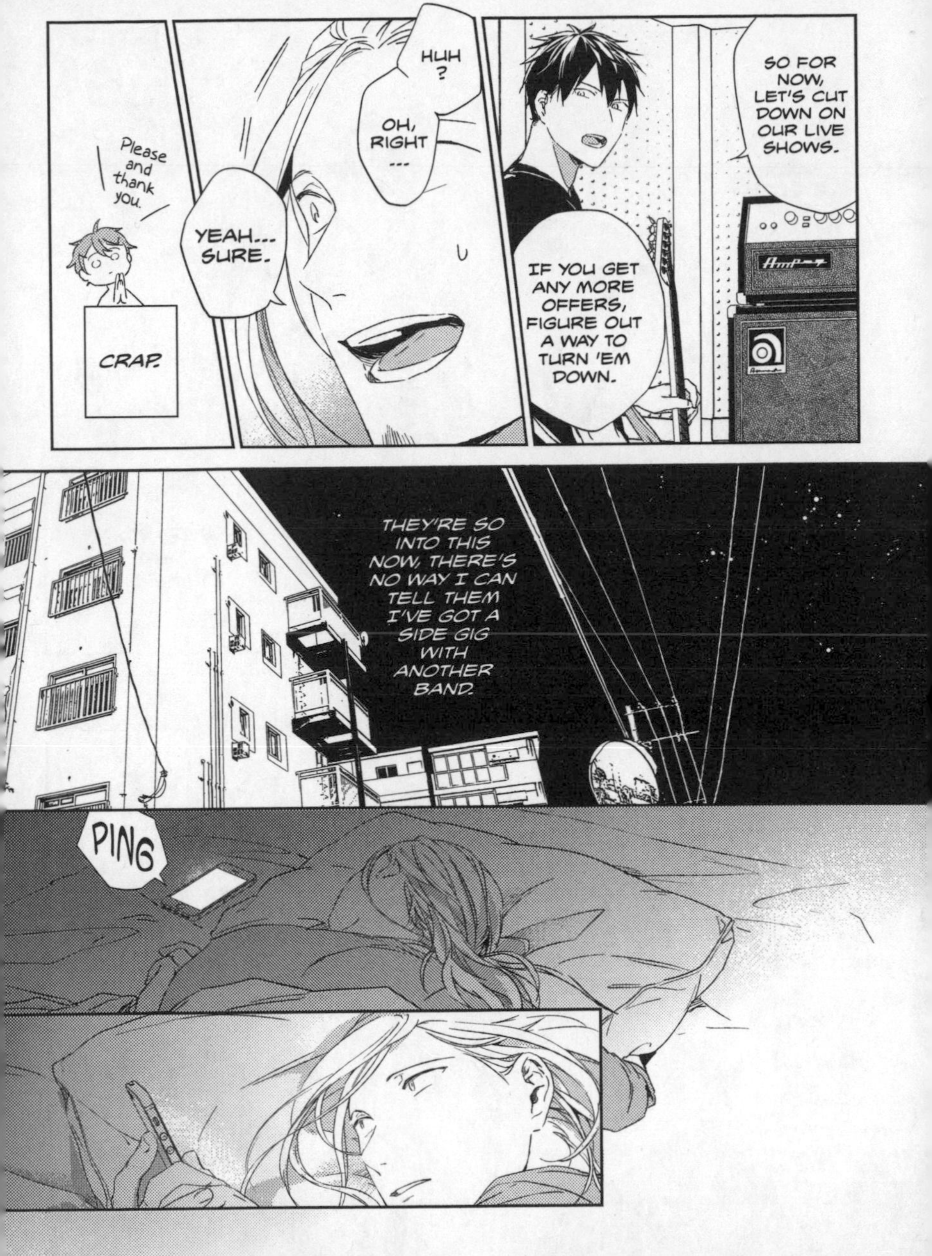
SO FOR NOW, LET'S CUT DOWN ON OUR LIVE SHOWS.
IF YOU GET ANY MORE OFFERS, FIGURE OUT A WAY TO TURN 'EM DOWN.
HUH?
OH, RIGHT...
YEAH... SURE.
Please and thank you.
CRAP.
THEY'RE SO INTO THIS NOW, THERE'S NO WAY I CAN TELL THEM I'VE GOT A SIDE GIG WITH ANOTHER BAND.
PING

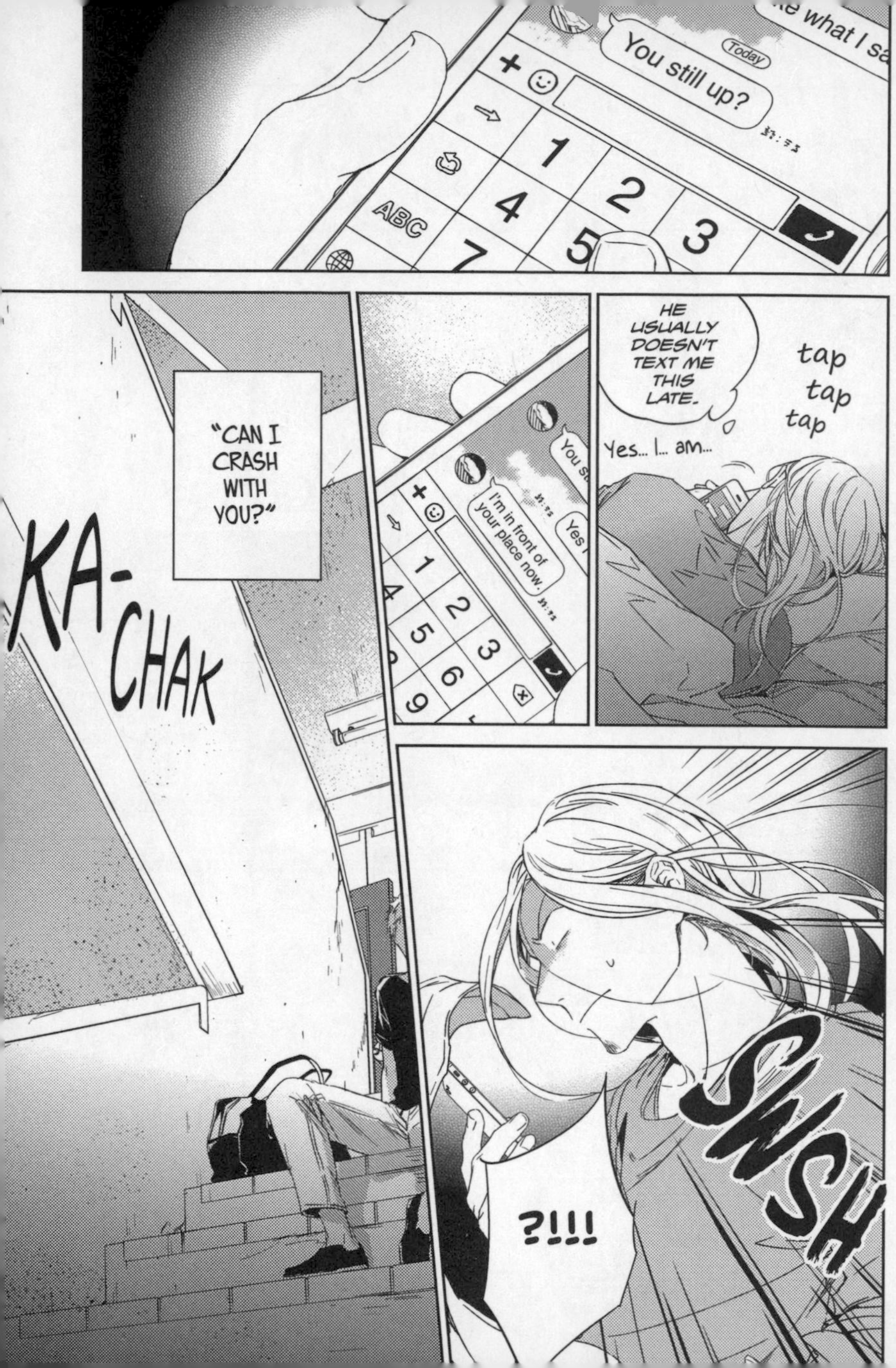
Today
You still up?
HE USUALLY DOESN'T TEXT ME THIS LATE.
tap tap tap
Yes... I... am...
I'm in front of your place now.
"CAN I CRASH WITH YOU?"
KA-CHAK
SWSH
?!!!

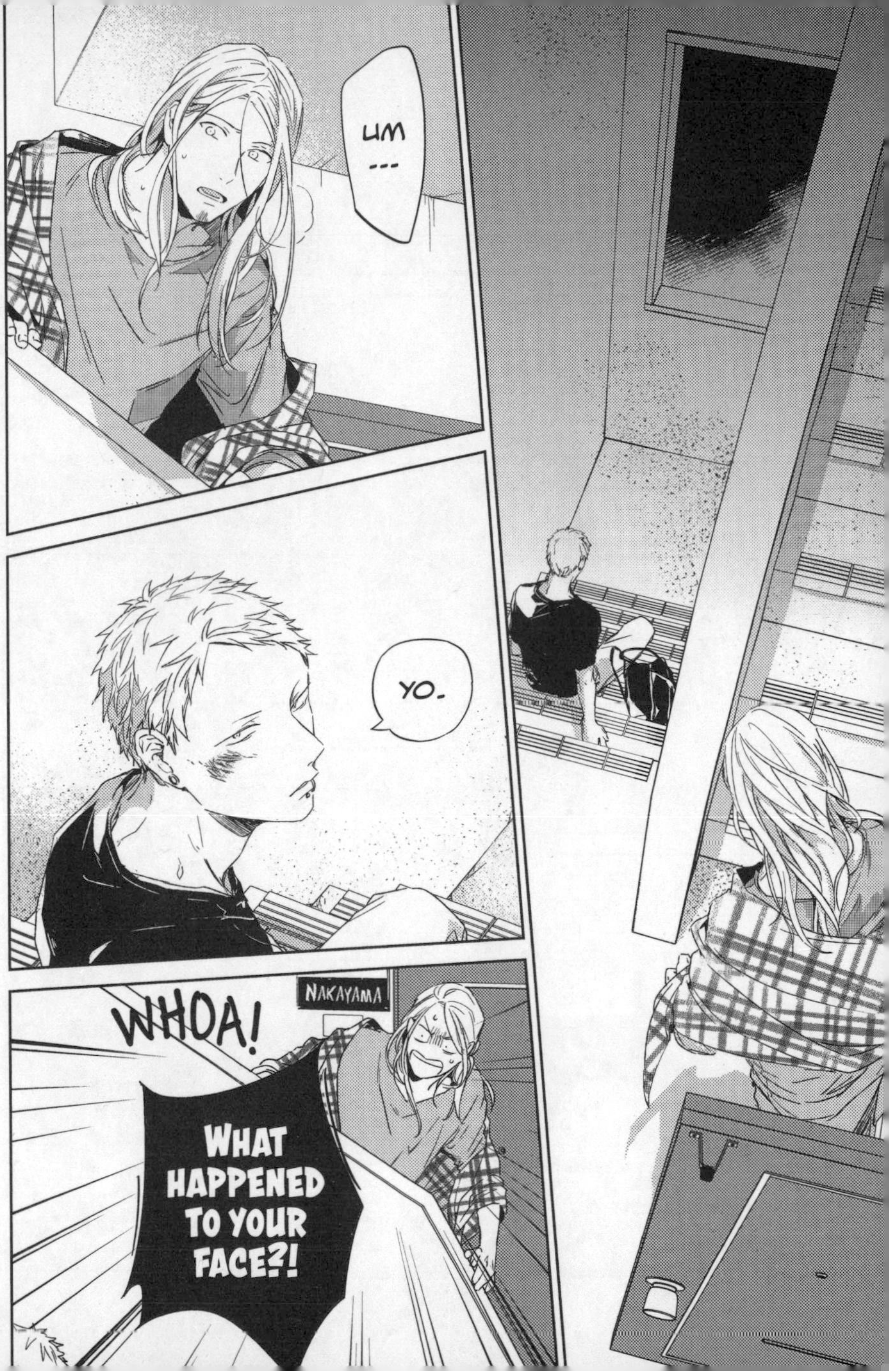
UM ---
YO.
NAKAYAMA
WHOA!
WHAT HAPPENED TO YOUR FACE?!

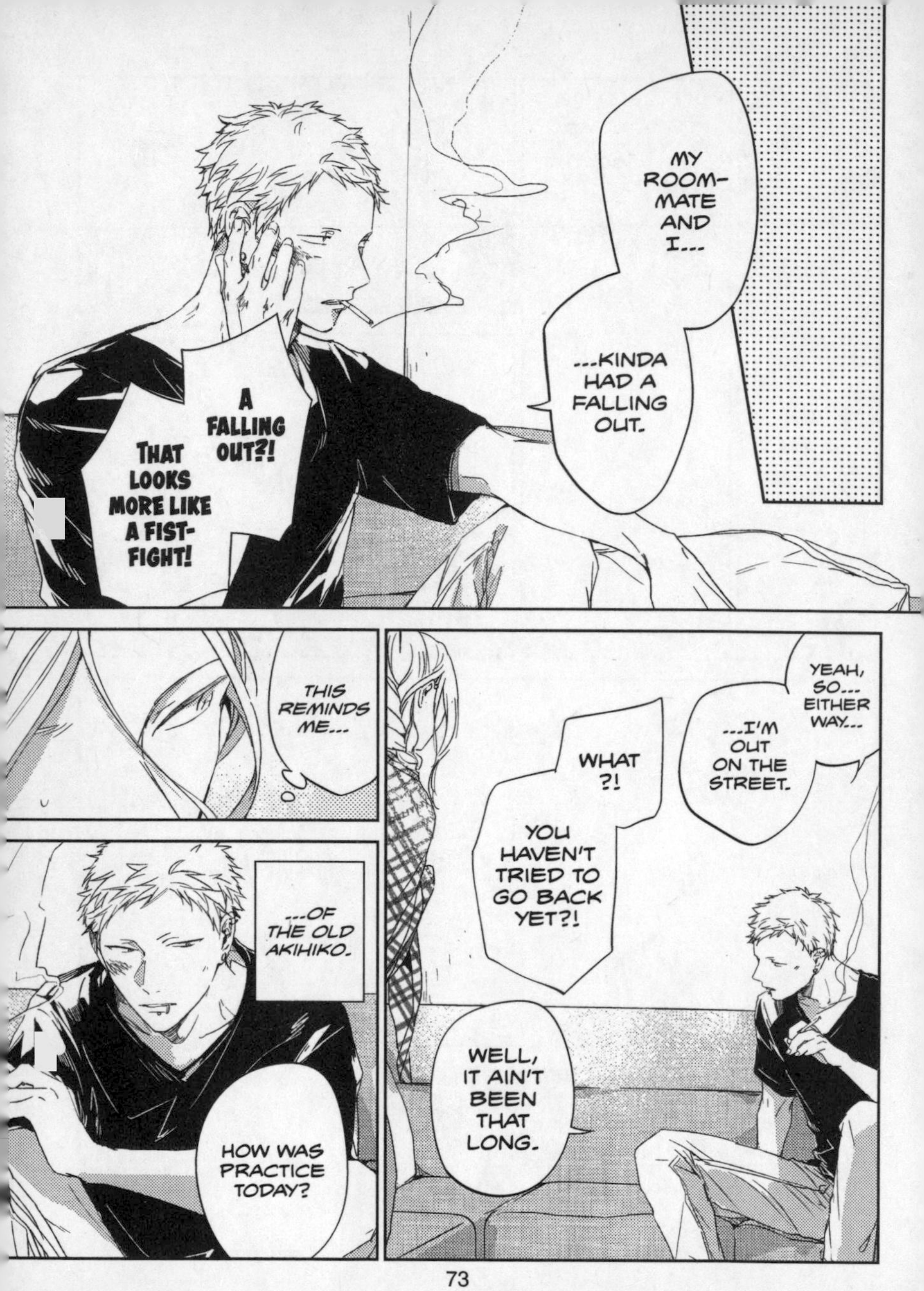
MY ROOM-MATE AND I...
...KINDA HAD A FALLING OUT.
A FALLING OUT?!
THAT LOOKS MORE LIKE A FIST-FIGHT!
YEAH, SO... EITHER WAY...
...I'M OUT ON THE STREET.
WHAT?!
YOU HAVEN'T TRIED TO GO BACK YET?!
WELL, IT AIN'T BEEN THAT LONG.
THIS REMINDS ME...
...OF THE OLD AKIHIKO.
HOW WAS PRACTICE TODAY?

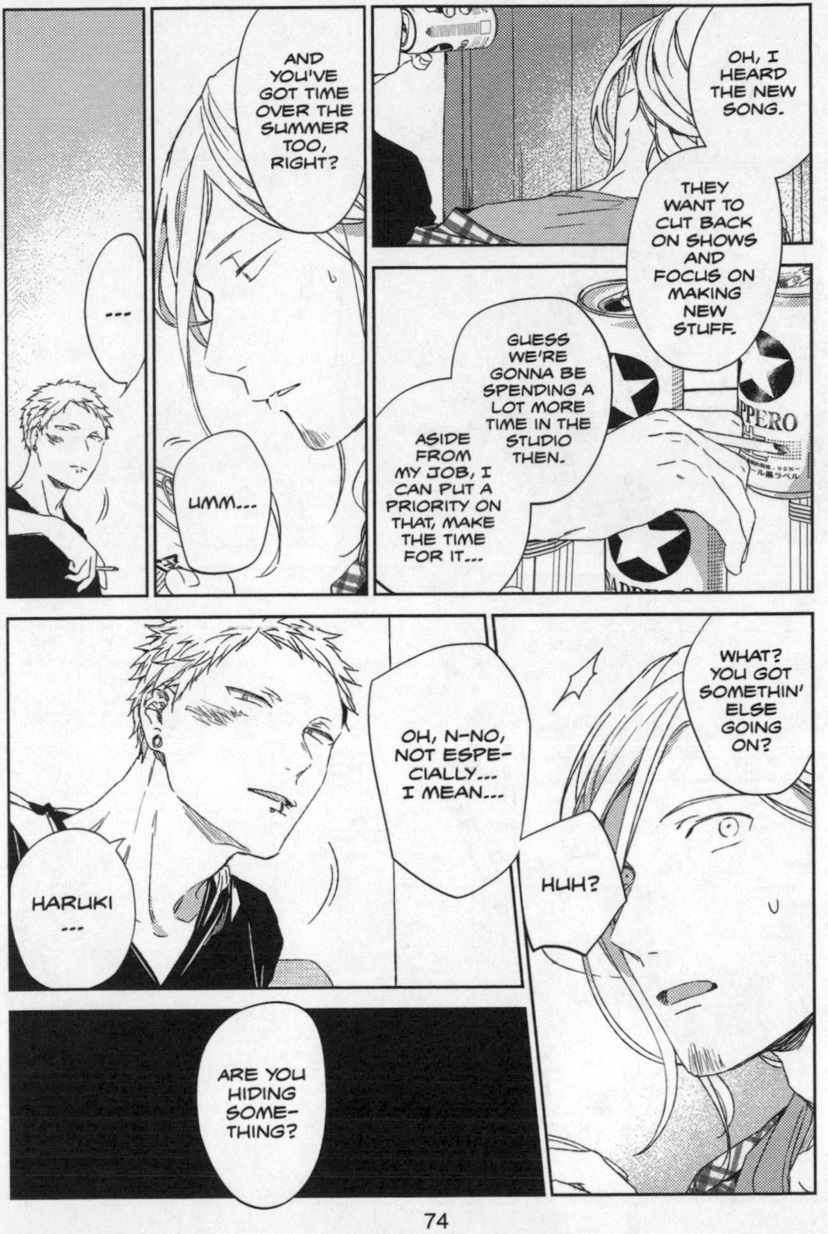
OH, I HEARD THE NEW SONG.
THEY WANT TO CUT BACK ON SHOWS AND FOCUS ON MAKING NEW STUFF.
GUESS WE'RE GONNA BE SPENDING A LOT MORE TIME IN THE STUDIO THEN.
ASIDE FROM MY JOB, I CAN PUT A PRIORITY ON THAT, MAKE THE TIME FOR IT...
AND YOU'VE GOT TIME OVER THE SUMMER TOO, RIGHT?
UMM...
...
WHAT? YOU GOT SOMETHIN' ELSE GOING ON?
HUH?
OH, N-NO, NOT ESPECIALLY... I MEAN...
HARUKI...
ARE YOU HIDING SOMETHING?

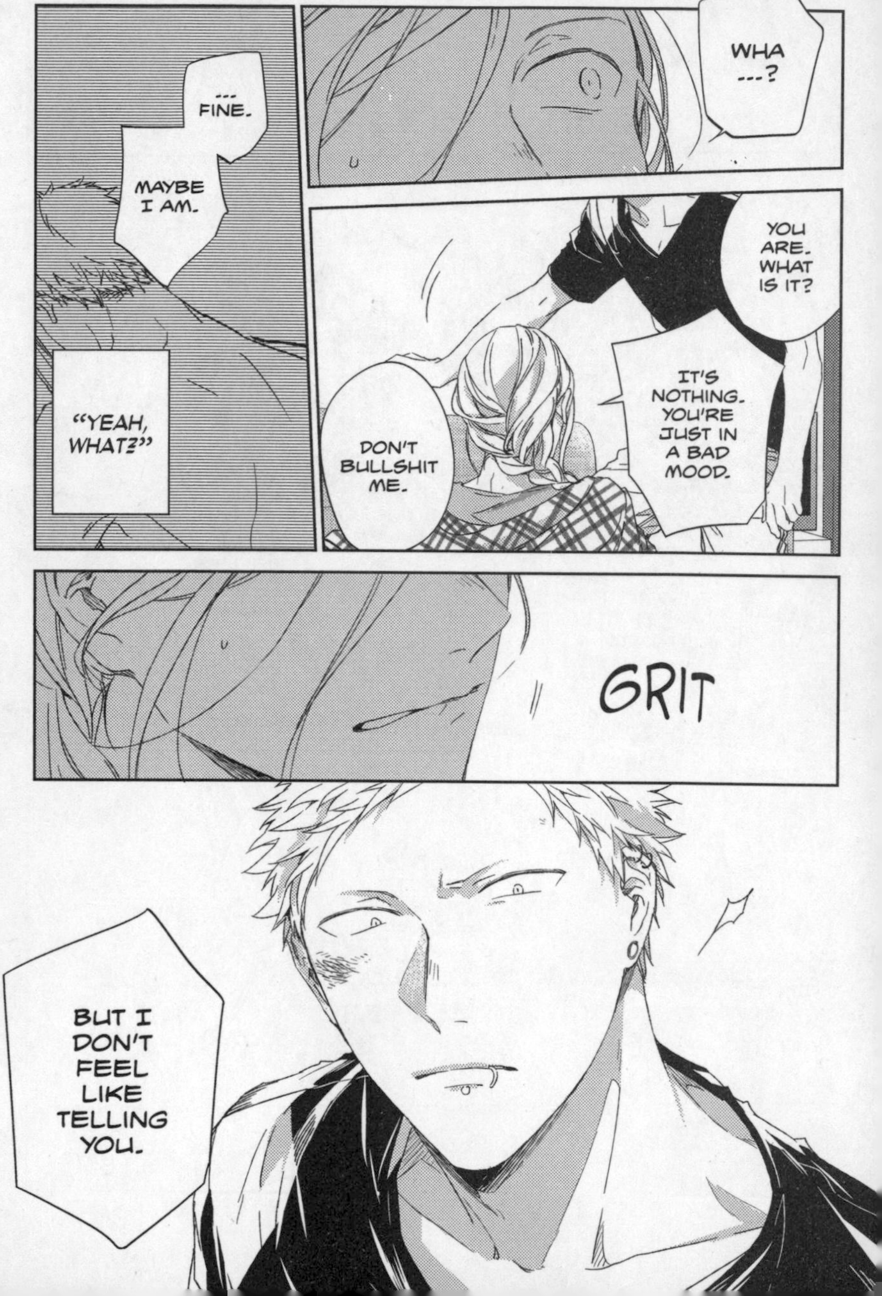
WHA ---?
YOU ARE. WHAT IS IT?
IT'S NOTHING. YOU'RE JUST IN A BAD MOOD.
DON'T BULLSHIT ME.
... FINE.
MAYBE I AM.
"YEAH, WHAT?"
GRIT
BUT I DON'T FEEL LIKE TELLING YOU.

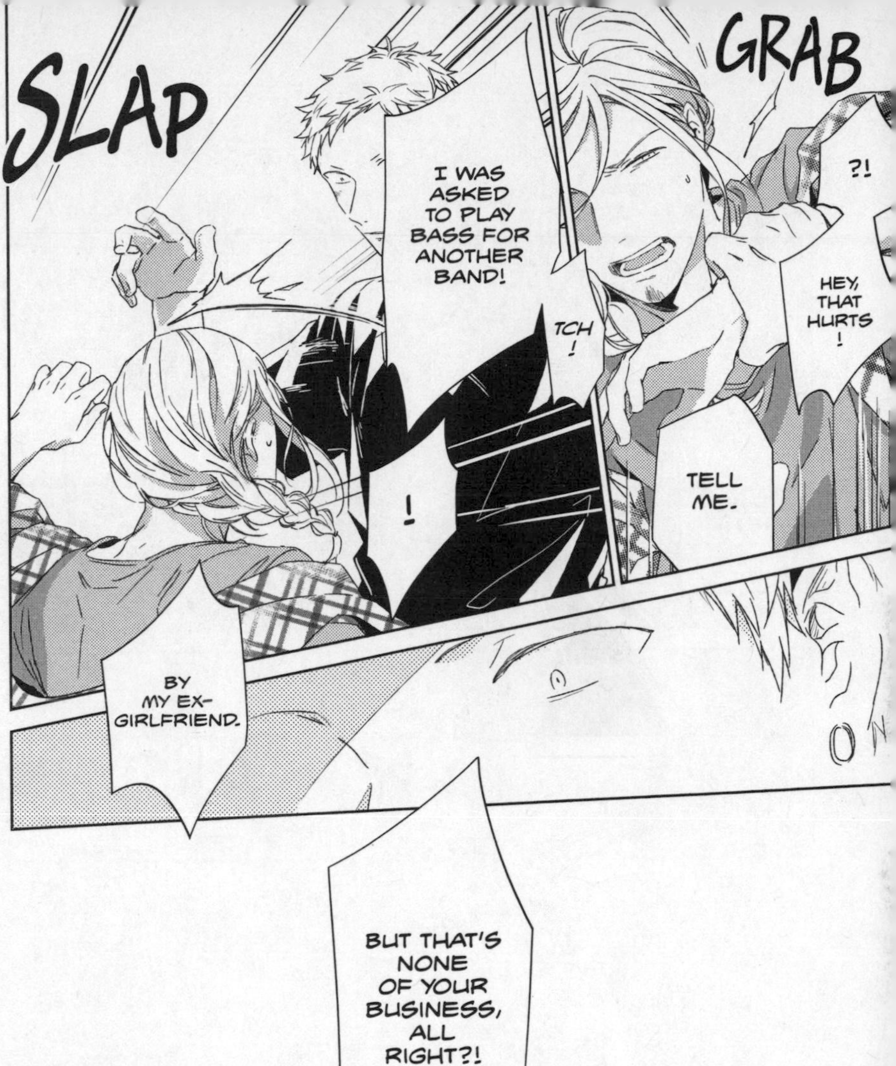
GRAB
?!
HEY, THAT HURTS!
TELL ME.
TCH!
I WAS ASKED TO PLAY BASS FOR ANOTHER BAND!
SLAP
!
BY MY EX-GIRLFRIEND.
BUT THAT'S NONE OF YOUR BUSINESS, ALL RIGHT?!

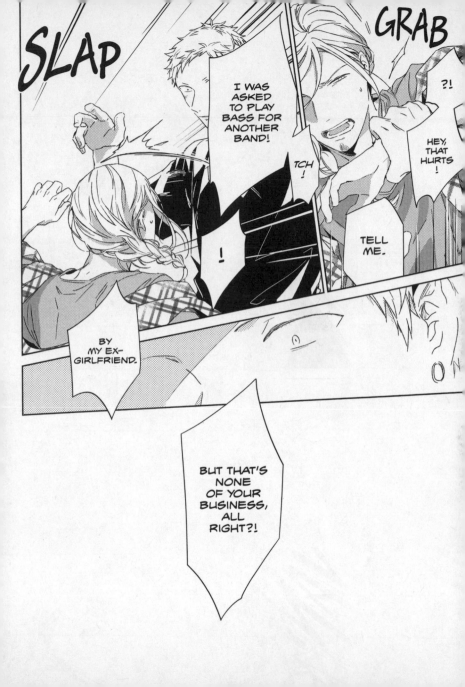

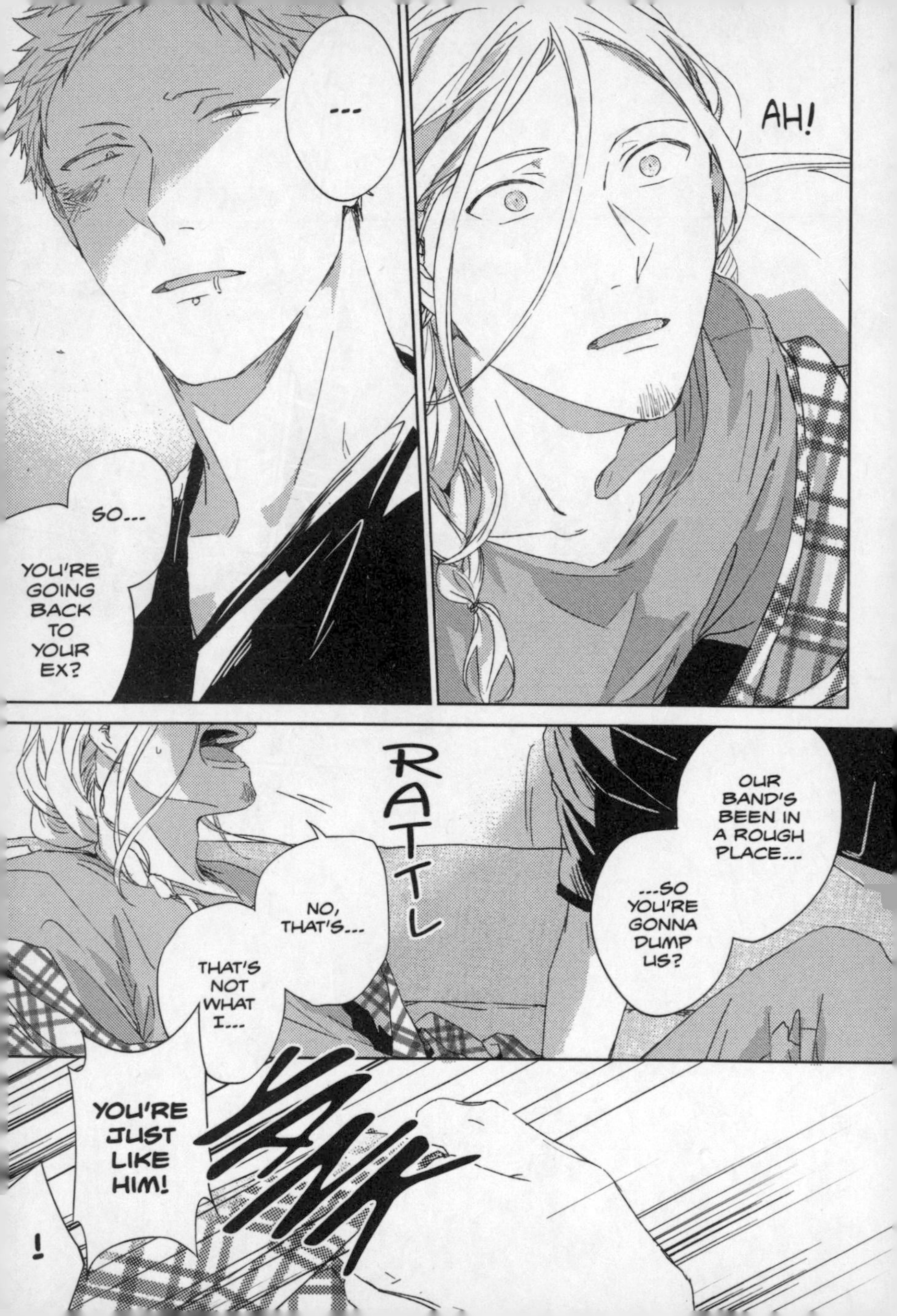
AH!
...
SO...
YOU'RE GOING BACK TO YOUR EX?
OUR BAND'S BEEN IN A ROUGH PLACE...
...SO YOU'RE GONNA DUMP US?
RATTL
NO, THAT'S...
THAT'S NOT WHAT I...
YOU'RE JUST LIKE HIM!
YANK
!

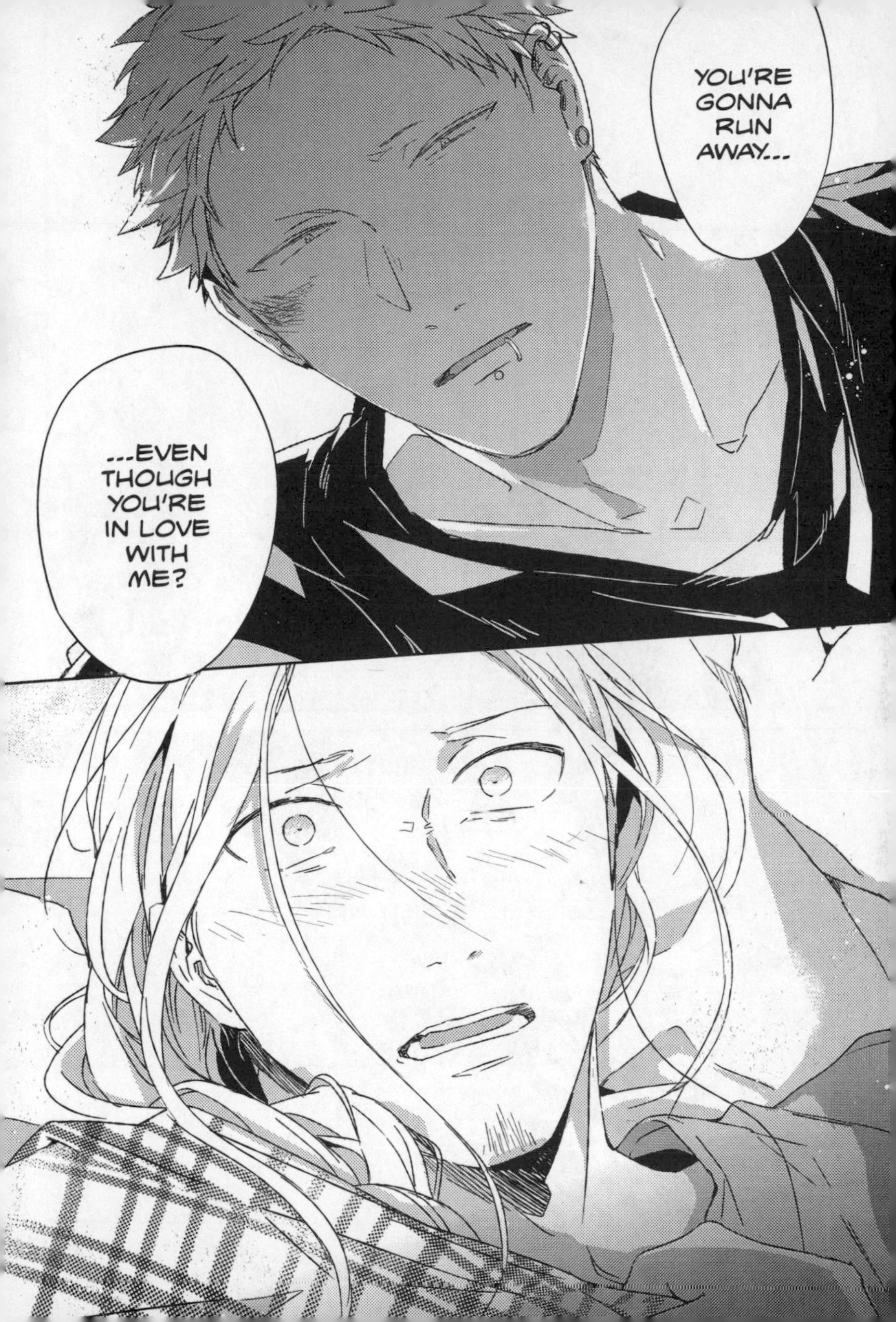
YOU'RE GONNA RUN AWAY...
...EVEN THOUGH YOU'RE IN LOVE WITH ME?

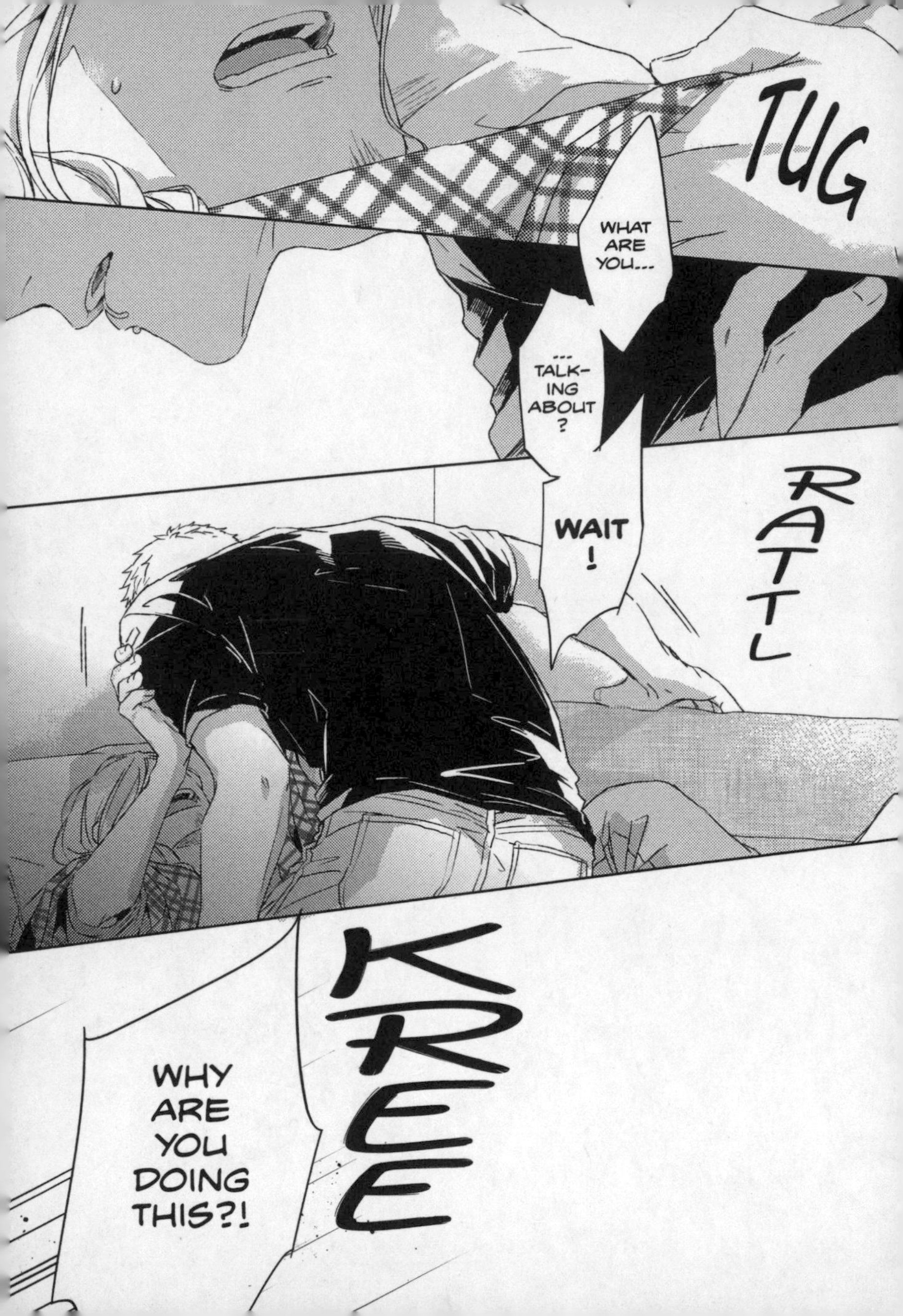
TUG
WHAT ARE YOU...
...TALKING ABOUT?
RATTL
WAIT!
KREE
WHY ARE YOU DOING THIS?!

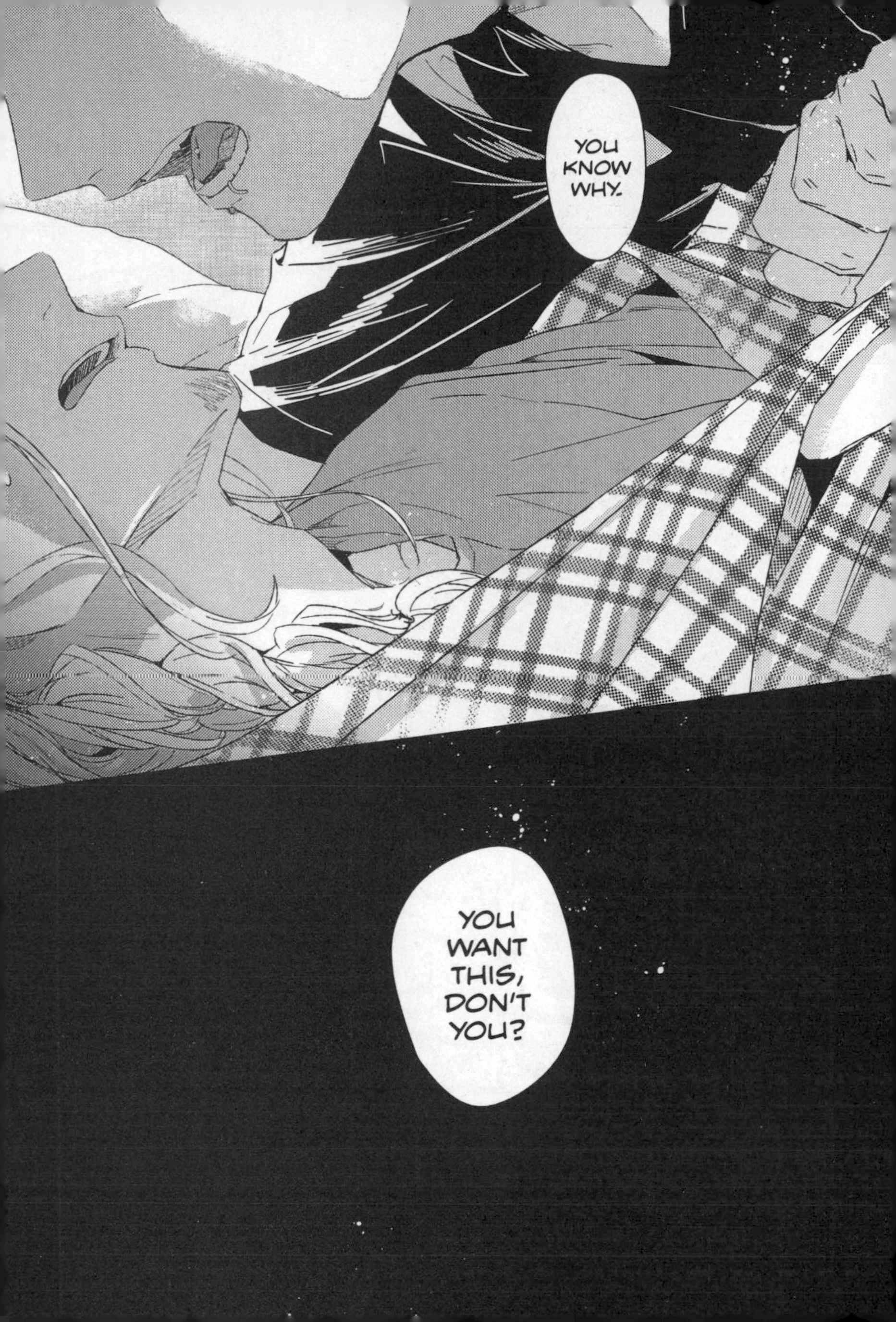
YOU KNOW WHY.
YOU WANT THIS, DON'T YOU?

given

by Natsuki Kizu

given

by Natsuki Kizu

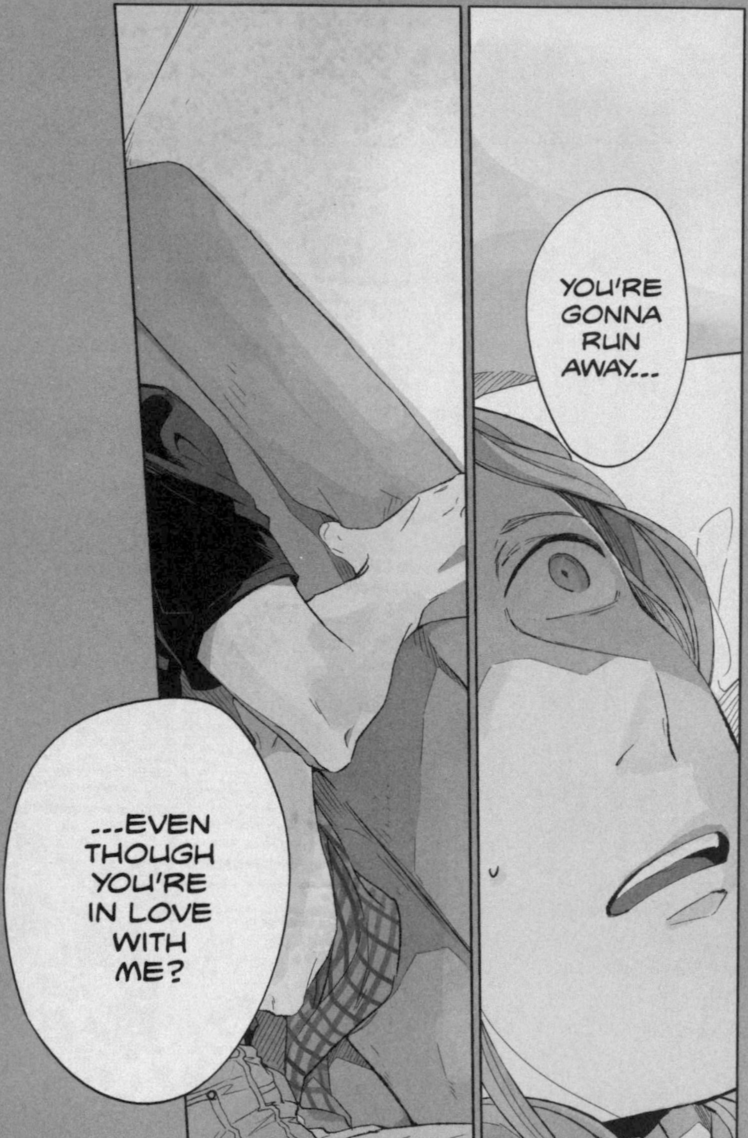
YOU'RE GONNA RUN AWAY...
...EVEN THOUGH YOU'RE IN LOVE WITH ME?

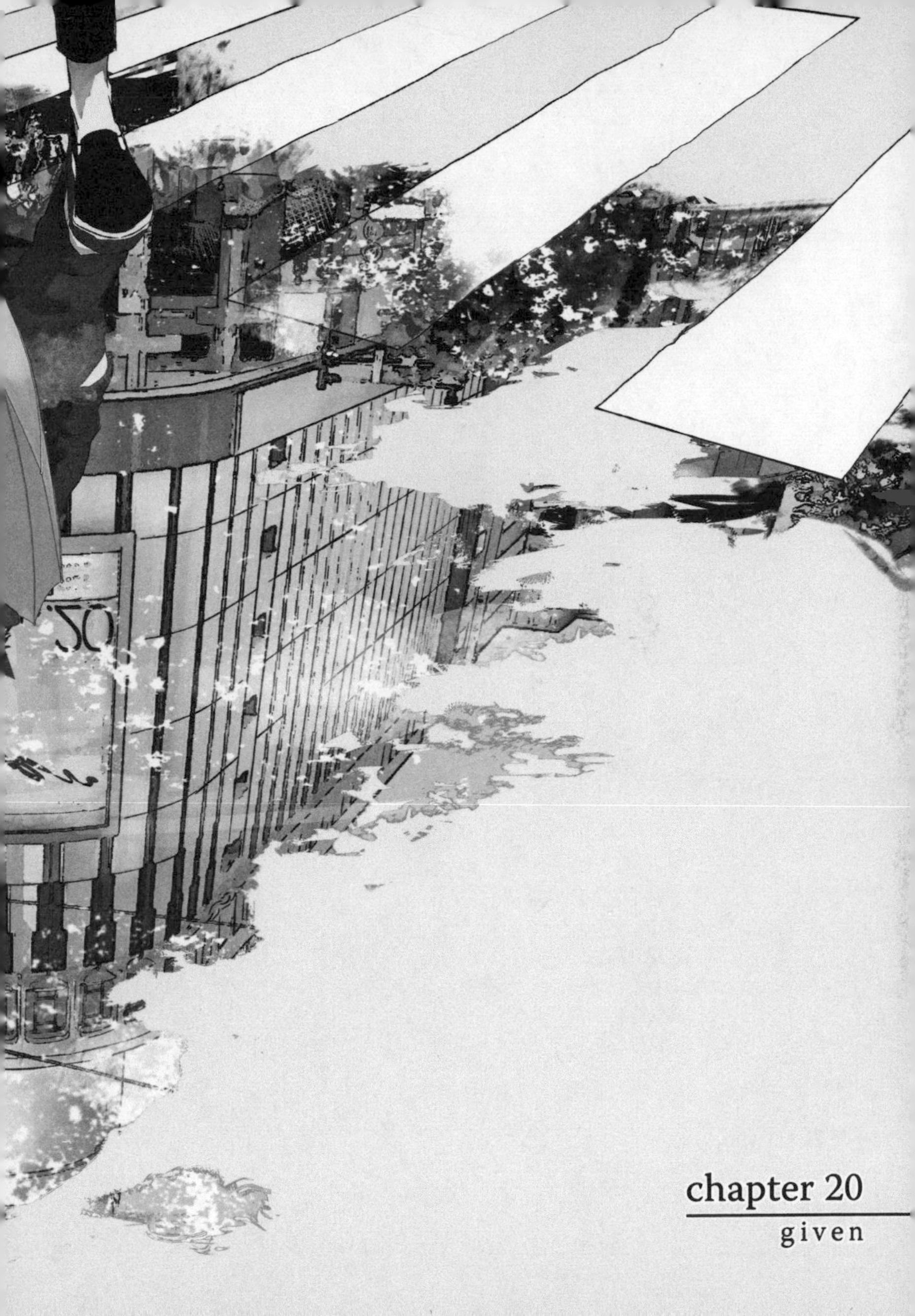

chapter 20
given

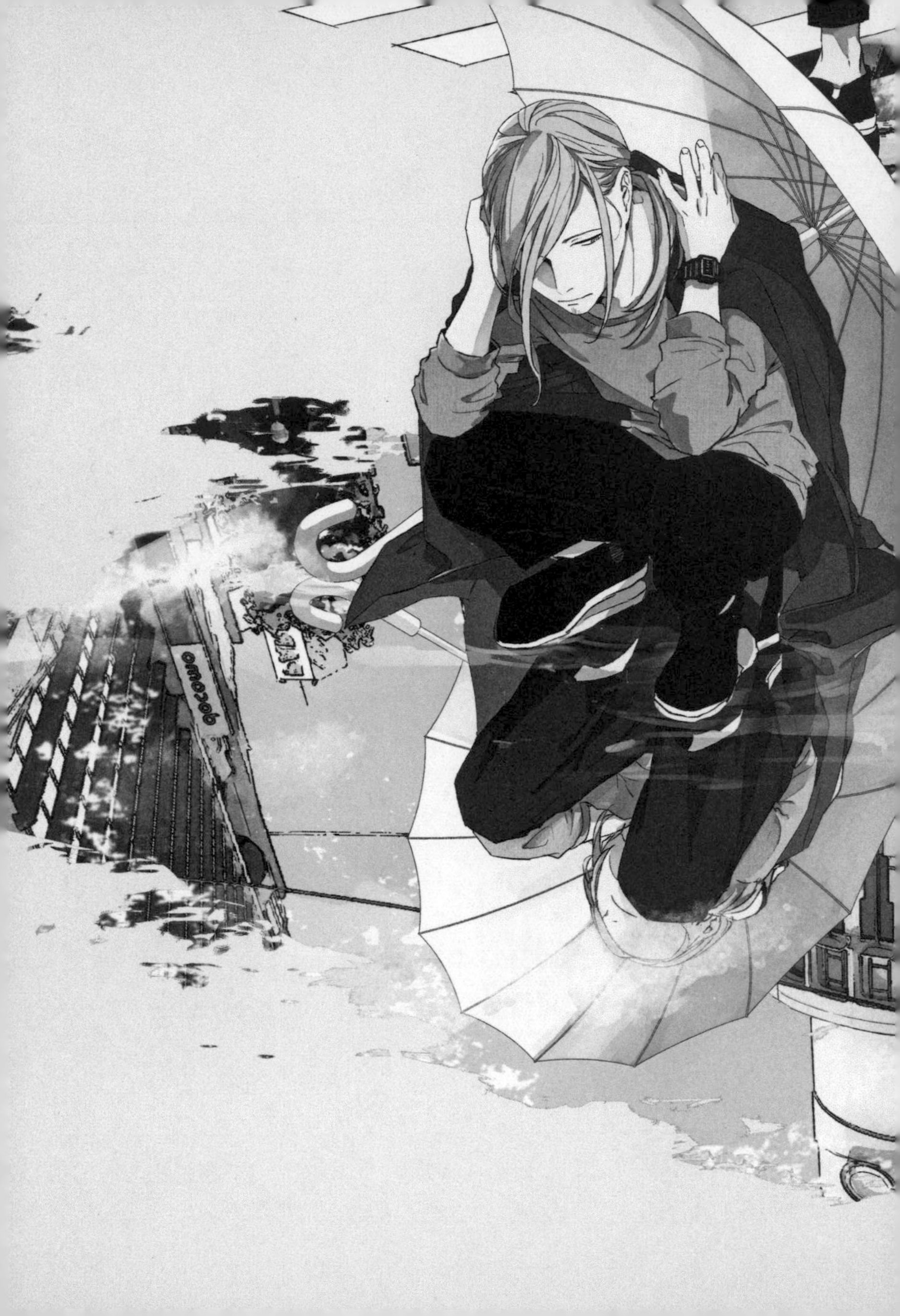

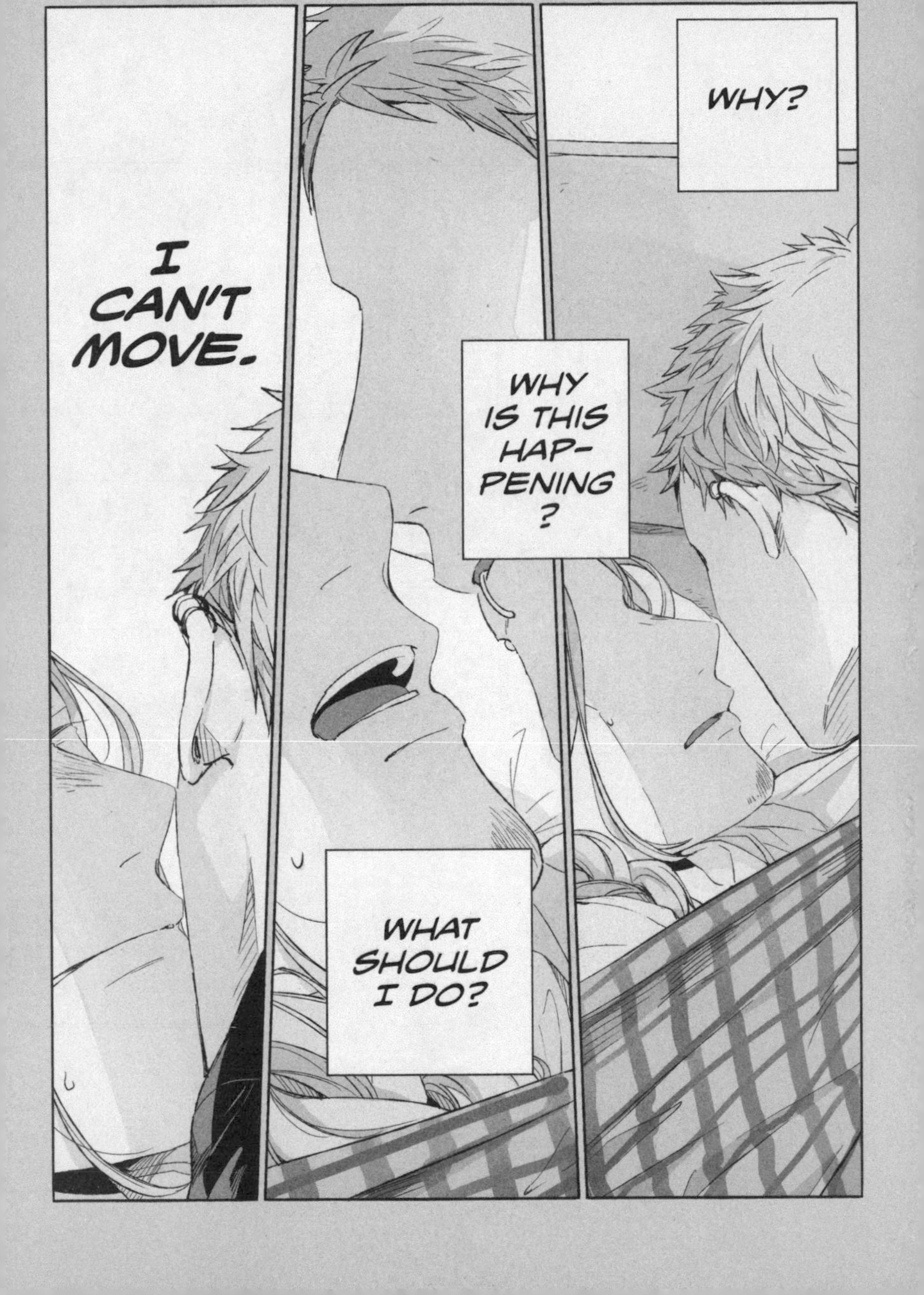
WHY?
WHY IS THIS HAP-PENING?
WHAT SHOULD I DO?
I CAN'T MOVE.

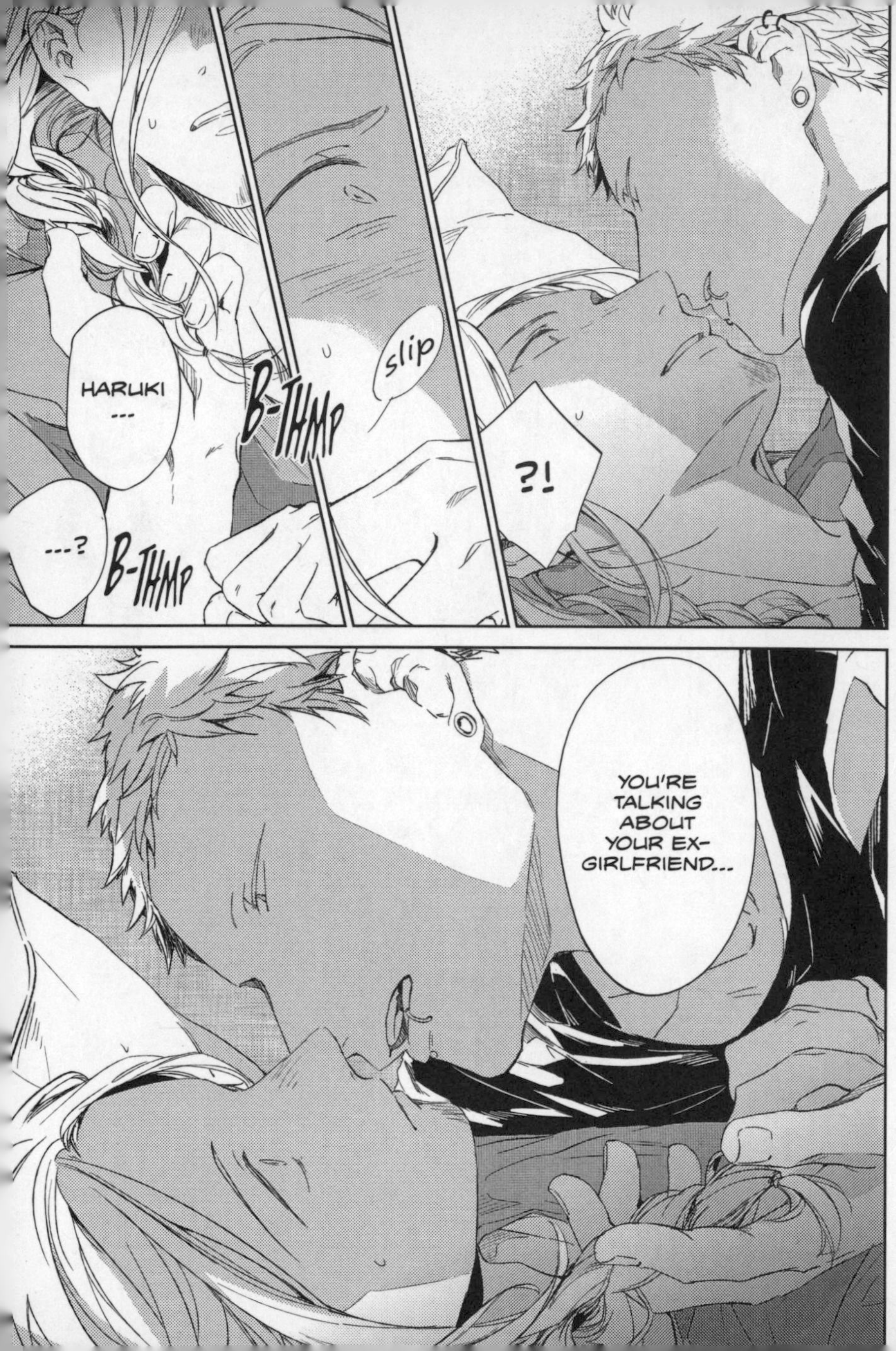
?!
slip
B-THMP
HARUKI ---
---?
B-THMP
YOU'RE TALKING ABOUT YOUR EX-GIRLFRIEND...

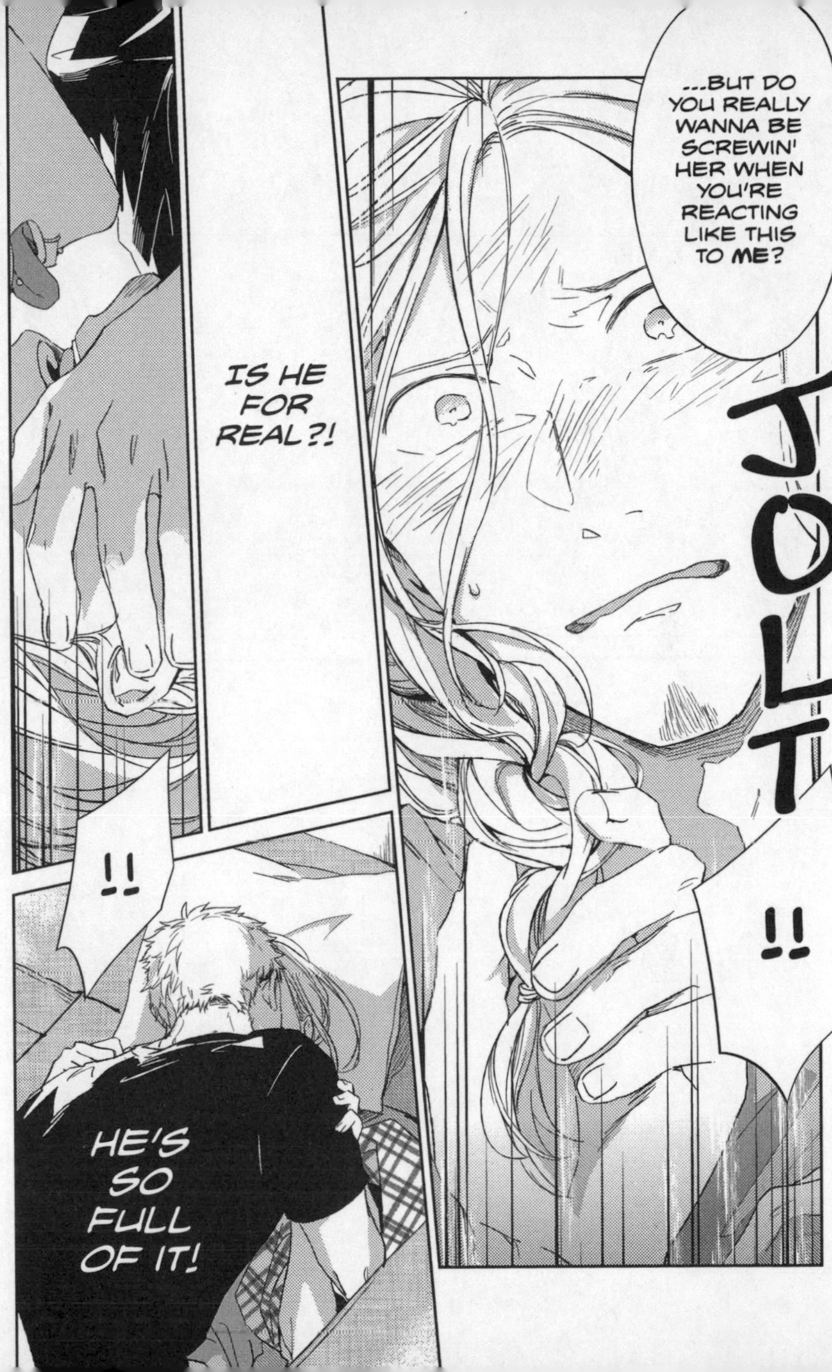
...BUT DO YOU REALLY WANNA BE SCREWIN' HER WHEN YOU'RE REACTING LIKE THIS TO ME?
JOLT
!!
IS HE FOR REAL?!
!!
HE'S SO FULL OF IT!

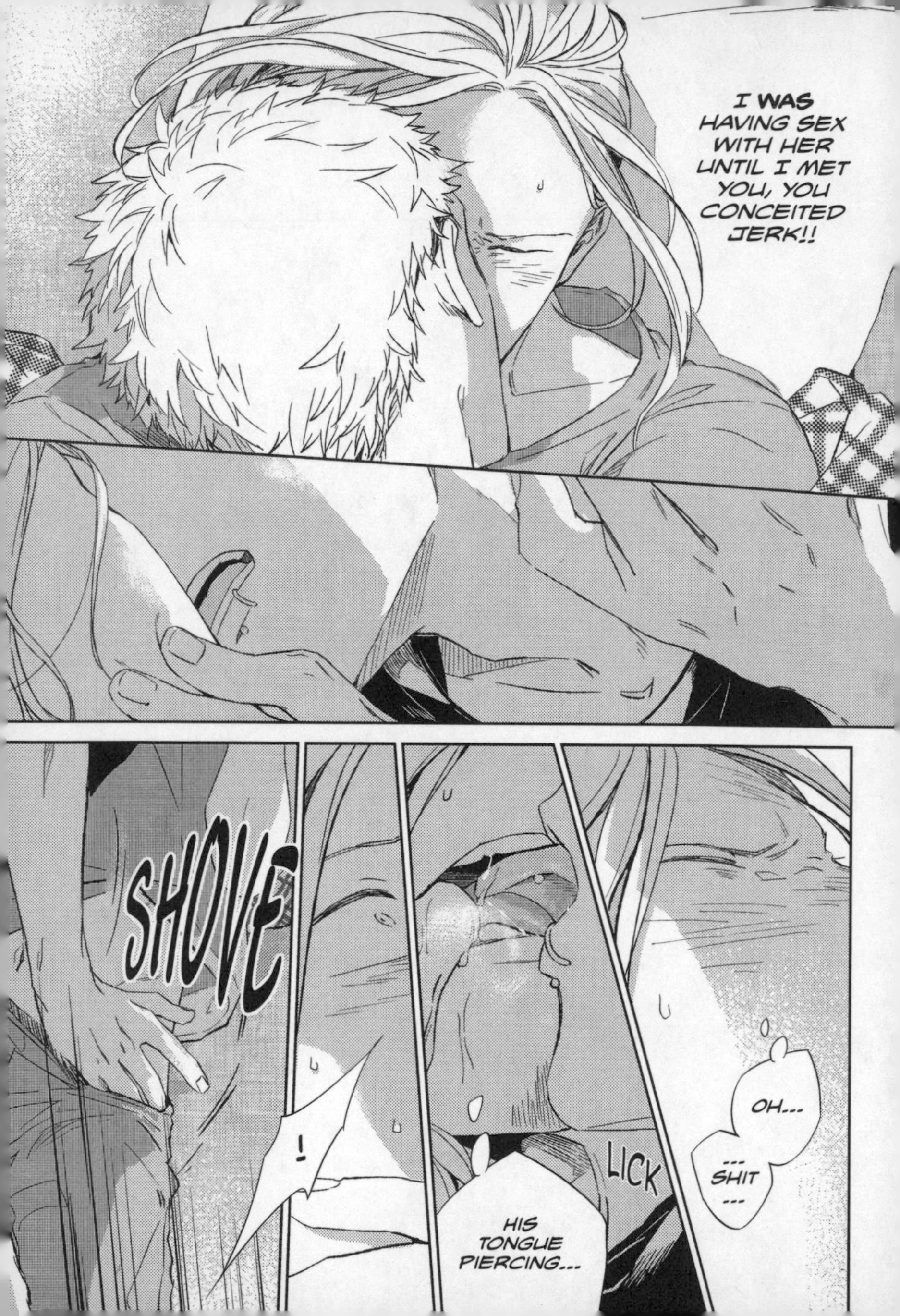
I WAS HAVING SEX WITH HER UNTIL I MET YOU, YOU CONCEITED JERK!!
OH...
...SHIT...
LICK
HIS TONGUE PIERCING...
!
SHOVE

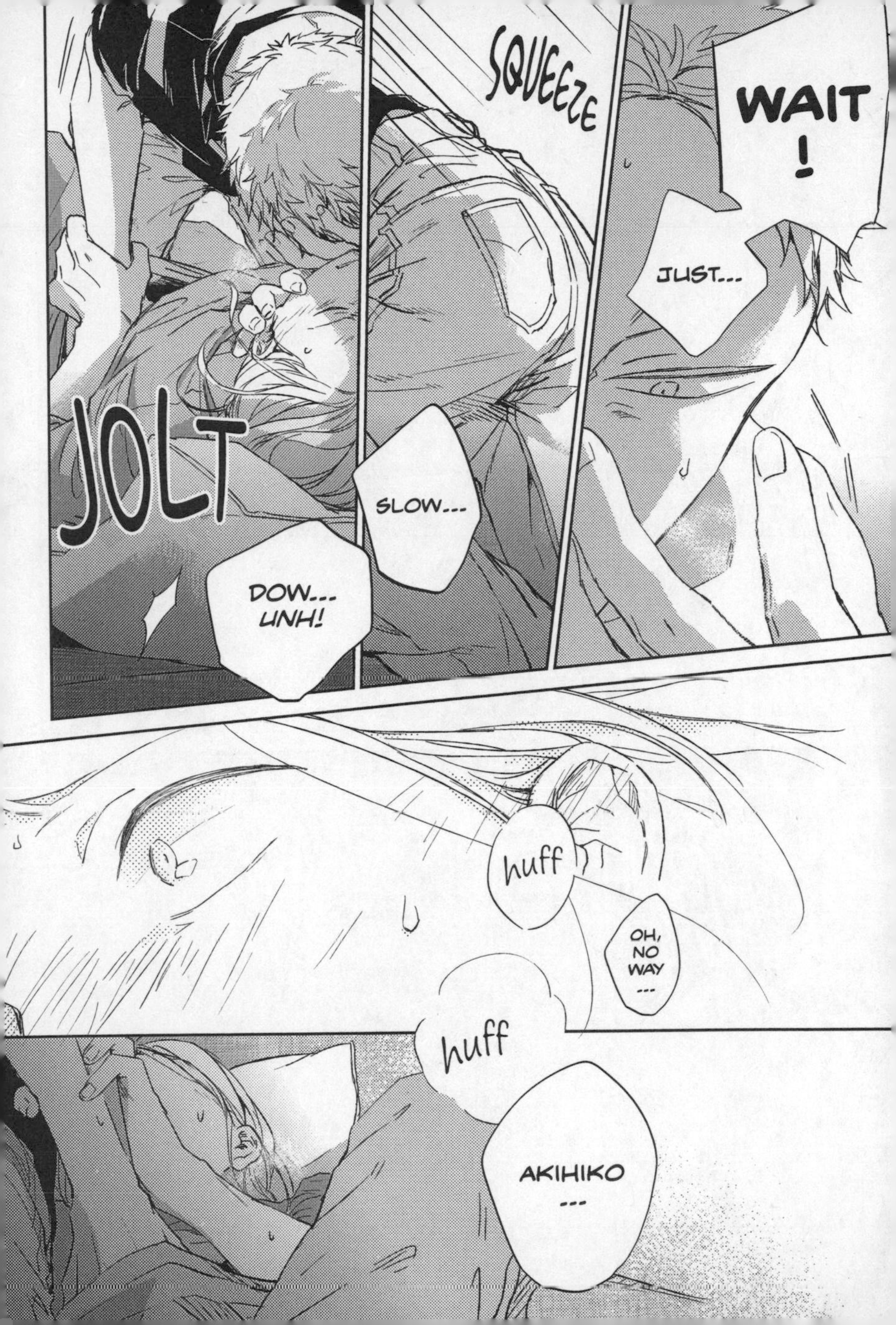
WAIT !
JUST...
SQUEEZE
SLOW...
JOLT
DOW... UNH!
huff
OH, NO WAY ...
huff
AKIHIKO ...

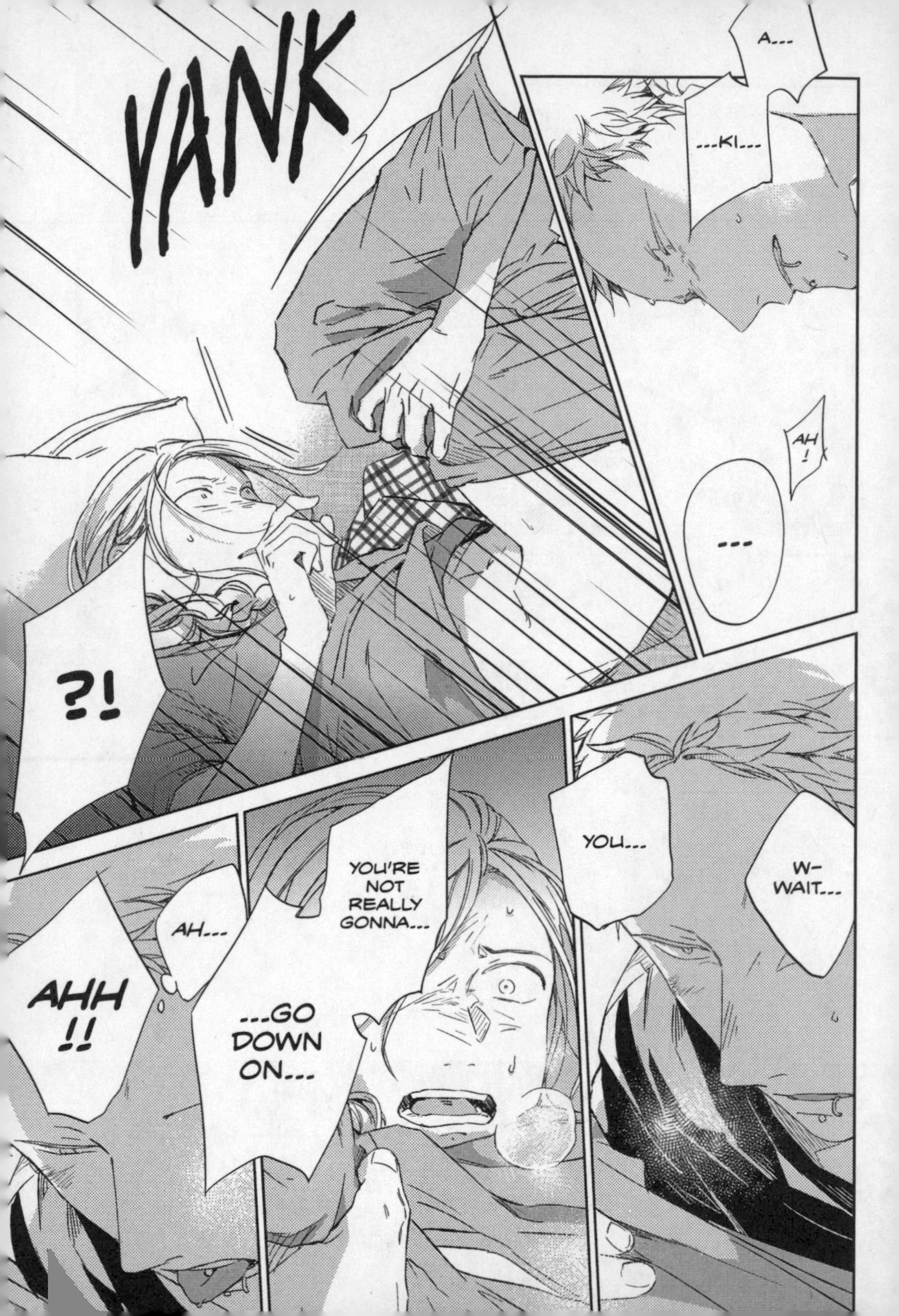
A...
...KI...
AH!
...
YANK
?!
W-WAIT...
YOU...
YOU'RE NOT REALLY GONNA...
...GO DOWN ON...
AH...
AHH!!

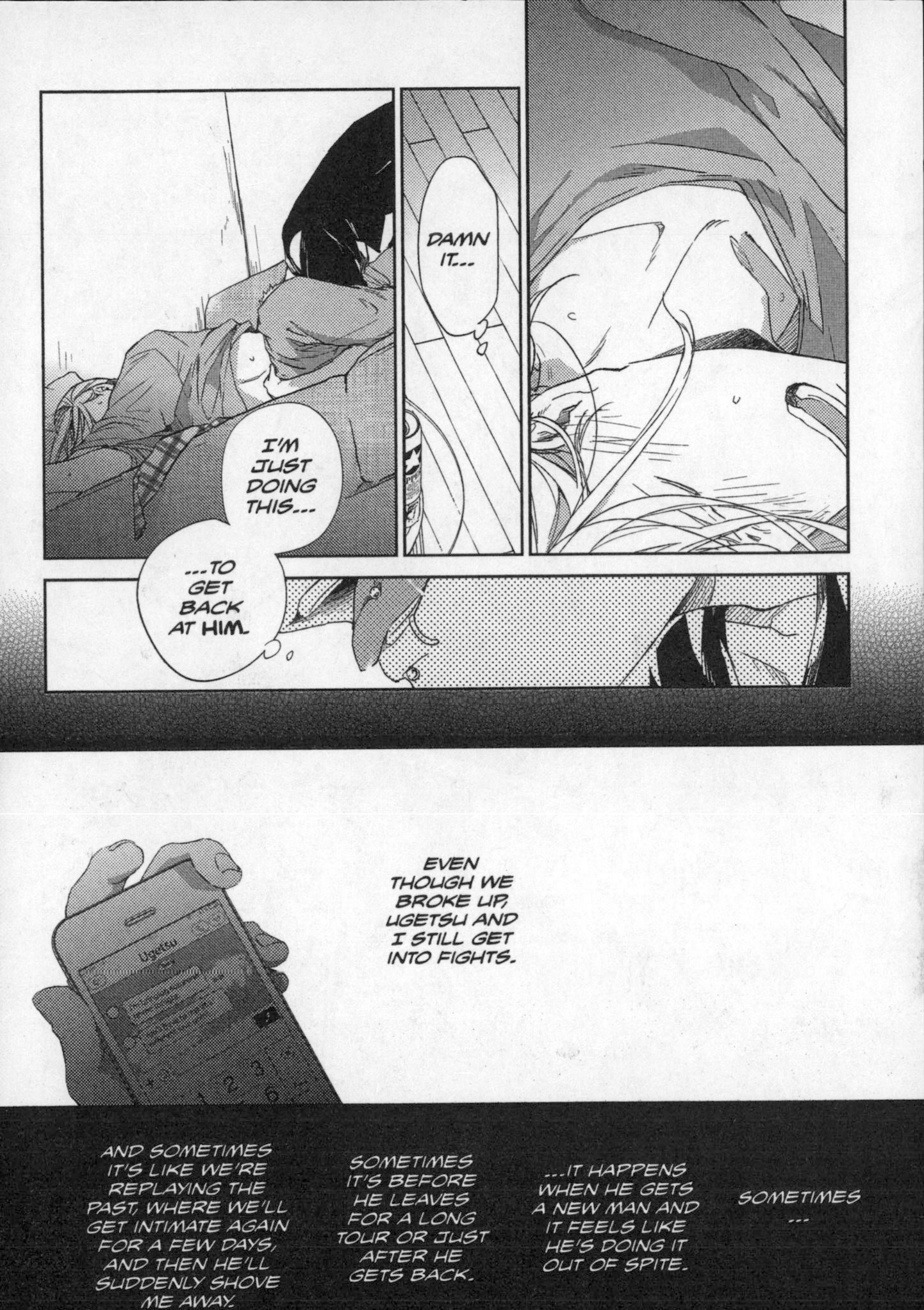
DAMN IT...
I'M JUST DOING THIS...
...TO GET BACK AT HIM.
EVEN THOUGH WE BROKE UP, UGETSU AND I STILL GET INTO FIGHTS.
Ugetsu
SOMETIMES ...
...IT HAPPENS WHEN HE GETS A NEW MAN AND IT FEELS LIKE HE'S DOING IT OUT OF SPITE.
SOMETIMES IT'S BEFORE HE LEAVES FOR A LONG TOUR OR JUST AFTER HE GETS BACK.
AND SOMETIMES IT'S LIKE WE'RE REPLAYING THE PAST, WHERE WE'LL GET INTIMATE AGAIN FOR A FEW DAYS, AND THEN HE'LL SUDDENLY SHOVE ME AWAY.

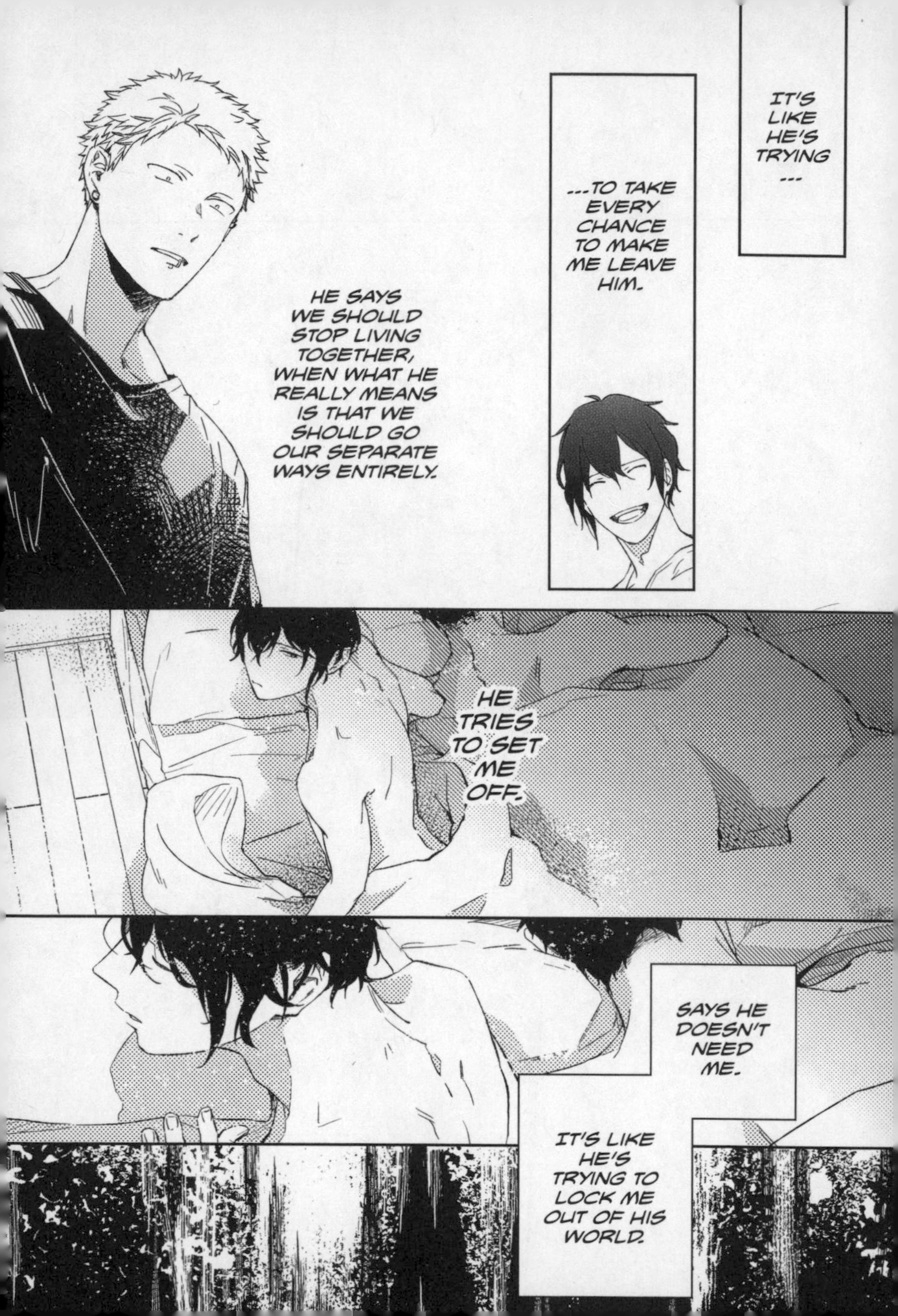
IT'S LIKE HE'S TRYING ---
---TO TAKE EVERY CHANCE TO MAKE ME LEAVE HIM.
HE SAYS WE SHOULD STOP LIVING TOGETHER, WHEN WHAT HE REALLY MEANS IS THAT WE SHOULD GO OUR SEPARATE WAYS ENTIRELY.
HE TRIES TO SET ME OFF.
SAYS HE DOESN'T NEED ME.
IT'S LIKE HE'S TRYING TO LOCK ME OUT OF HIS WORLD.

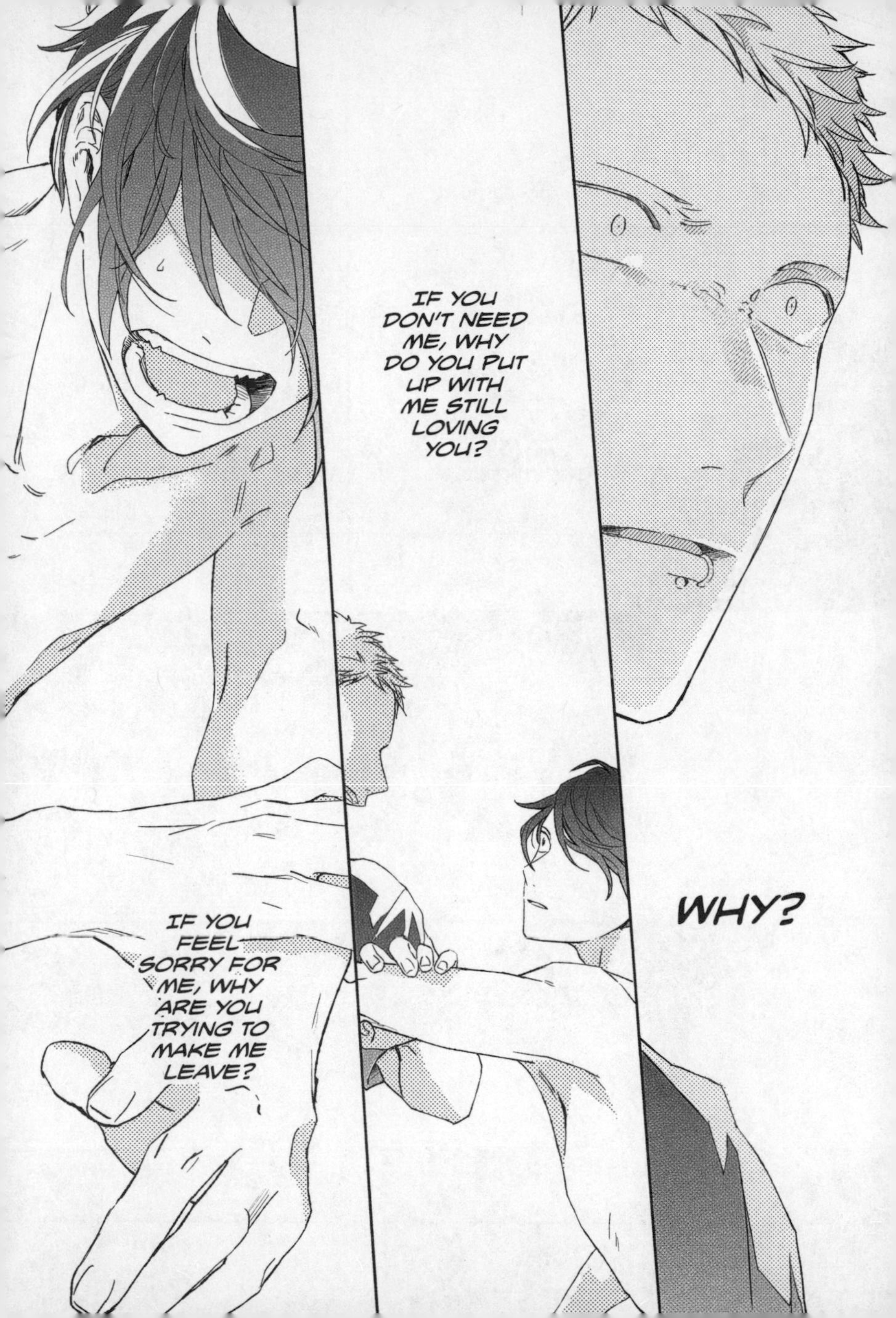
IF YOU DON'T NEED ME, WHY DO YOU PUT UP WITH ME STILL LOVING YOU?
IF YOU FEEL SORRY FOR ME, WHY ARE YOU TRYING TO MAKE ME LEAVE?
WHY?

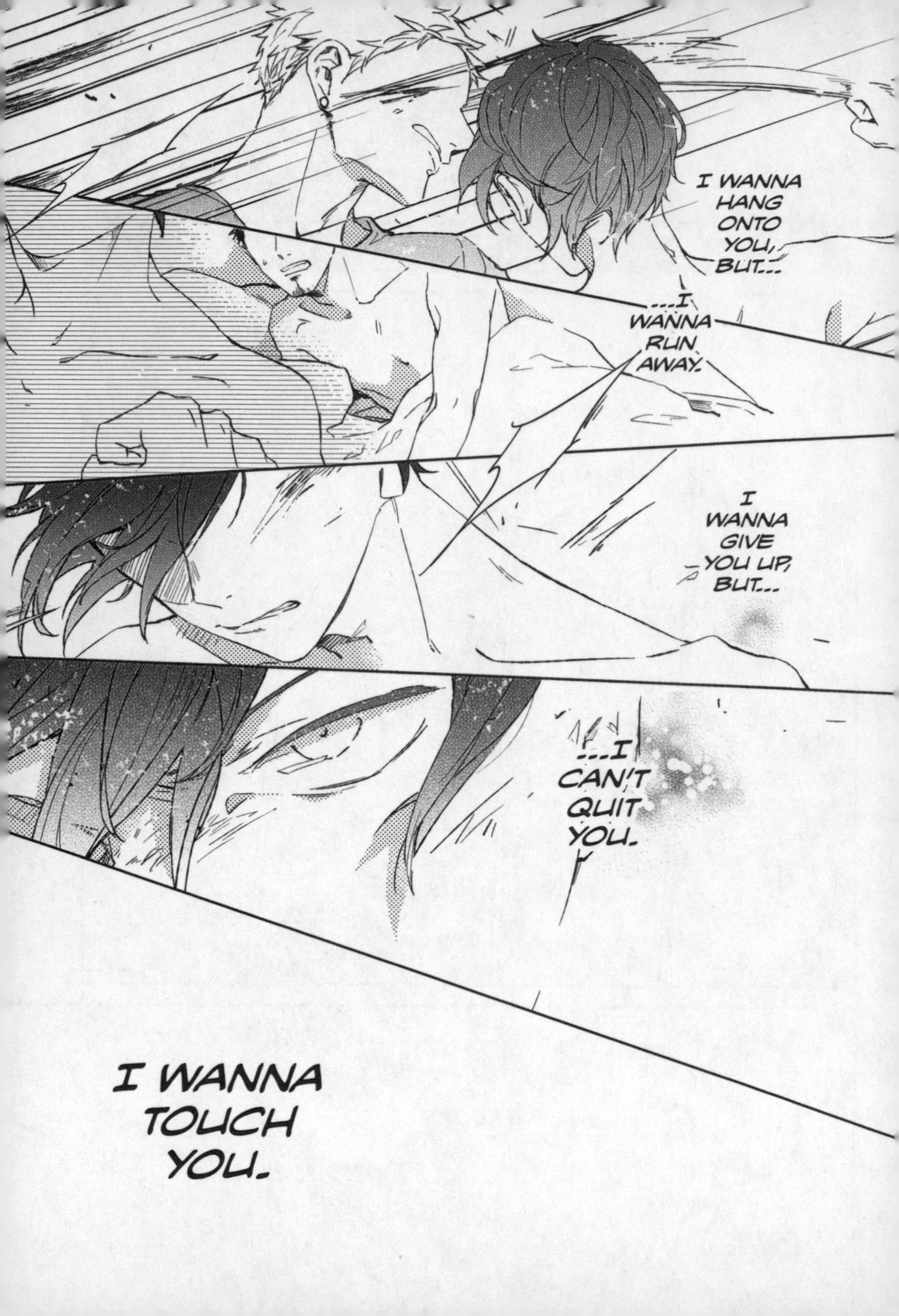
I WANNA HANG ONTO YOU, BUT...
...I WANNA RUN AWAY.
I WANNA GIVE YOU UP, BUT...
...I CAN'T QUIT YOU.
I WANNA TOUCH YOU.

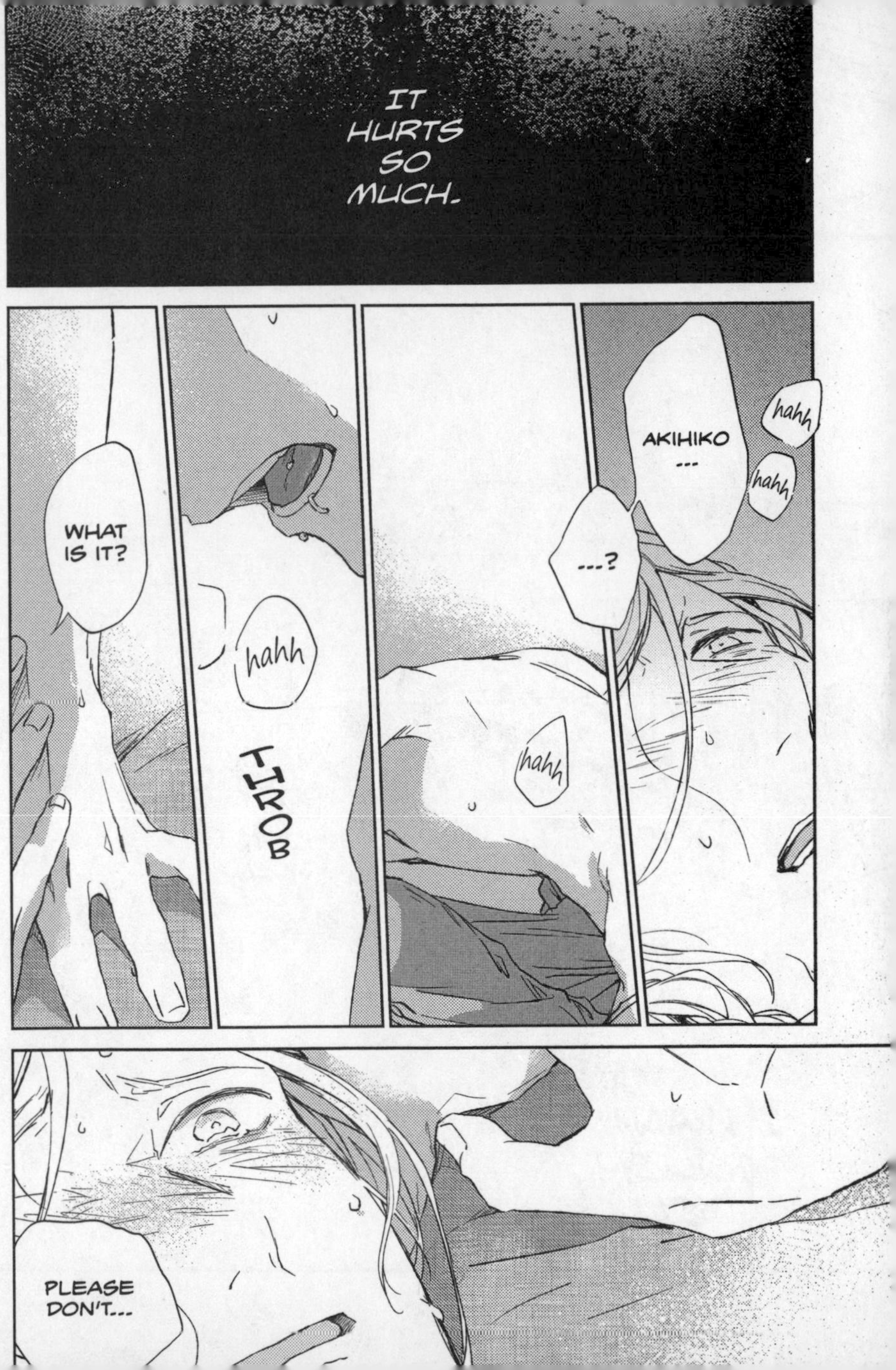
IT HURTS SO MUCH.
hahh
AKIHIKO ...
hahh
...?
hahh
hahh
THROB
WHAT IS IT?
PLEASE DON'T...

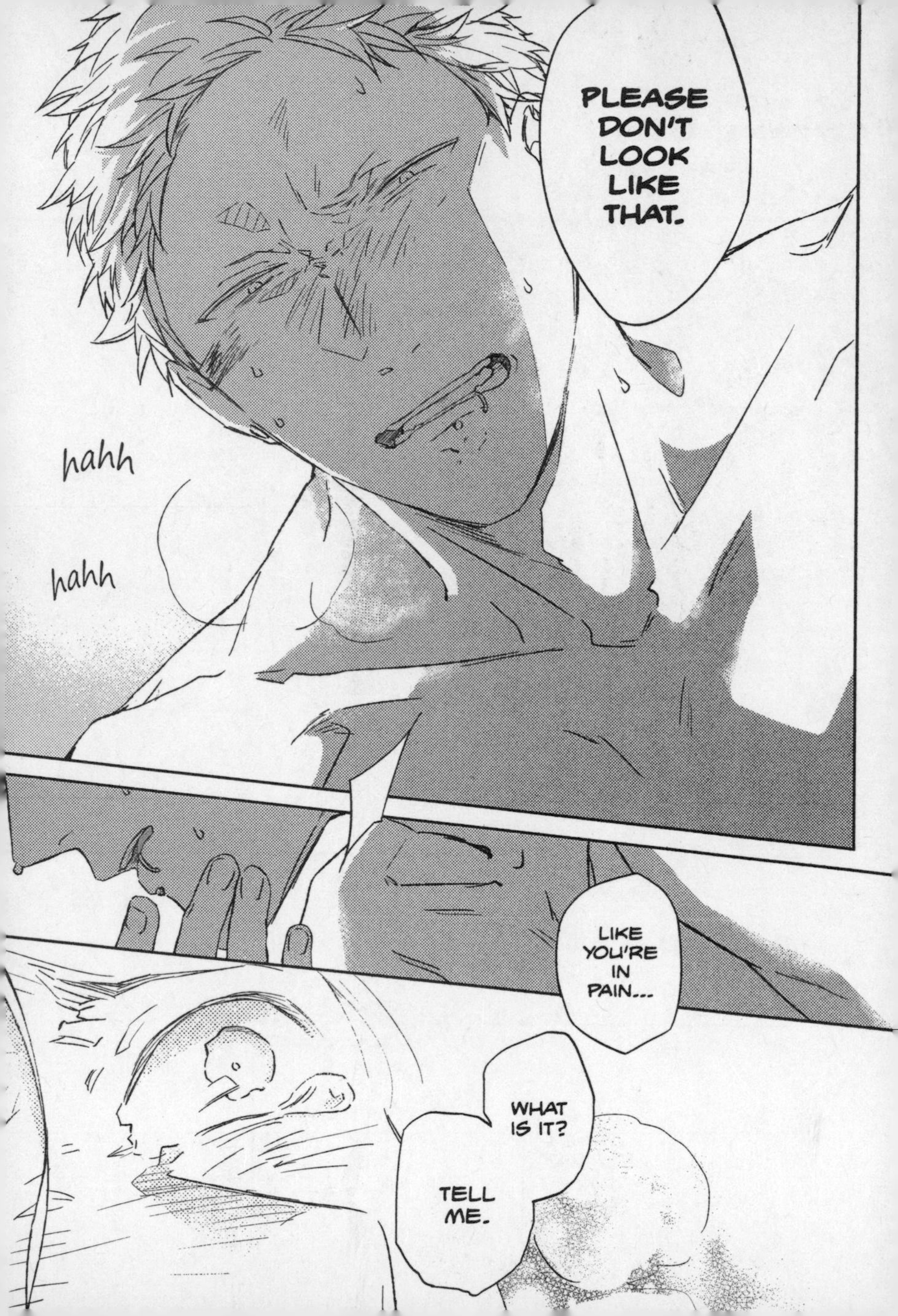
PLEASE DON'T LOOK LIKE THAT.
hahh
hahh
LIKE YOU'RE IN PAIN...
WHAT IS IT?
TELL ME.

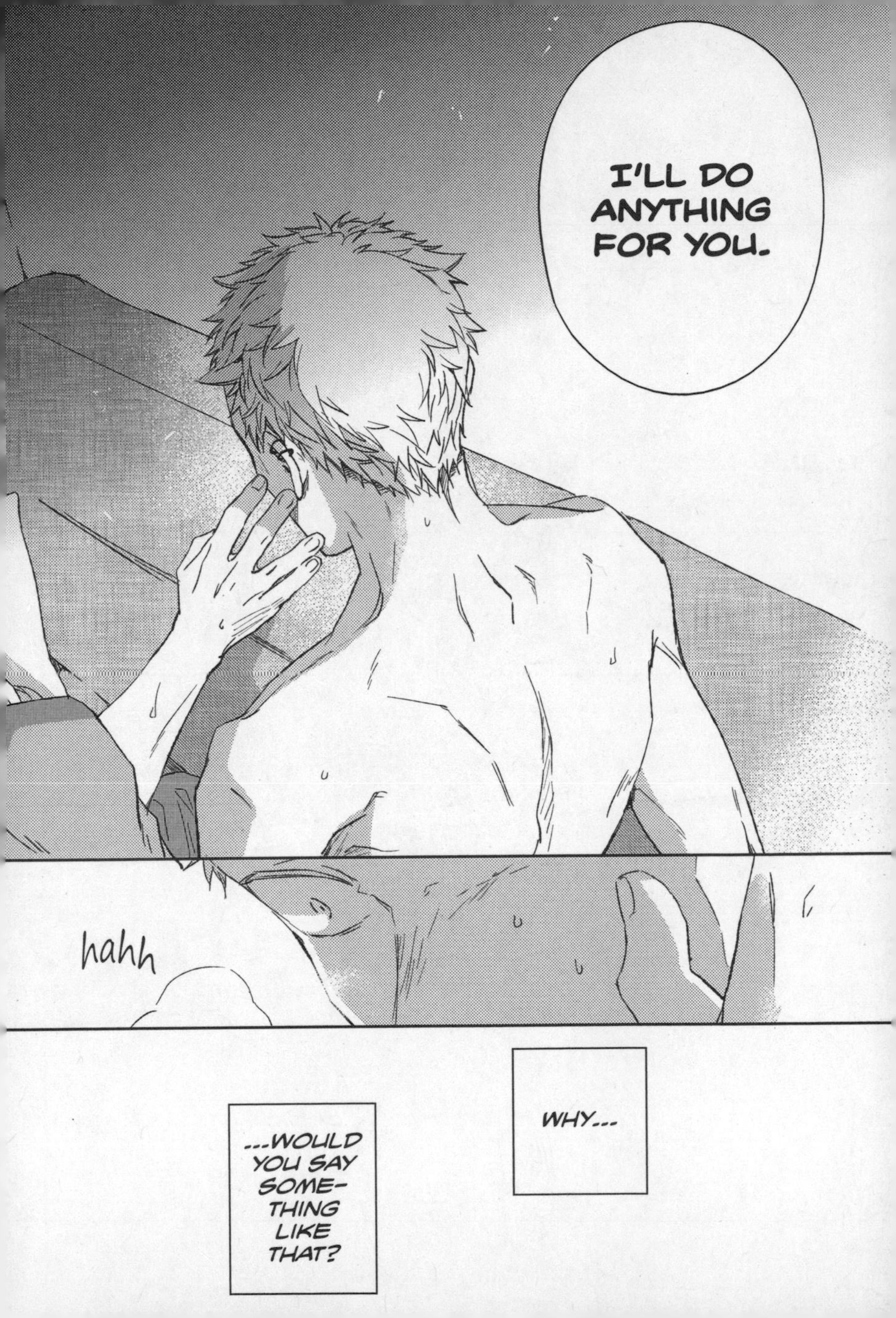
I'LL DO ANYTHING FOR YOU.
hahh
WHY...
...WOULD YOU SAY SOME-THING LIKE THAT?

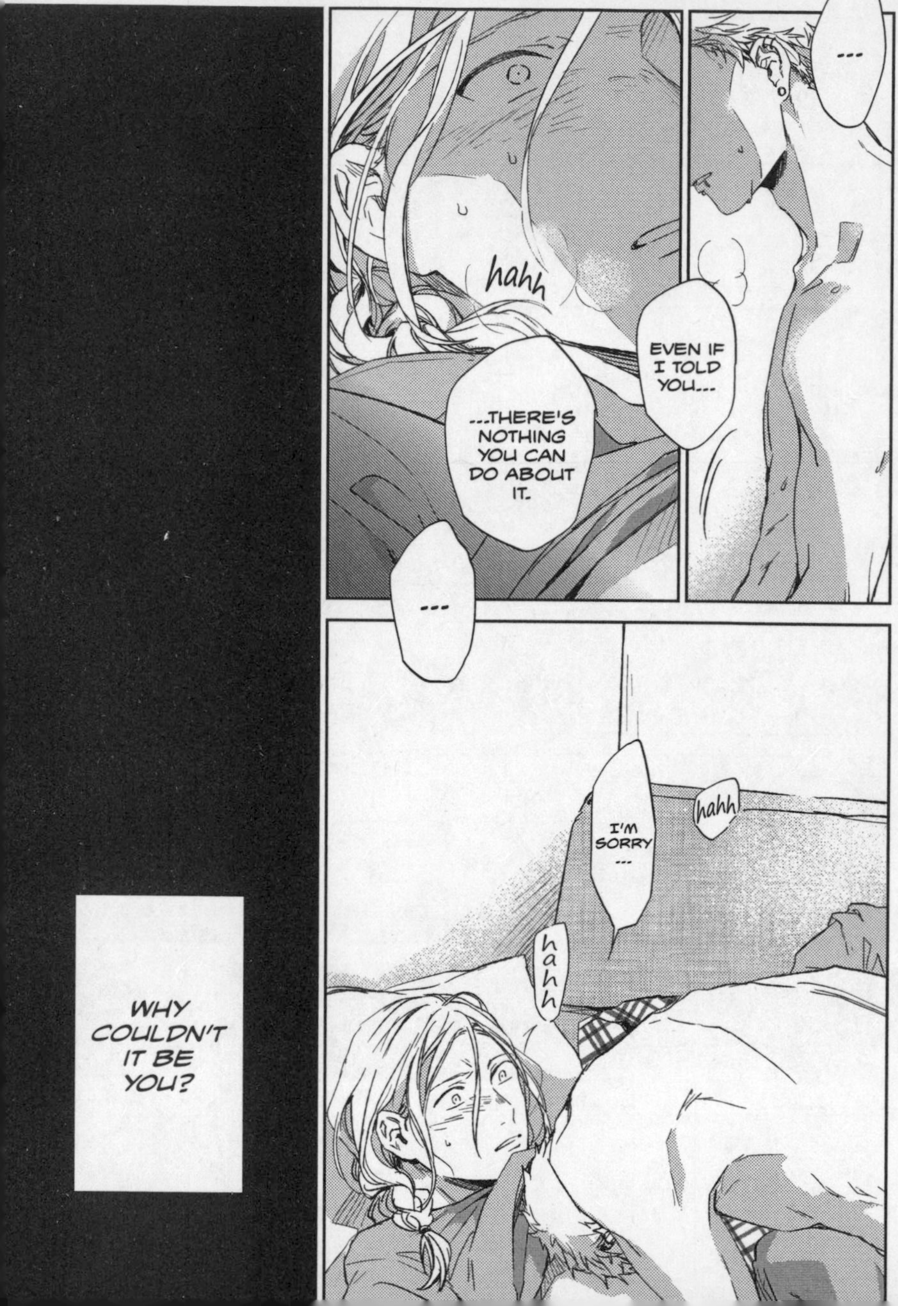
...
EVEN IF I TOLD YOU...
hahh
...THERE'S NOTHING YOU CAN DO ABOUT IT.
...
hahh
I'M SORRY ...
hahh
WHY COULDN'T IT BE YOU?

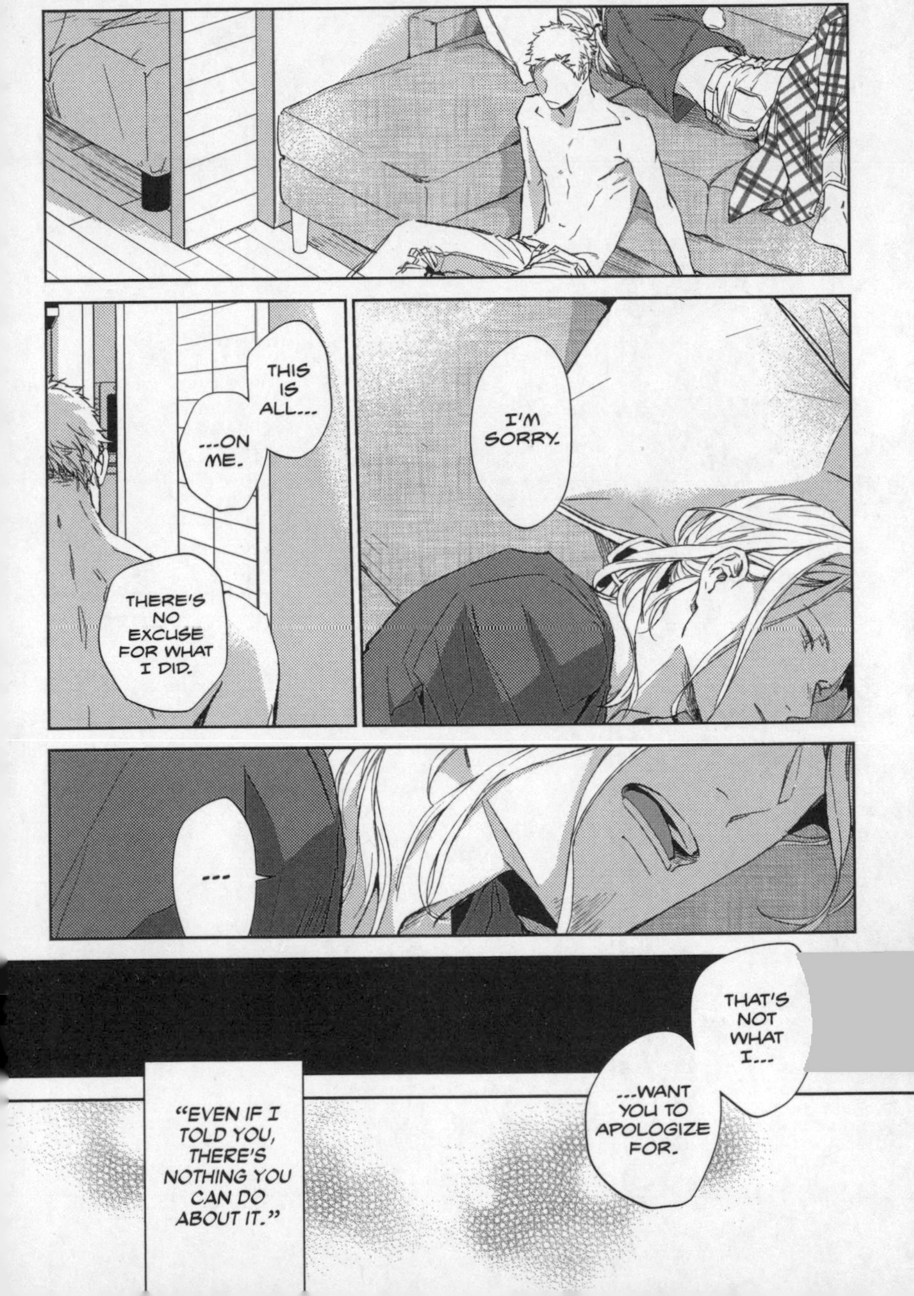
I'M SORRY.
THIS IS ALL...
...ON ME.
THERE'S NO EXCUSE FOR WHAT I DID.
...
THAT'S NOT WHAT I...
...WANT YOU TO APOLOGIZE FOR.
"EVEN IF I TOLD YOU, THERE'S NOTHING YOU CAN DO ABOUT IT."

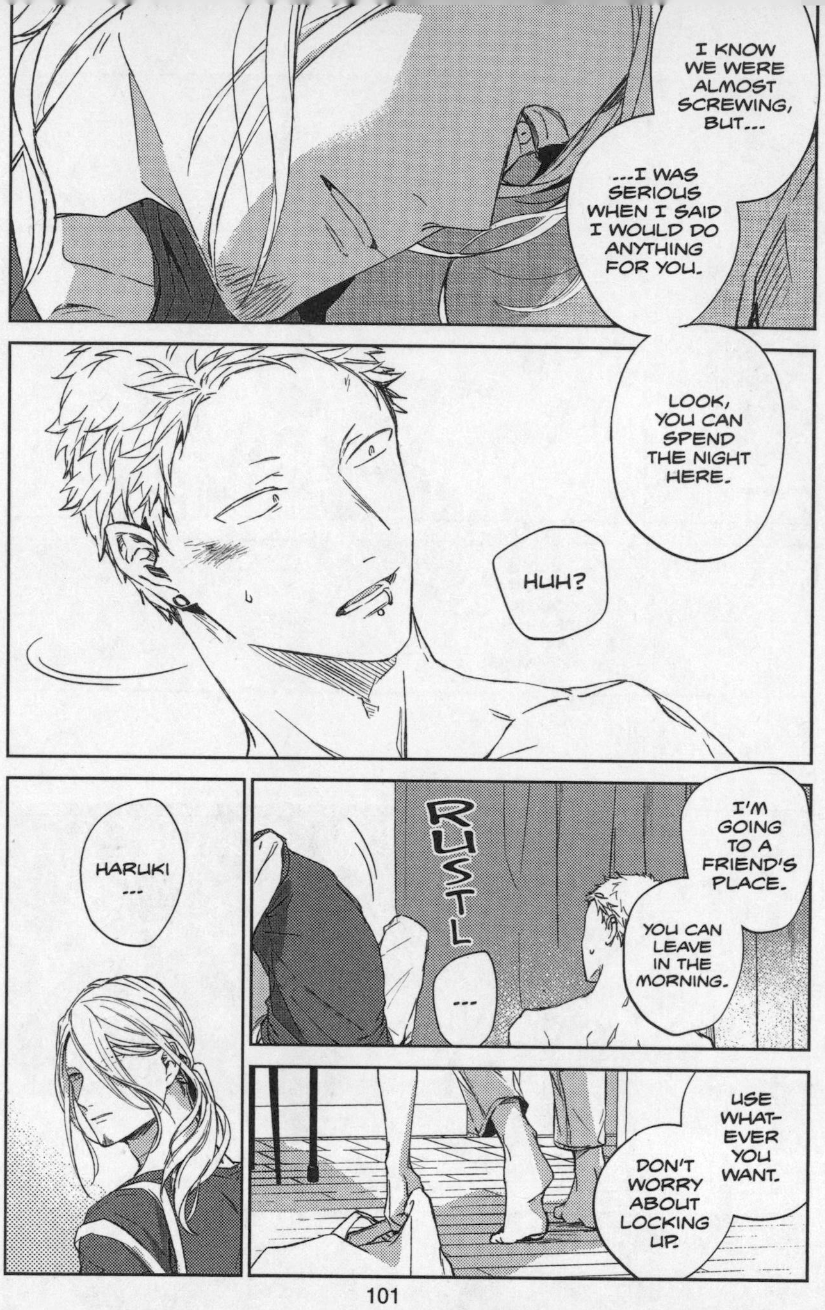
I KNOW WE WERE ALMOST SCREWING, BUT...
...I WAS SERIOUS WHEN I SAID I WOULD DO ANYTHING FOR YOU.
LOOK, YOU CAN SPEND THE NIGHT HERE.
HUH?
I'M GOING TO A FRIEND'S PLACE.
YOU CAN LEAVE IN THE MORNING.
RUSTL
...
USE WHAT-EVER YOU WANT.
DON'T WORRY ABOUT LOCKING UP.
HARUKI...

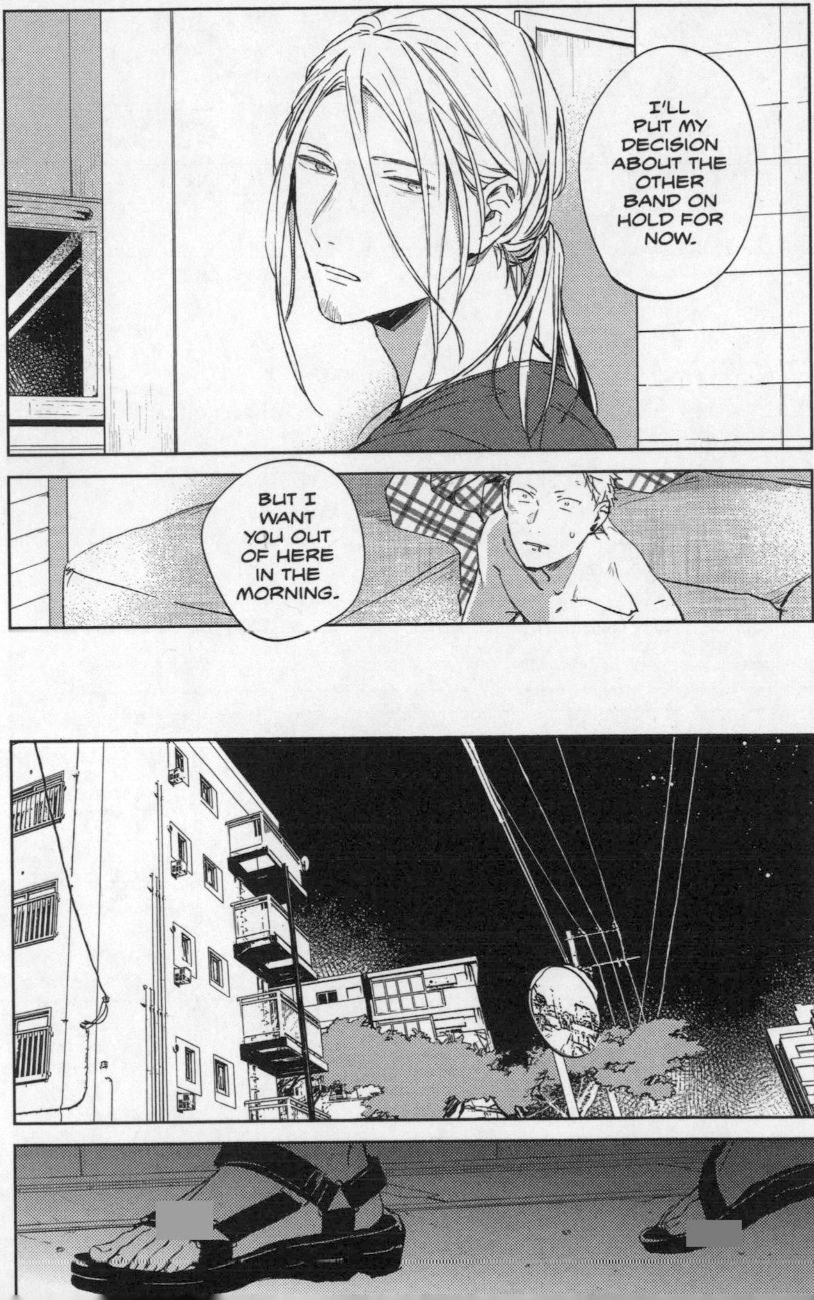
I'LL PUT MY DECISION ABOUT THE OTHER BAND ON HOLD FOR NOW.
BUT I WANT YOU OUT OF HERE IN THE MORNING.

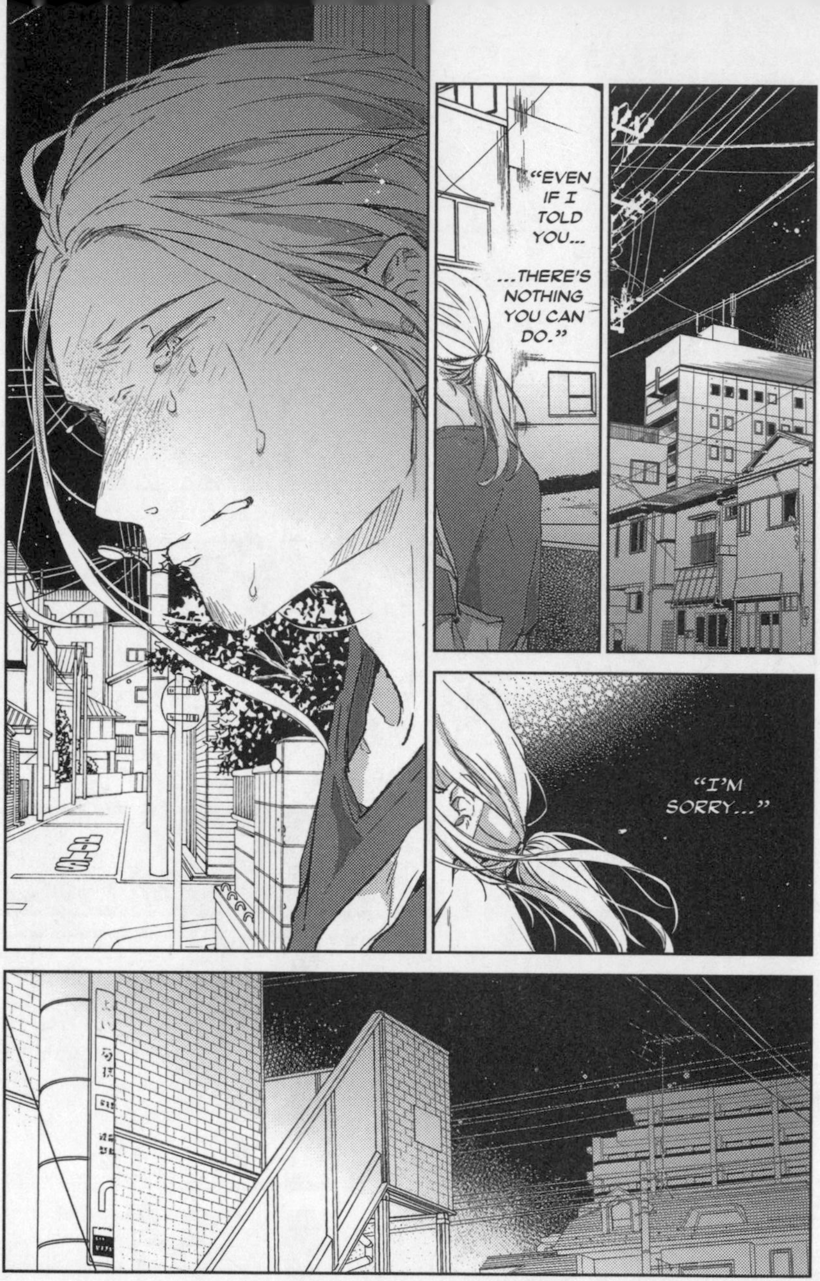
"EVEN IF I TOLD YOU...
...THERE'S NOTHING YOU CAN DO."
"I'M SORRY..."

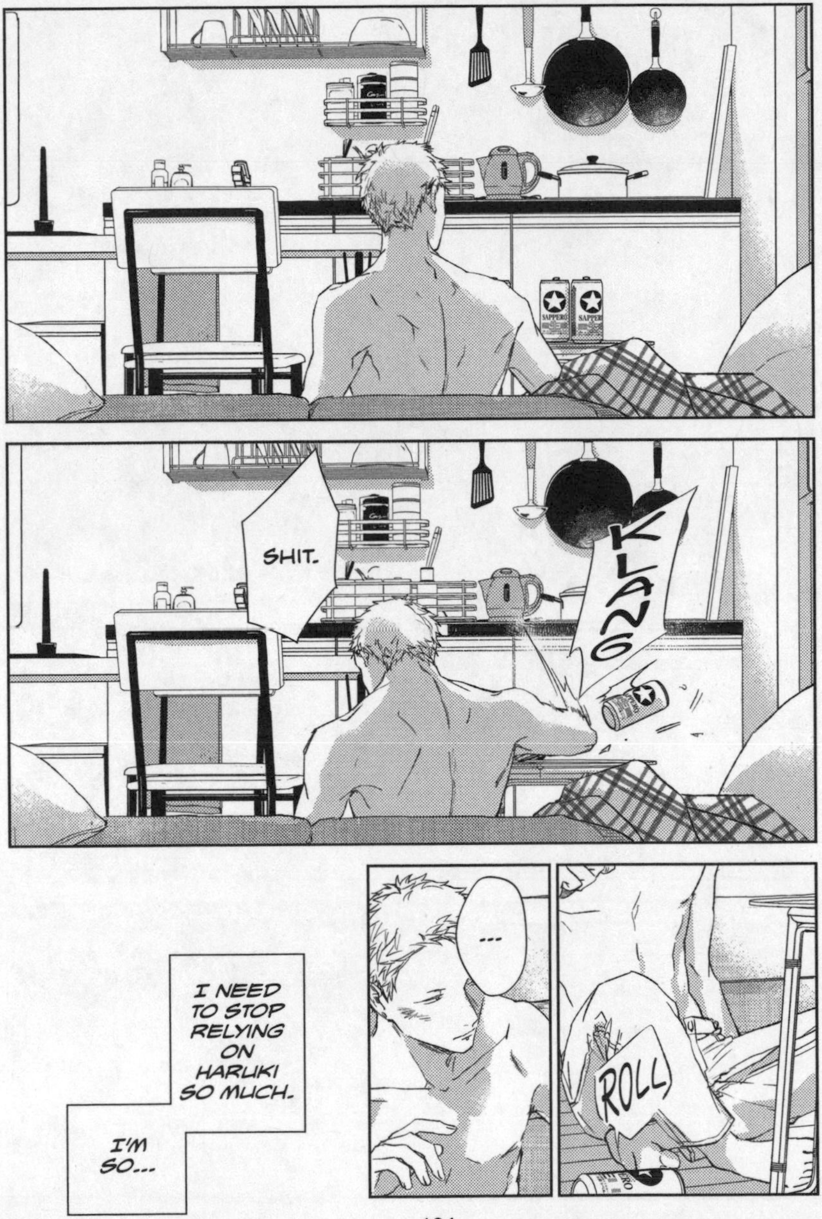
SHIT.
KLANG
ROLL
...
I NEED TO STOP RELYING ON HARUKI SO MUCH.
I'M SO...

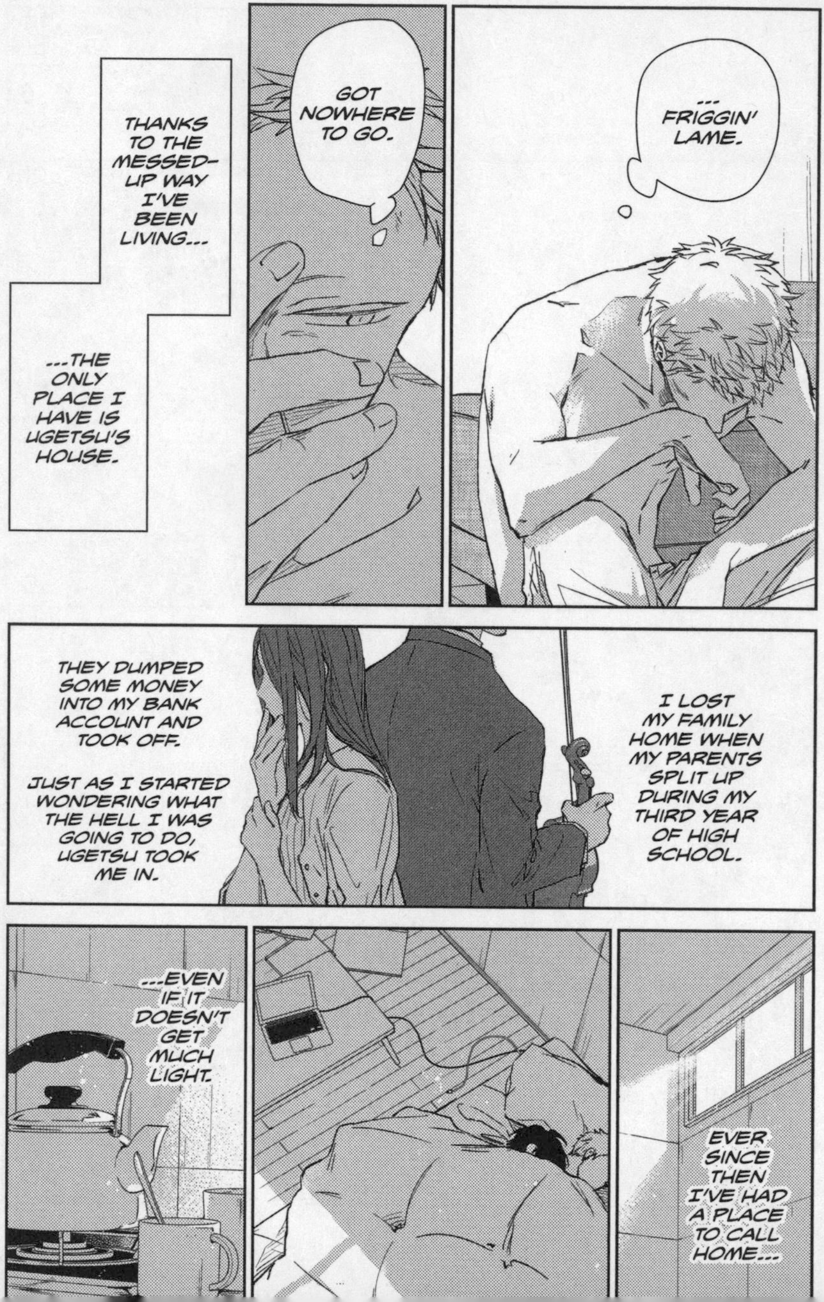
...FRIGGIN' LAME.
GOT NOWHERE TO GO.
THANKS TO THE MESSED-UP WAY I'VE BEEN LIVING...
...THE ONLY PLACE I HAVE IS UGETSU'S HOUSE.
I LOST MY FAMILY HOME WHEN MY PARENTS SPLIT UP DURING MY THIRD YEAR OF HIGH SCHOOL.
THEY DUMPED SOME MONEY INTO MY BANK ACCOUNT AND TOOK OFF.
JUST AS I STARTED WONDERING WHAT THE HELL I WAS GOING TO DO, UGETSU TOOK ME IN.
EVER SINCE THEN I'VE HAD A PLACE TO CALL HOME...
...EVEN IF IT DOESN'T GET MUCH LIGHT.

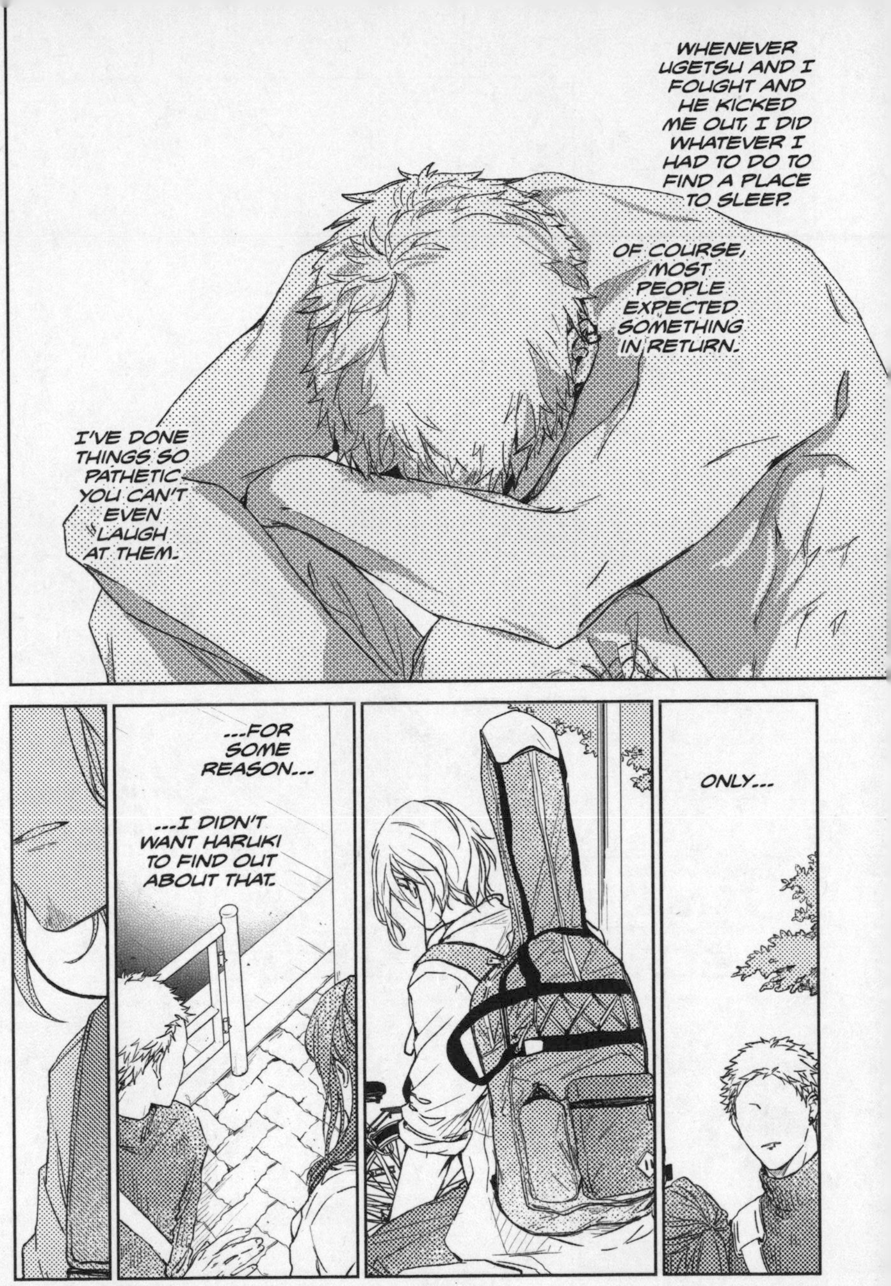
WHENEVER UGETSU AND I FOUGHT AND HE KICKED ME OUT, I DID WHATEVER I HAD TO DO TO FIND A PLACE TO SLEEP.
OF COURSE, MOST PEOPLE EXPECTED SOMETHING IN RETURN.
I'VE DONE THINGS SO PATHETIC YOU CAN'T EVEN LAUGH AT THEM.
ONLY...
...FOR SOME REASON...
...I DIDN'T WANT HARUKI TO FIND OUT ABOUT THAT.

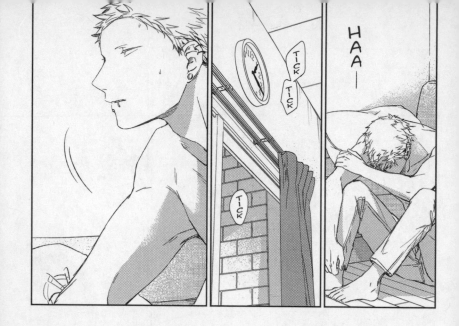

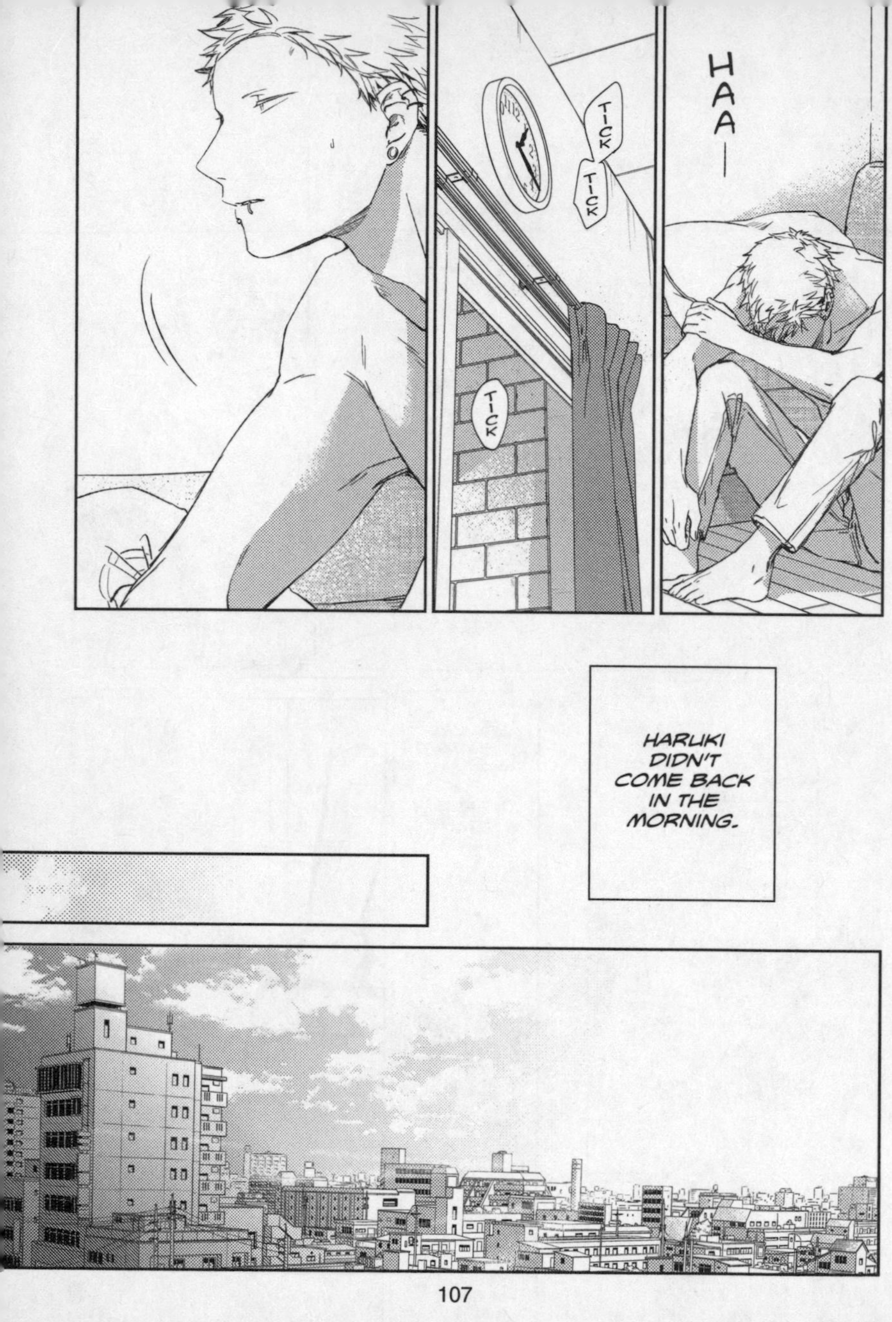

TICK
TICK
TICK

HAA―

HARUKI
DIDN'T
COME BACK
IN THE
MORNING.

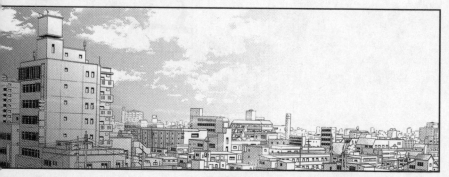

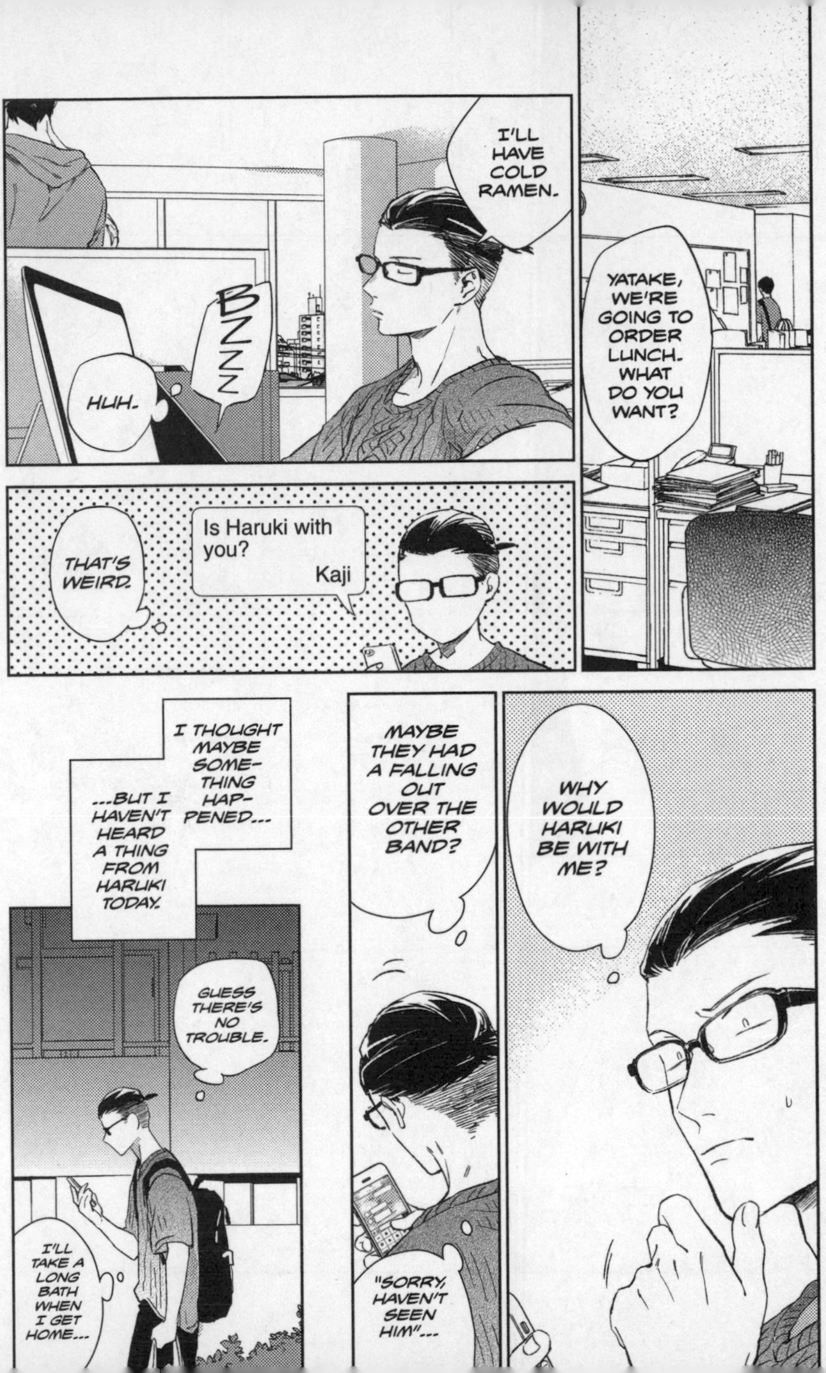
YATAKE, WE'RE GOING TO ORDER LUNCH. WHAT DO YOU WANT?
I'LL HAVE COLD RAMEN.
BZZZ
HUH.
Is Haruki with you?
Kaji
THAT'S WEIRD.
WHY WOULD HARUKI BE WITH ME?
MAYBE THEY HAD A FALLING OUT OVER THE OTHER BAND?
"SORRY, HAVEN'T SEEN HIM"...
I THOUGHT MAYBE SOME-THING HAP-PENED...
...BUT I HAVEN'T HEARD A THING FROM HARUKI TODAY.
GUESS THERE'S NO TROUBLE.
I'LL TAKE A LONG BATH WHEN I GET HOME...

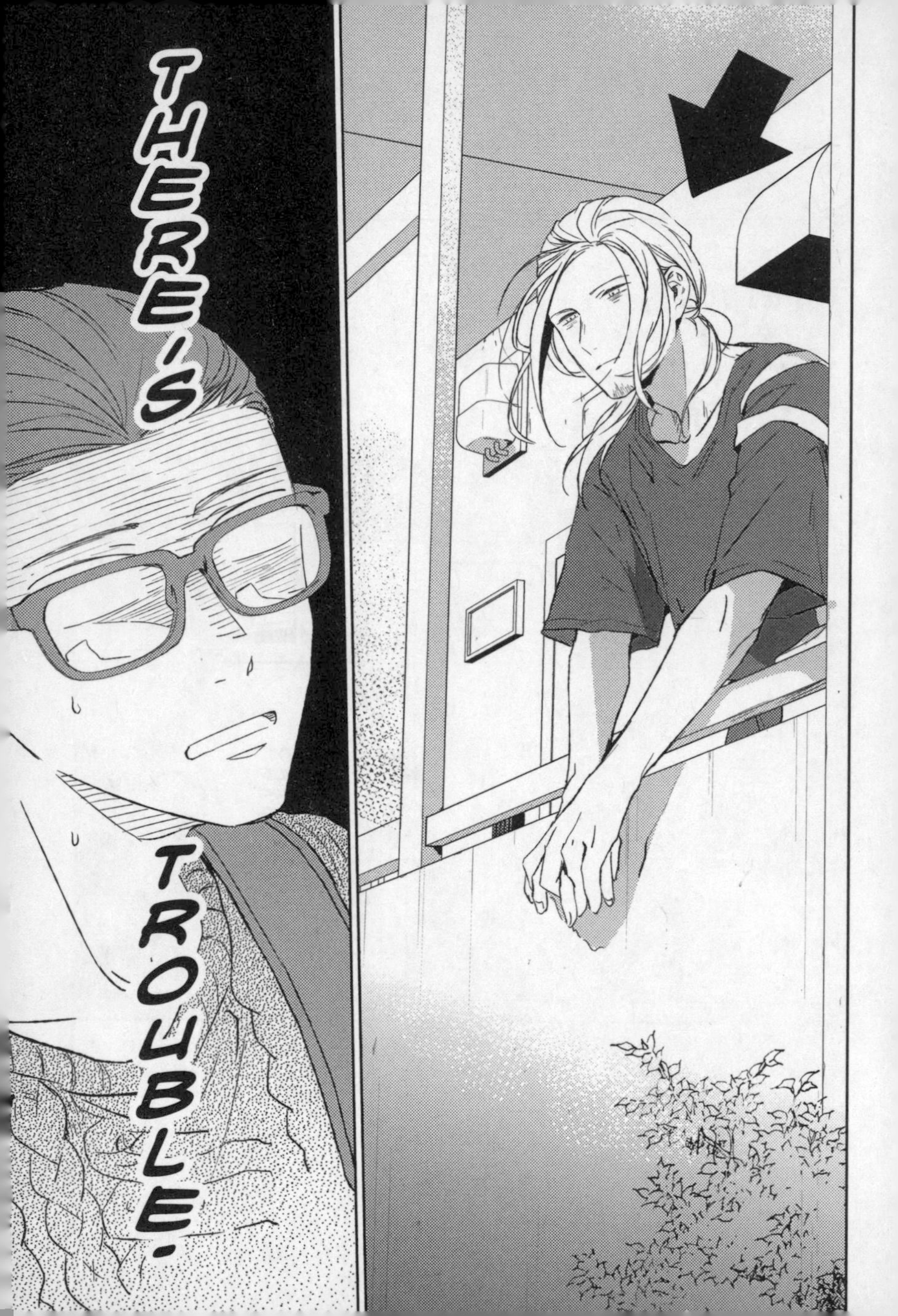
THERE'S TROUBLE.

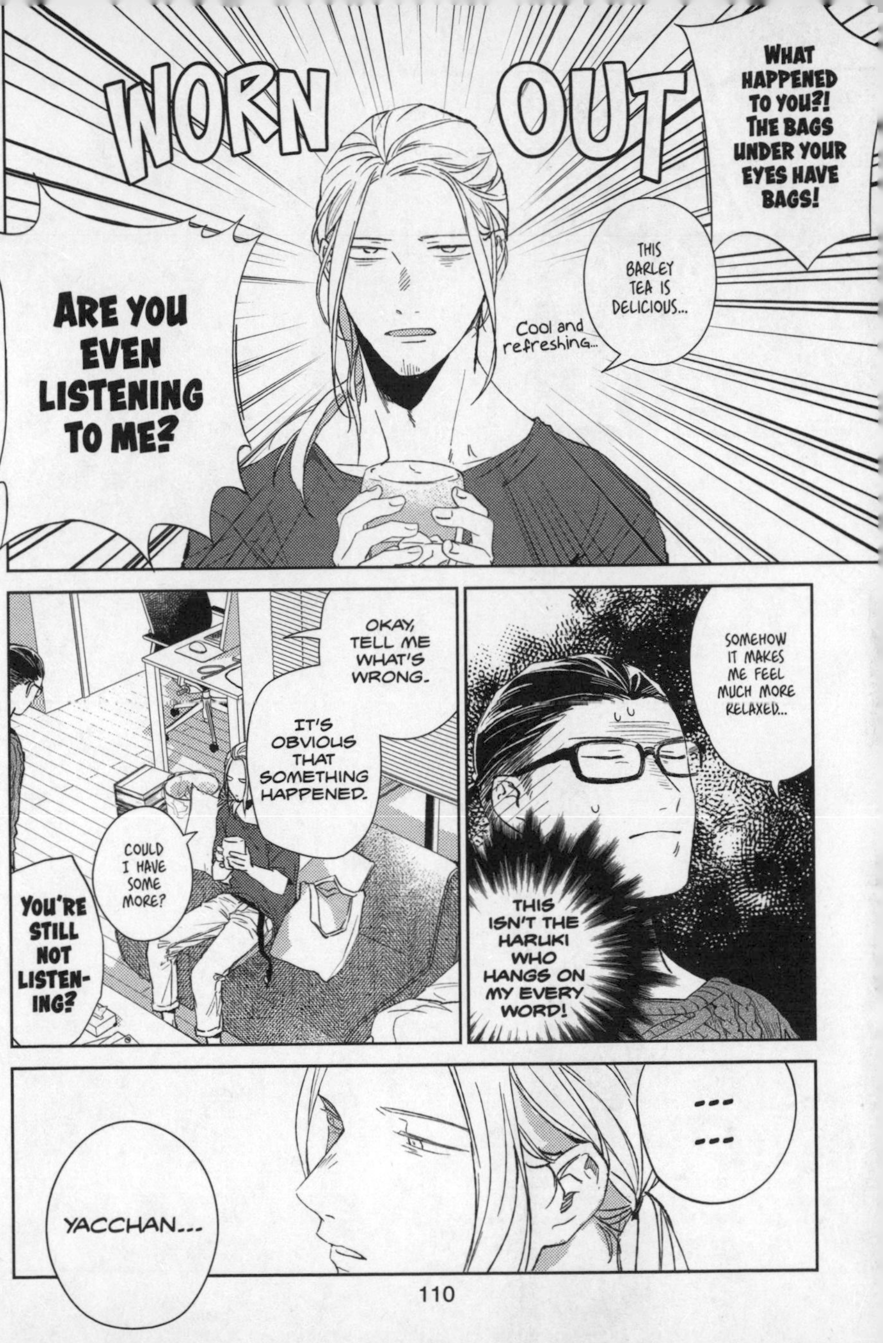
WHAT HAPPENED TO YOU?! THE BAGS UNDER YOUR EYES HAVE BAGS!
WORN OUT
THIS BARLEY TEA IS DELICIOUS...
Cool and refreshing...
ARE YOU EVEN LISTENING TO ME?
SOMEHOW IT MAKES ME FEEL MUCH MORE RELAXED...
THIS ISN'T THE HARUKI WHO HANGS ON MY EVERY WORD!
OKAY, TELL ME WHAT'S WRONG.
IT'S OBVIOUS THAT SOMETHING HAPPENED.
COULD I HAVE SOME MORE?
YOU'RE STILL NOT LISTEN-ING?
... ...
YACCHAN...

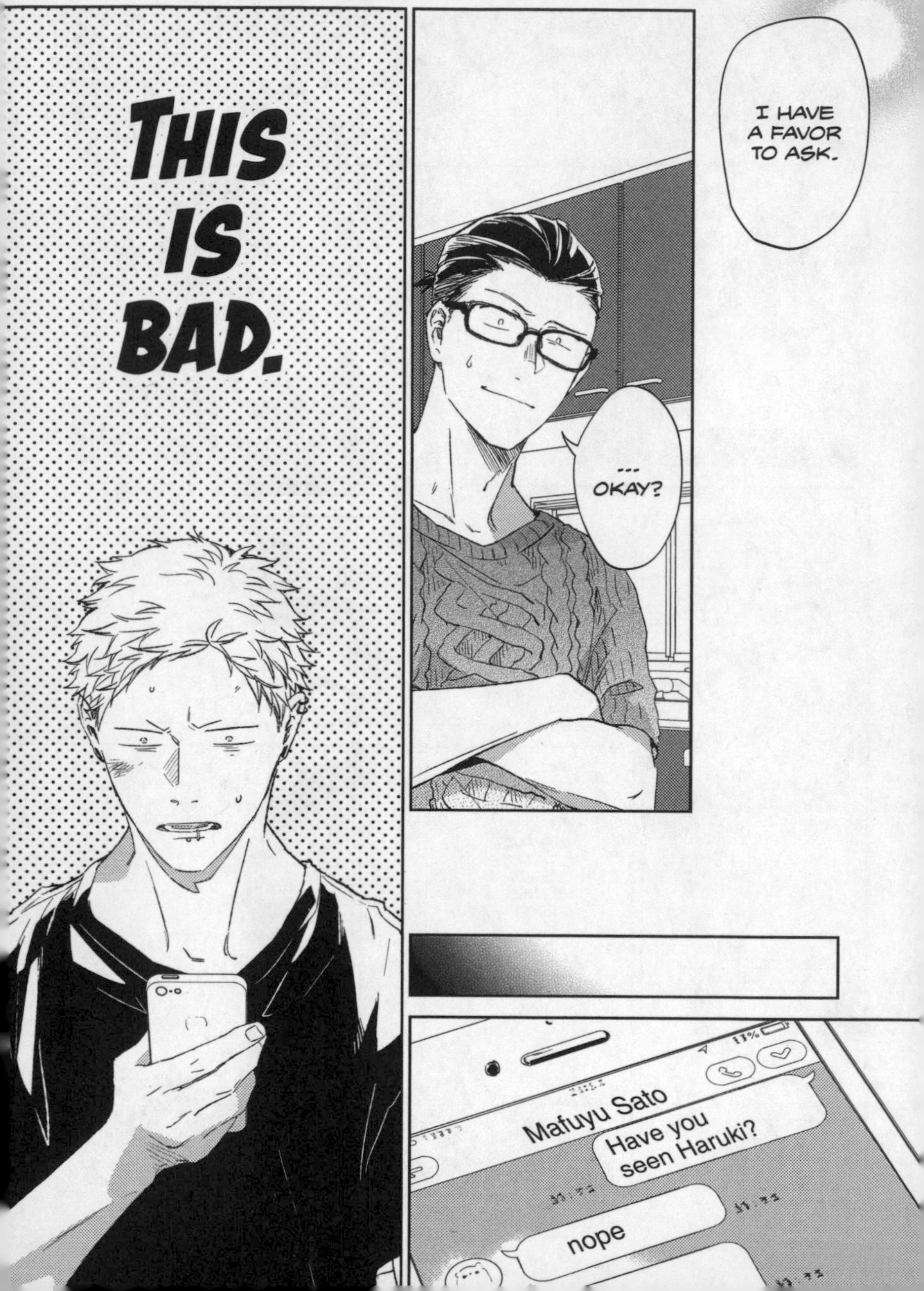
I HAVE A FAVOR TO ASK.
...OKAY?
Mafuyu Sato
Have you seen Haruki?
nope
THIS IS BAD.

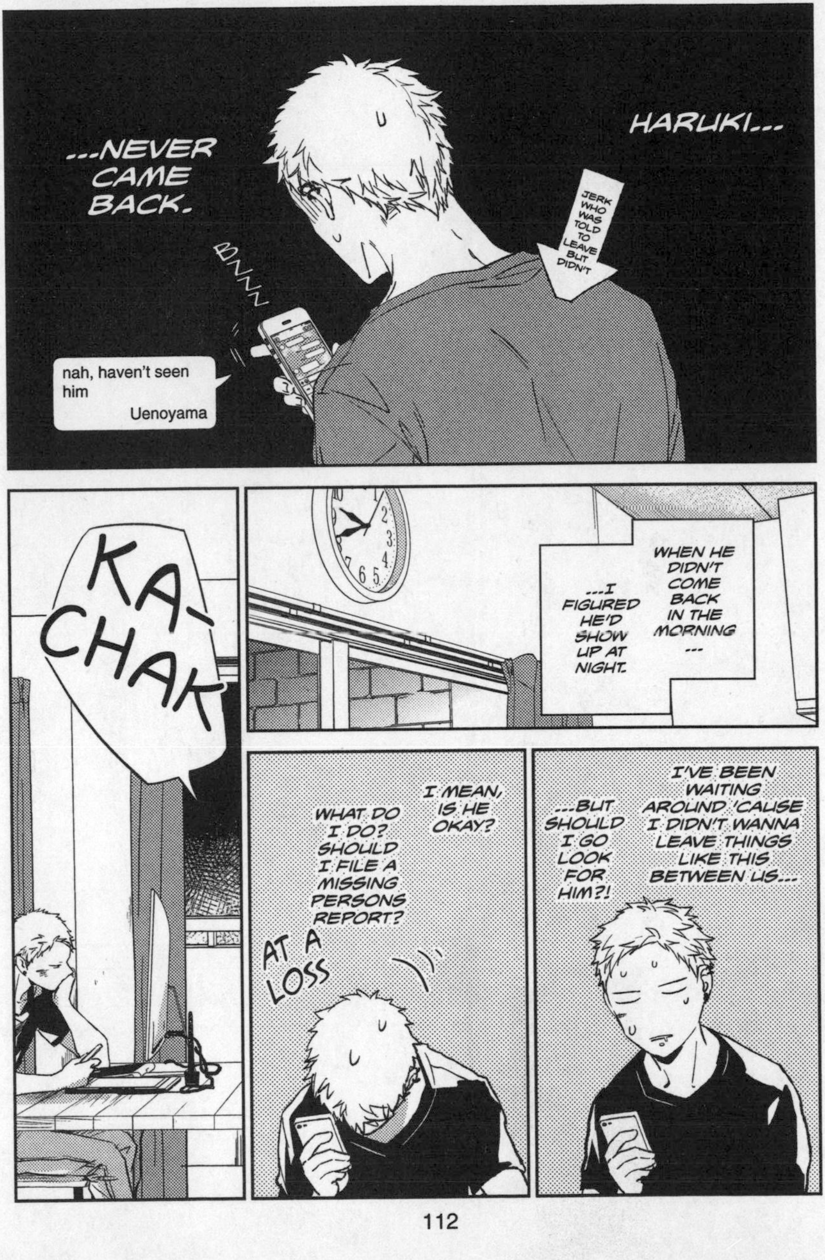
HARUKI...
...NEVER CAME BACK.
JERK WHO WAS TOLD TO LEAVE BUT DIDN'T
BZZZZ
nah, haven't seen him
Uenoyama
WHEN HE DIDN'T COME BACK IN THE MORNING...
...I FIGURED HE'D SHOW UP AT NIGHT.
I'VE BEEN WAITING AROUND 'CAUSE I DIDN'T WANNA LEAVE THINGS LIKE THIS BETWEEN US...
...BUT SHOULD I GO LOOK FOR HIM?!
I MEAN, IS HE OKAY?
WHAT DO I DO? SHOULD I FILE A MISSING PERSONS REPORT?
AT A LOSS
KA-CHAK

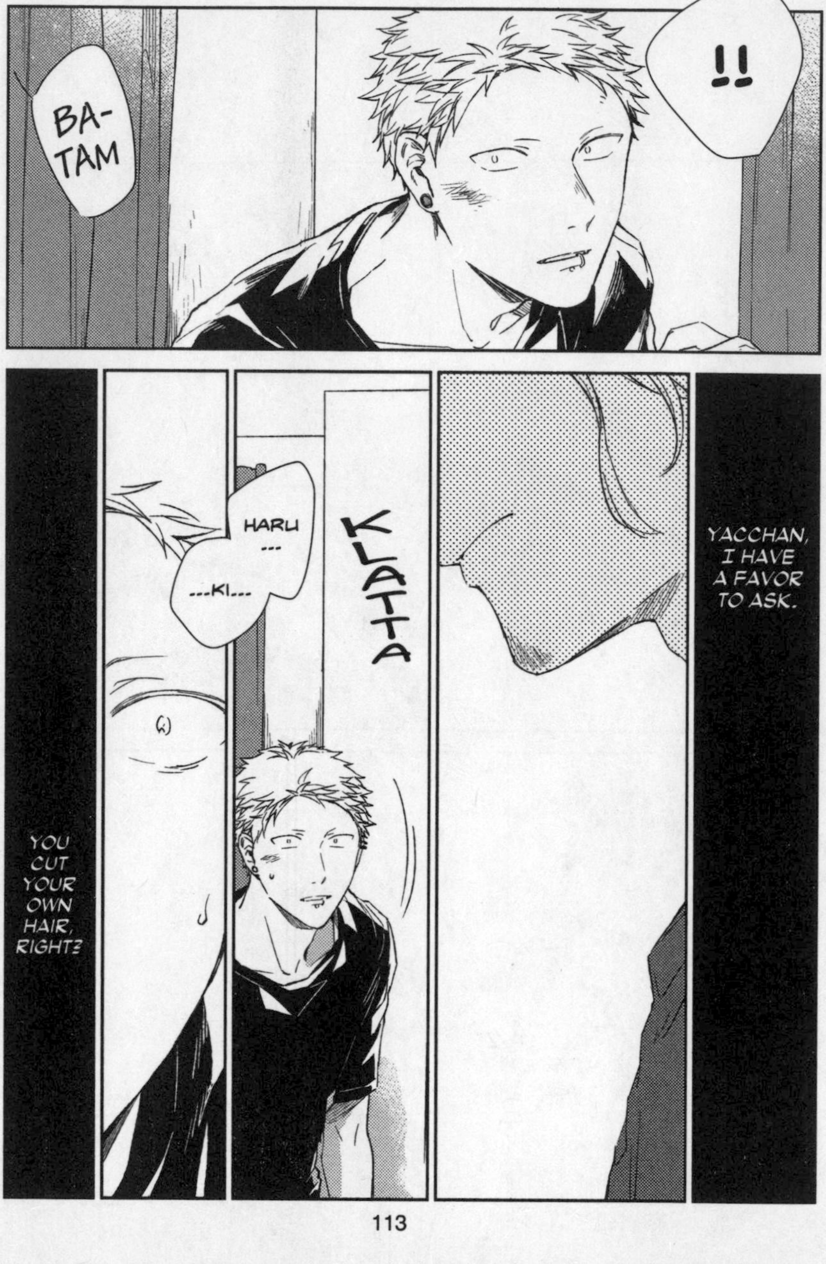
!!
BA-TAM
YACCHAN, I HAVE A FAVOR TO ASK.
KLATTA
HARU ---
---KI---
YOU CUT YOUR OWN HAIR, RIGHT?

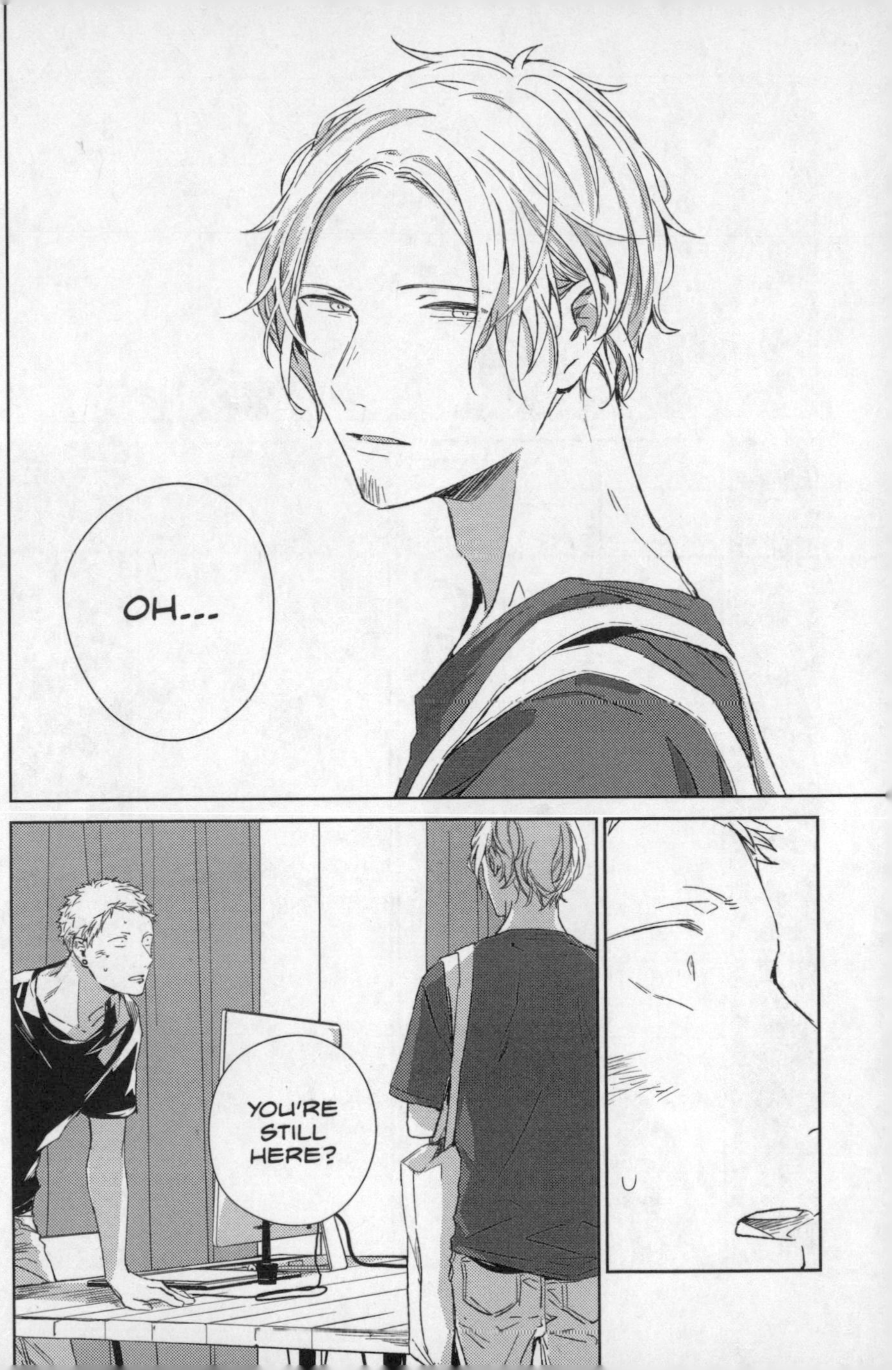
OH...
YOU'RE STILL HERE?

given

by Natsuki Kizu

given

by Natsuki Kizu

chapter 21

given

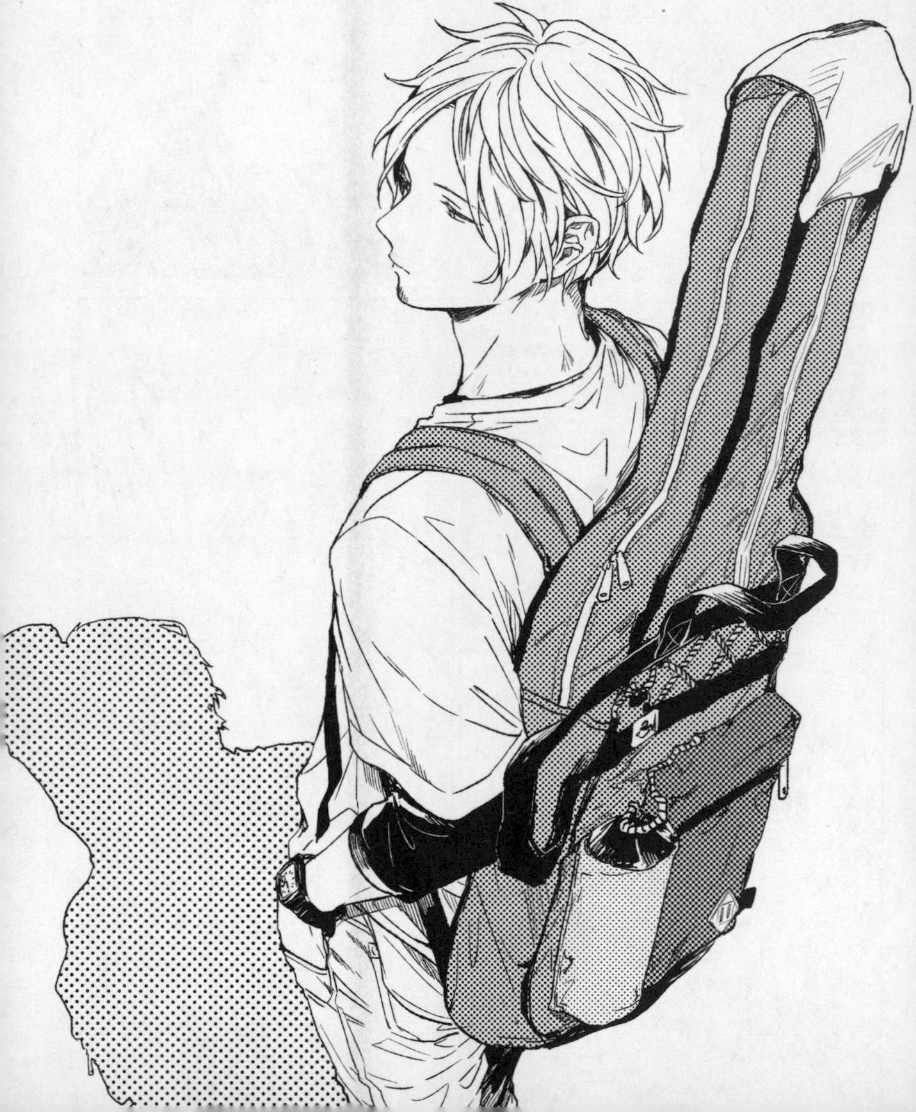

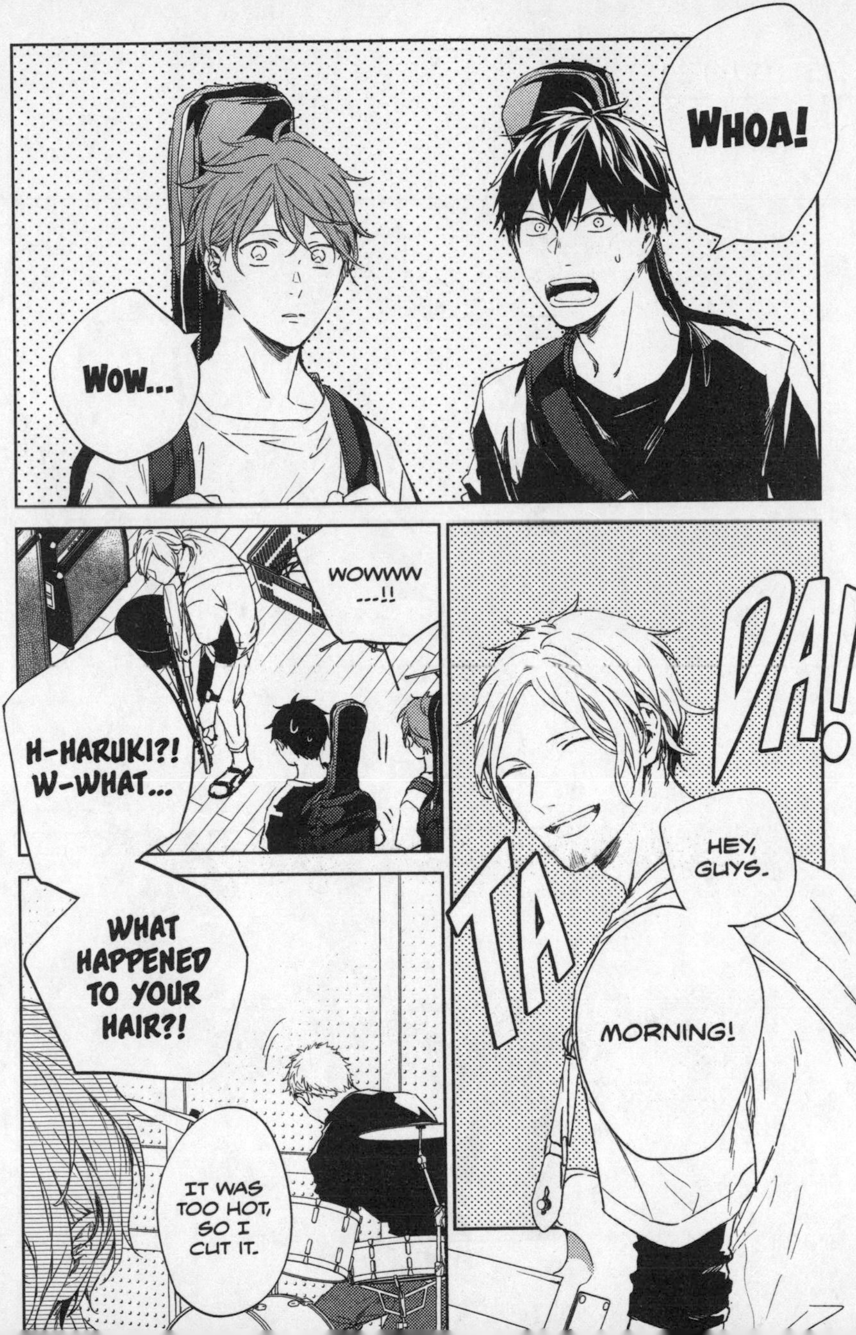
WHOA!
WOW...
TA DA!
HEY, GUYS.
MORNING!
WOWWW ---!!
H-HARUKI?! W-WHAT...
WHAT HAPPENED TO YOUR HAIR?!
IT WAS TOO HOT, SO I CUT IT.

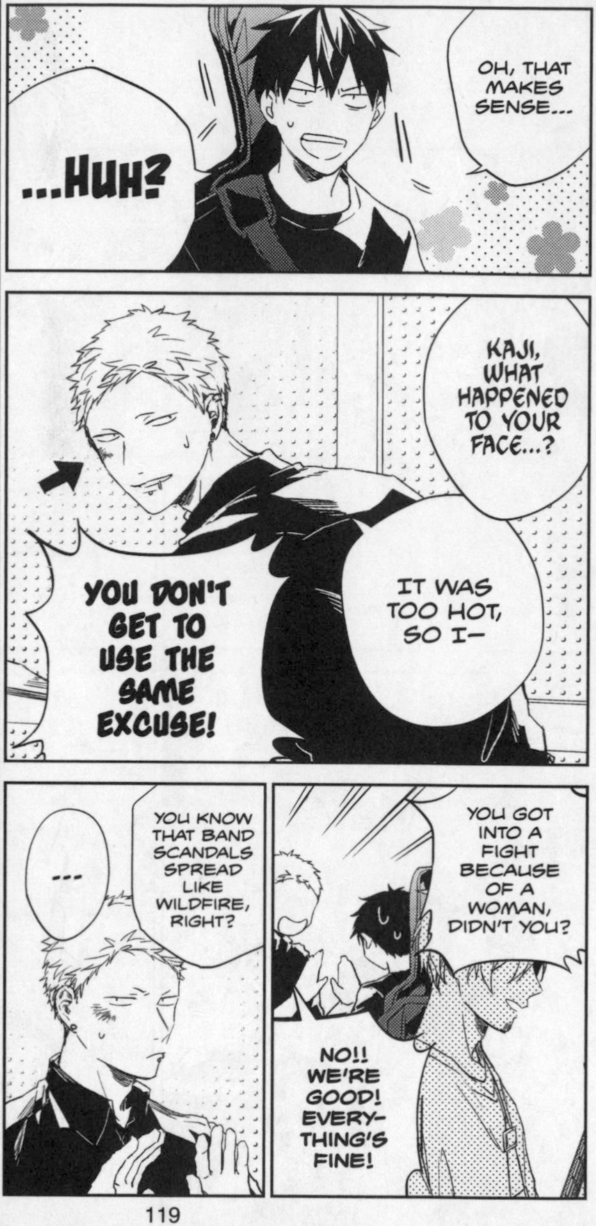
OH, THAT MAKES SENSE...
...HUH?
KAJI, WHAT HAPPENED TO YOUR FACE...?
IT WAS TOO HOT, SO I—
YOU DON'T GET TO USE THE SAME EXCUSE!
YOU GOT INTO A FIGHT BECAUSE OF A WOMAN, DIDN'T YOU?
NO!! WE'RE GOOD! EVERY-THING'S FINE!
YOU KNOW THAT BAND SCANDALS SPREAD LIKE WILDFIRE, RIGHT?
...

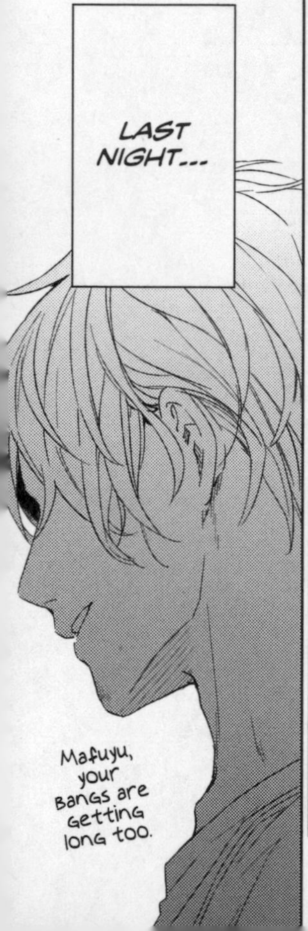
LAST NIGHT...
Mafuyu, your bangs are getting long too.

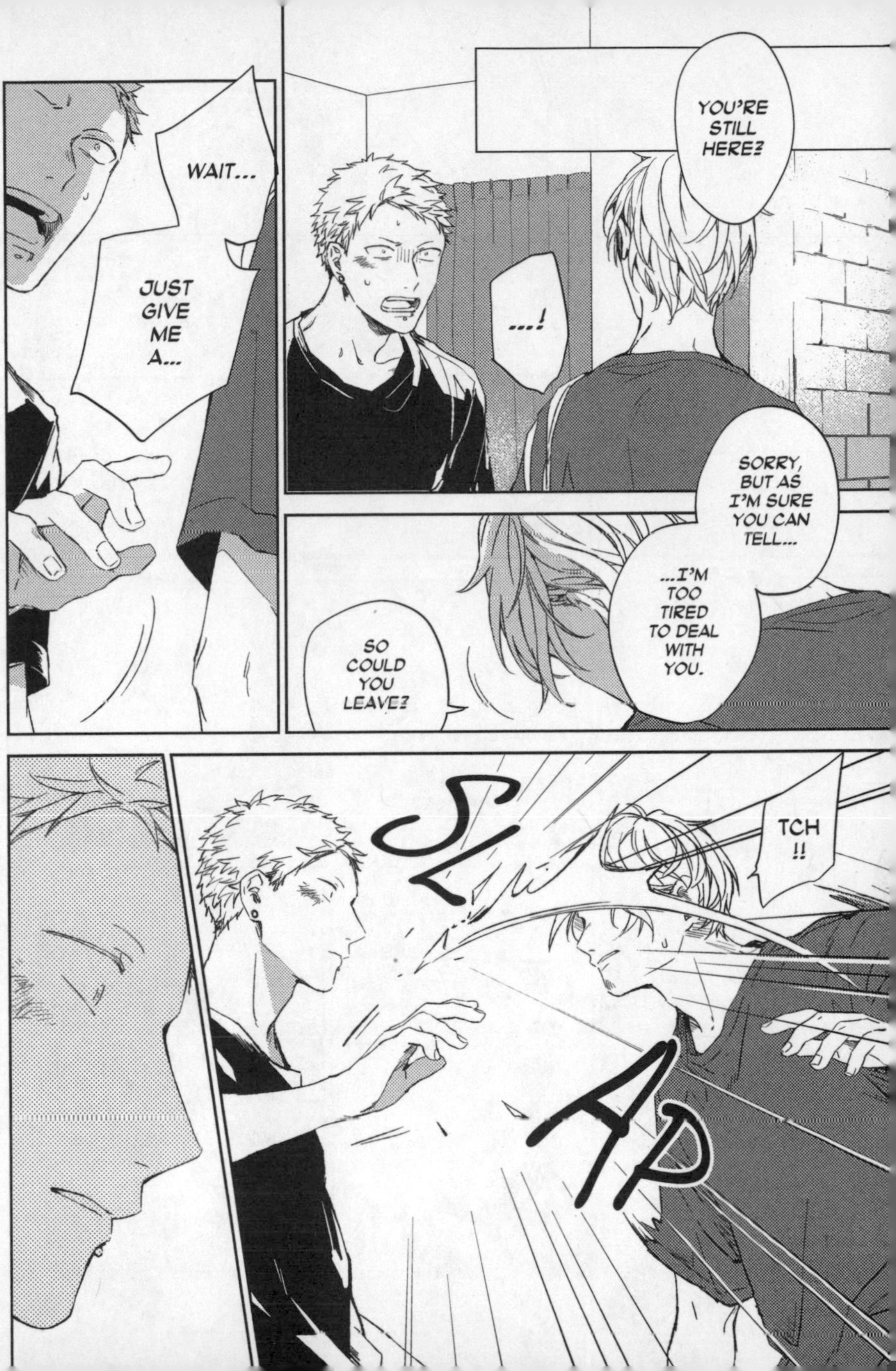
YOU'RE STILL HERE?
...!
SORRY, BUT AS I'M SURE YOU CAN TELL...
...I'M TOO TIRED TO DEAL WITH YOU.
SO COULD YOU LEAVE?
WAIT...
JUST GIVE ME A...
TCH !!
SLAP

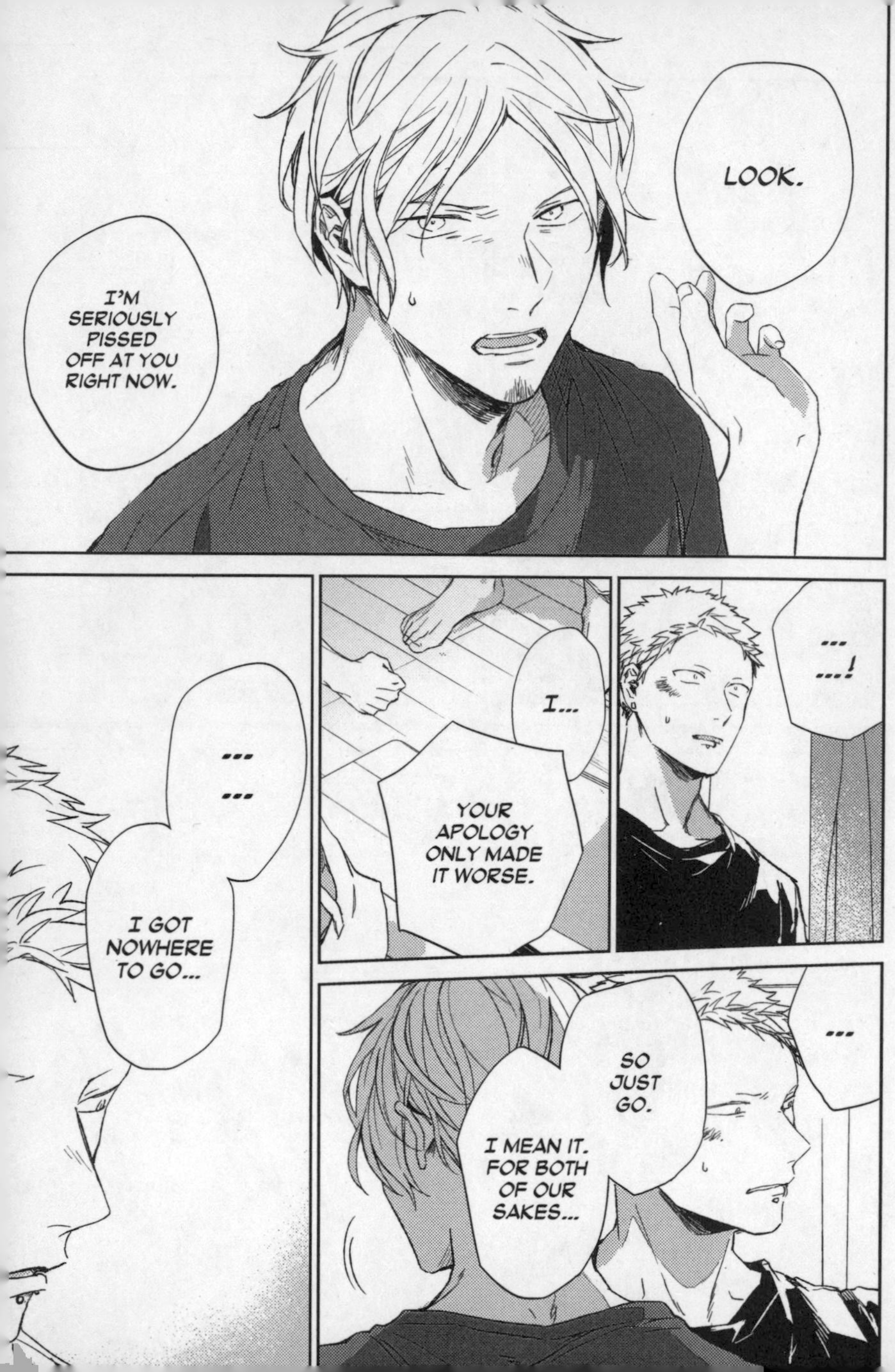
LOOK.
I'M SERIOUSLY PISSED OFF AT YOU RIGHT NOW.
... ...!
I...
YOUR APOLOGY ONLY MADE IT WORSE.
...
SO JUST GO.
I MEAN IT. FOR BOTH OF OUR SAKES...
... ...
I GOT NOWHERE TO GO...

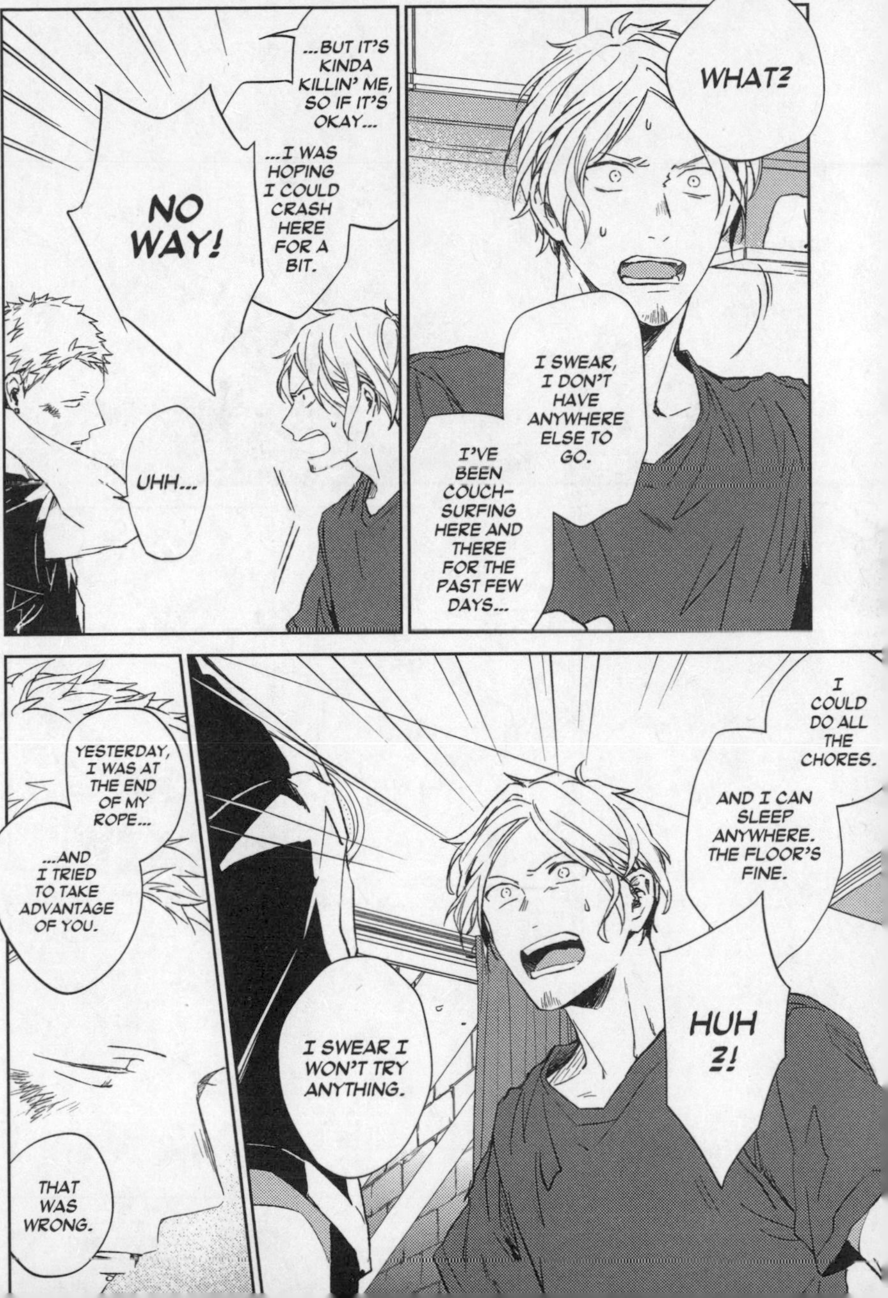
WHAT?
I SWEAR, I DON'T HAVE ANYWHERE ELSE TO GO.
I'VE BEEN COUCH-SURFING HERE AND THERE FOR THE PAST FEW DAYS...
...BUT IT'S KINDA KILLIN' ME, SO IF IT'S OKAY...
...I WAS HOPING I COULD CRASH HERE FOR A BIT.
NO WAY!
UHH...
I COULD DO ALL THE CHORES.
AND I CAN SLEEP ANYWHERE. THE FLOOR'S FINE.
HUH?!
I SWEAR I WON'T TRY ANYTHING.
YESTERDAY, I WAS AT THE END OF MY ROPE...
...AND I TRIED TO TAKE ADVANTAGE OF YOU.
THAT WAS WRONG.

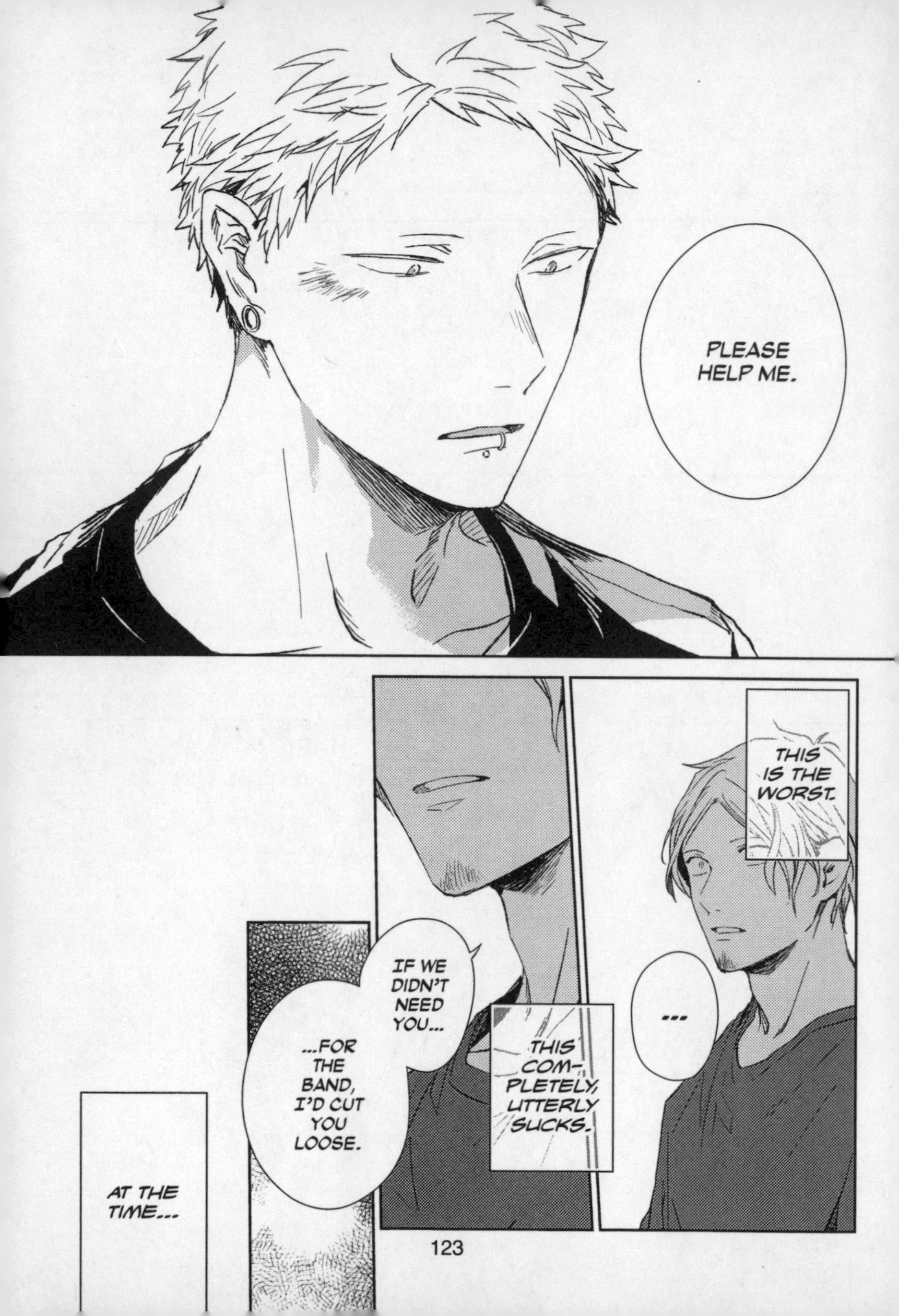
PLEASE HELP ME.
THIS IS THE WORST.
...
THIS COM-PLETELY, UTTERLY SUCKS.
IF WE DIDN'T NEED YOU...
...FOR THE BAND, I'D CUT YOU LOOSE.
AT THE TIME...

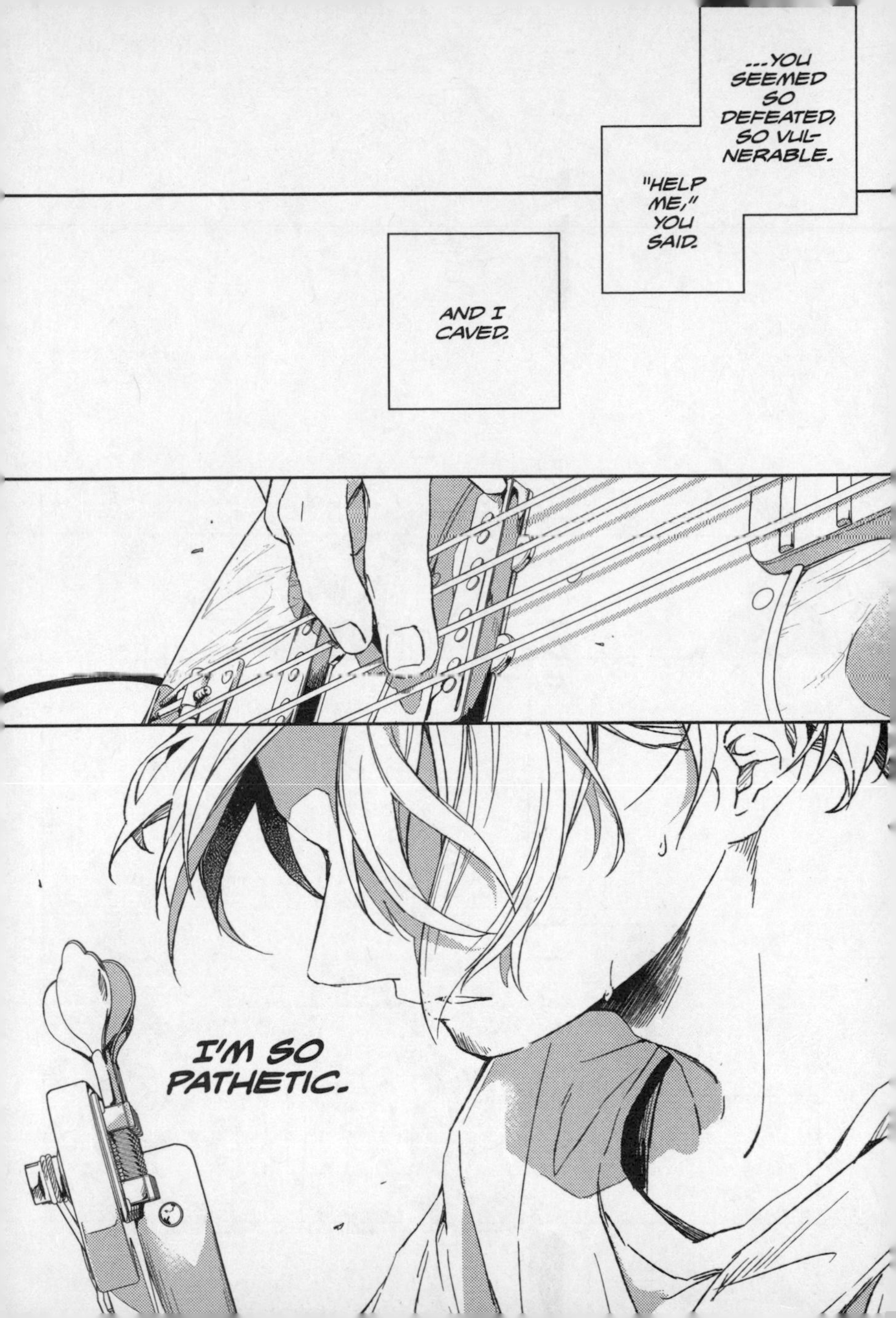
...YOU SEEMED SO DEFEATED, SO VUL-NERABLE.
"HELP ME," YOU SAID.
AND I CAVED.
I'M SO PATHETIC.

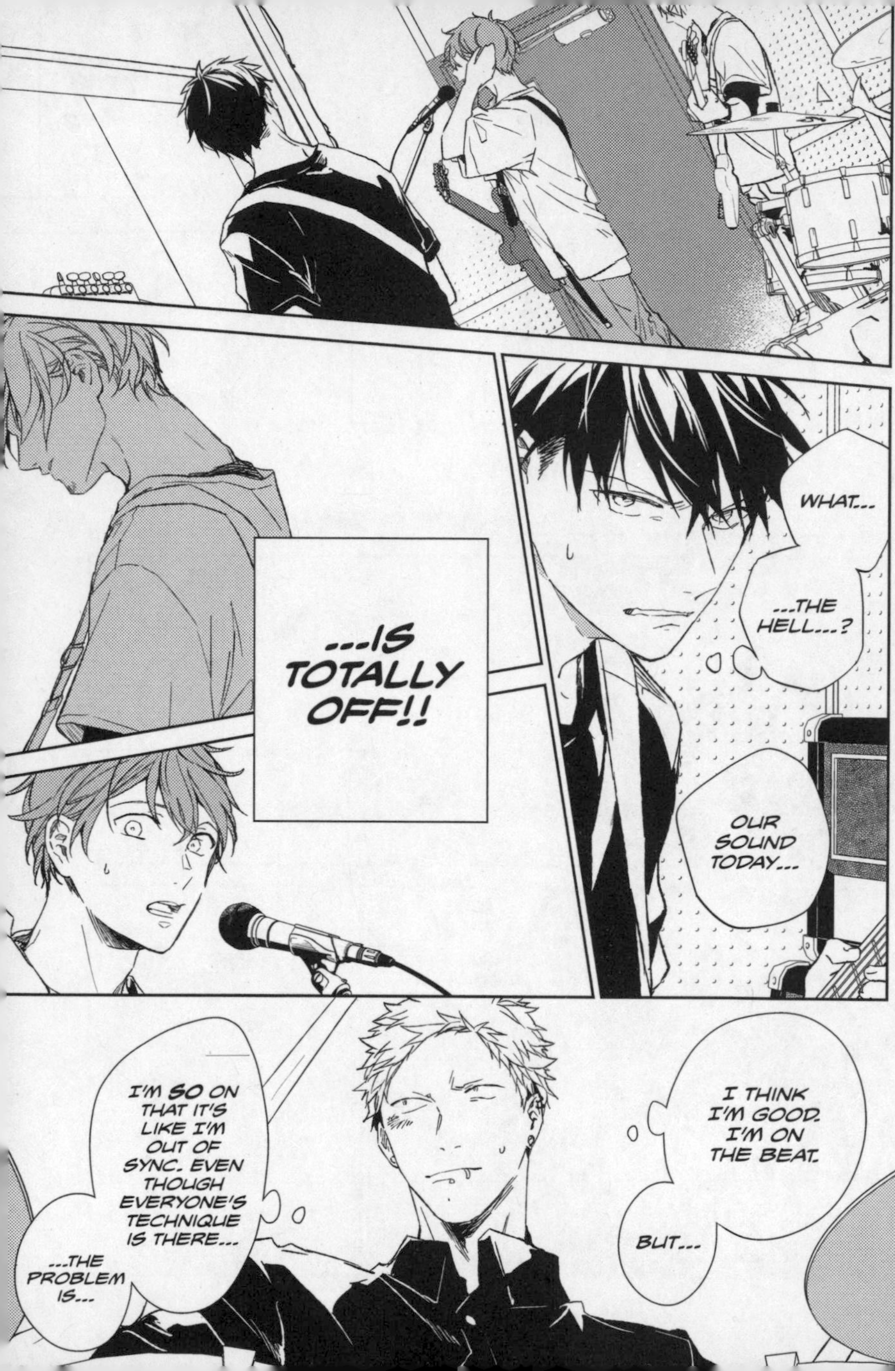
WHAT...
...THE HELL...?
OUR SOUND TODAY...
...IS TOTALLY OFF!!
I THINK I'M GOOD. I'M ON THE BEAT.
BUT...
I'M SO ON THAT IT'S LIKE I'M OUT OF SYNC. EVEN THOUGH EVERYONE'S TECHNIQUE IS THERE...
...THE PROBLEM IS...

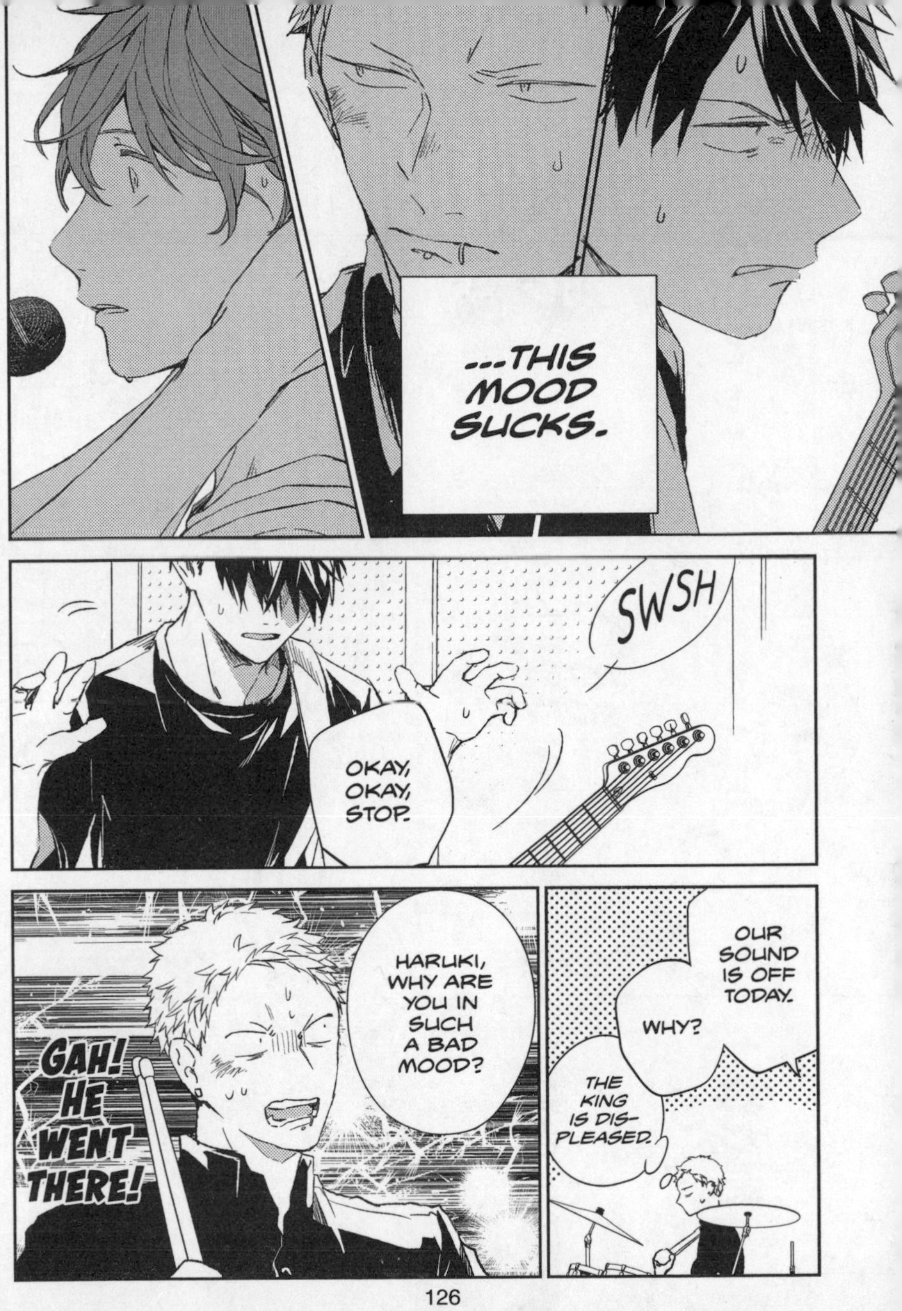
...THIS MOOD SUCKS.
SWSH
OKAY, OKAY, STOP.
OUR SOUND IS OFF TODAY.
WHY?
THE KING IS DIS-PLEASED.
HARUKI, WHY ARE YOU IN SUCH A BAD MOOD?
GAH! HE WENT THERE!

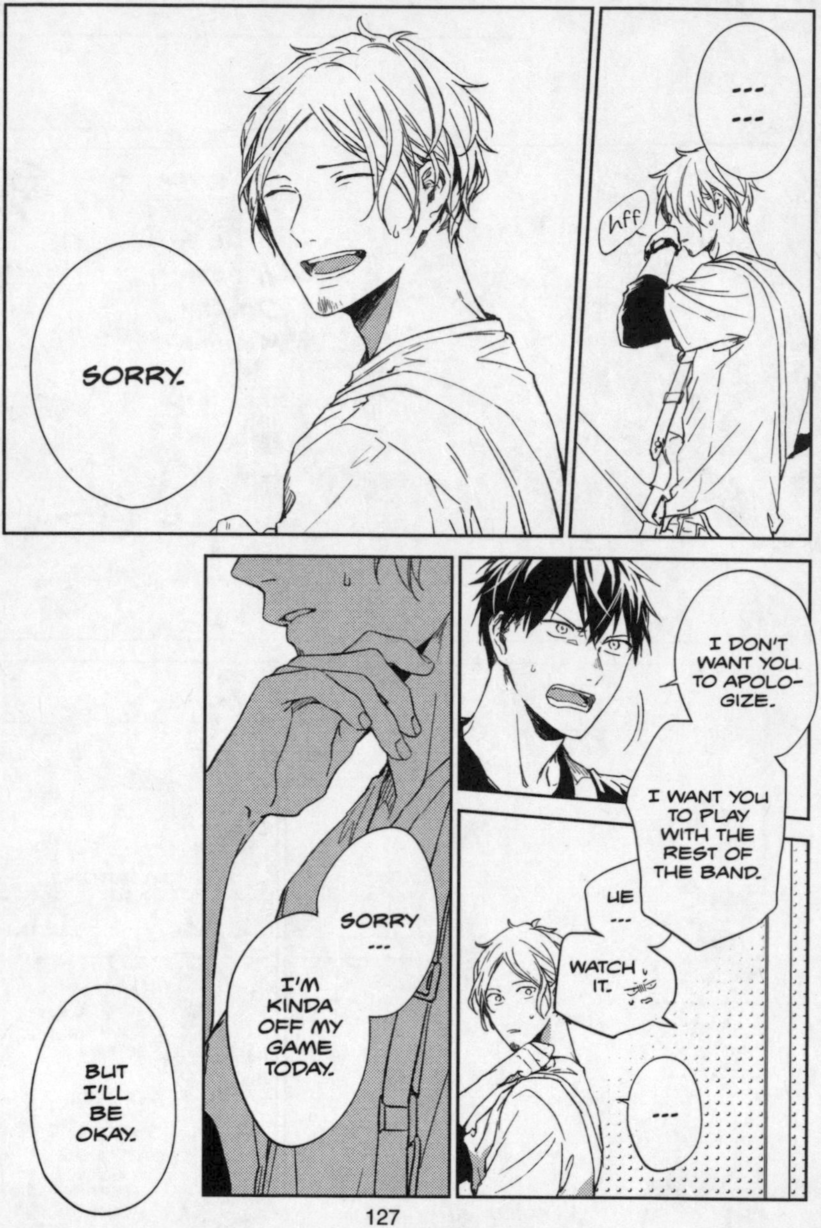

... ...
hff
SORRY.
I DON'T WANT YOU TO APOLOGIZE.
I WANT YOU TO PLAY WITH THE REST OF THE BAND.
UE ... WATCH IT.
...
SORRY ... I'M KINDA OFF MY GAME TODAY.
BUT I'LL BE OKAY.

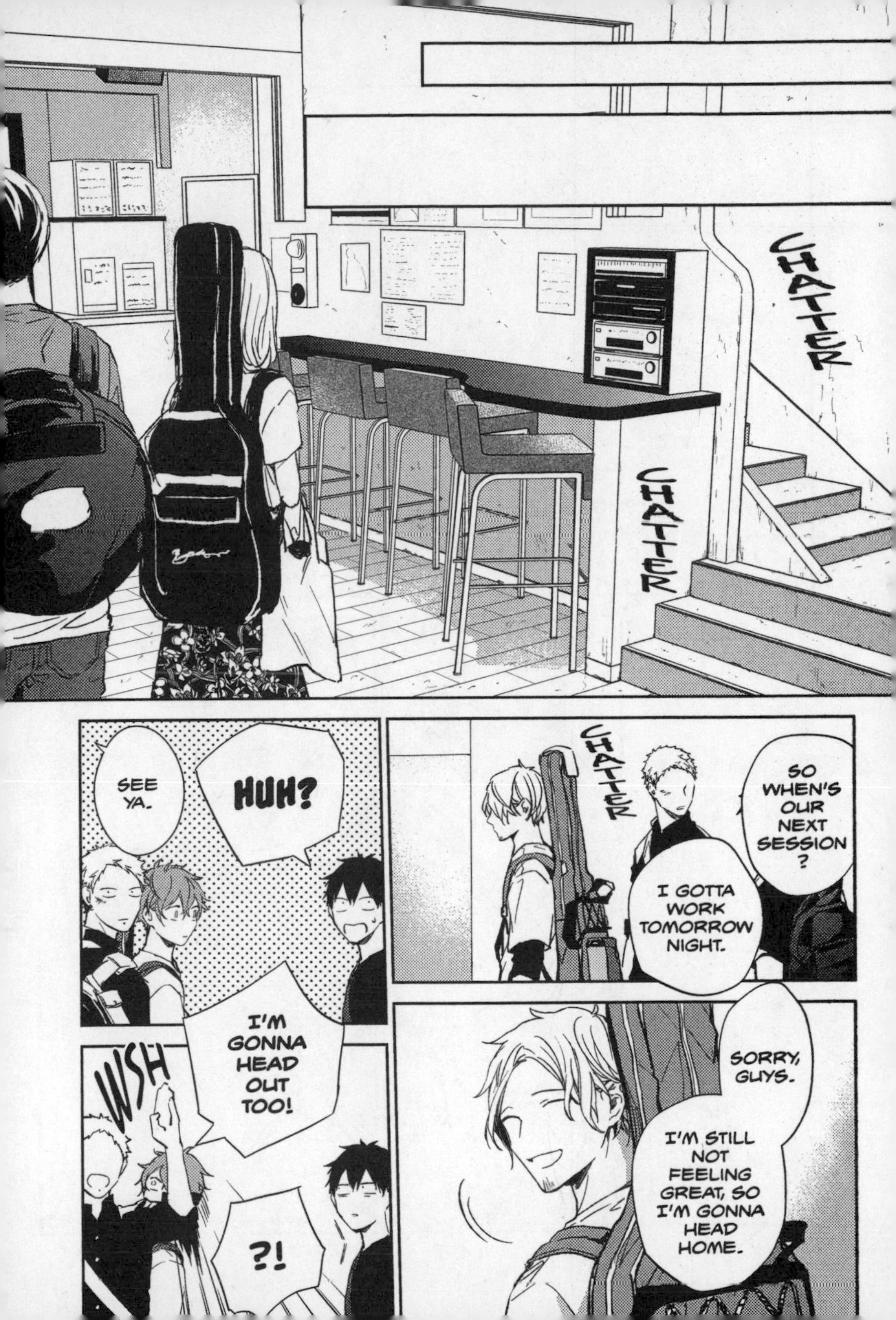
CHATTER
CHATTER
CHATTER
SO WHEN'S OUR NEXT SESSION?
I GOTTA WORK TOMORROW NIGHT.
HUH?
SEE YA.
SORRY, GUYS.
I'M STILL NOT FEELING GREAT, SO I'M GONNA HEAD HOME.
I'M GONNA HEAD OUT TOO!
WSH
?!

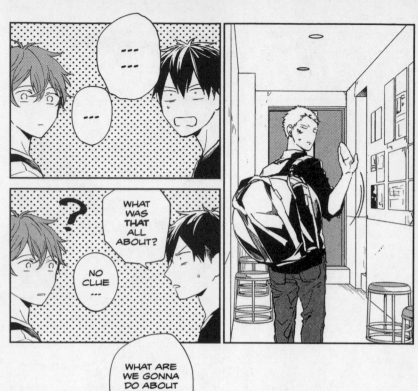

··· ··· ···

WHAT WAS THAT ALL ABOUT?

NO CLUE ···

WHAT ARE WE GONNA DO ABOUT THE NEXT STUDIO SESSION?

NO CLUE...

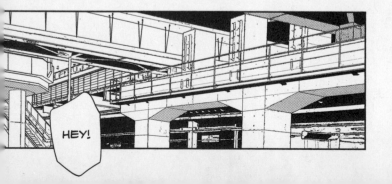

HEY!

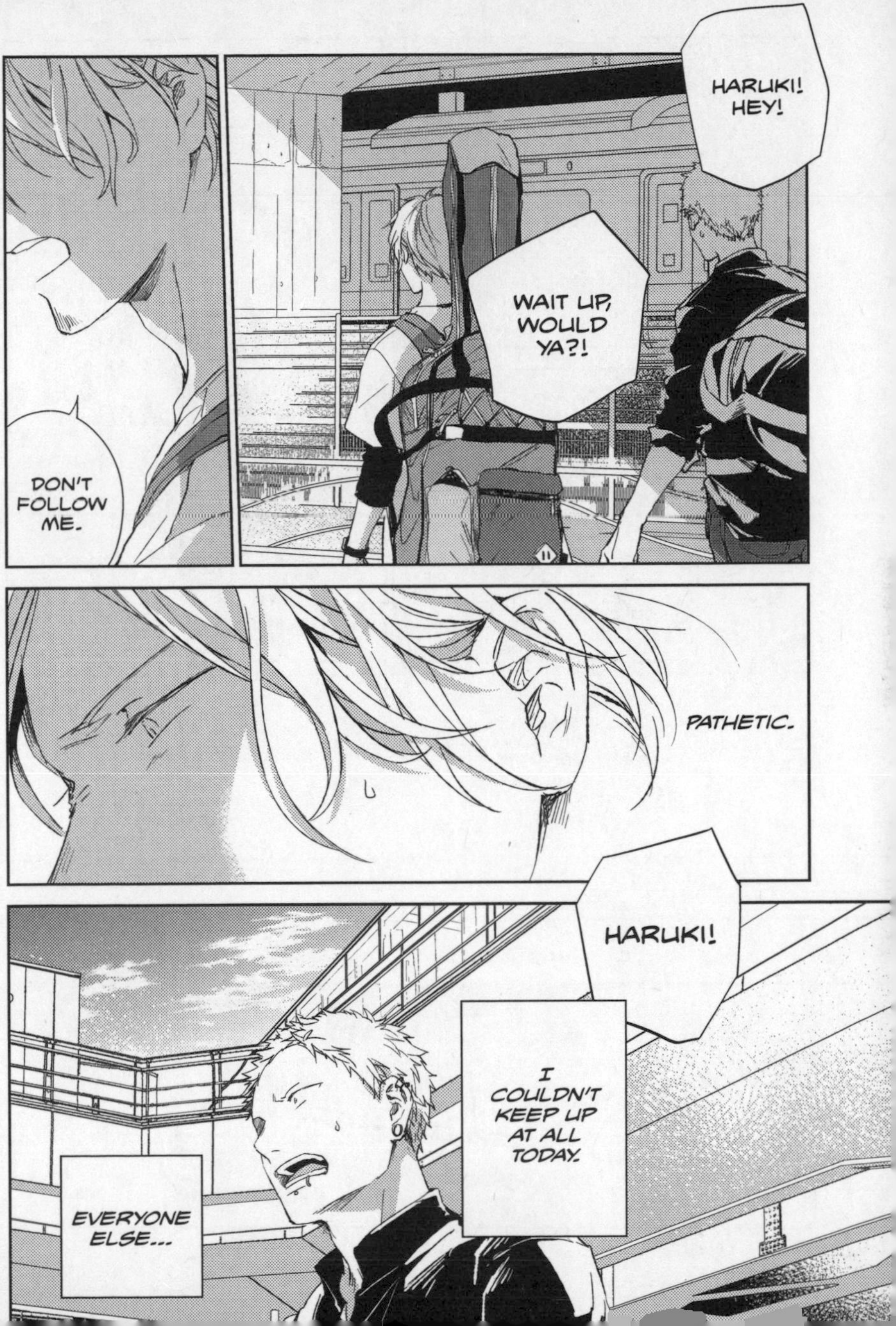
HARUKI! HEY!
WAIT UP, WOULD YA?!
DON'T FOLLOW ME.
PATHETIC.
HARUKI!
I COULDN'T KEEP UP AT ALL TODAY.
EVERYONE ELSE...

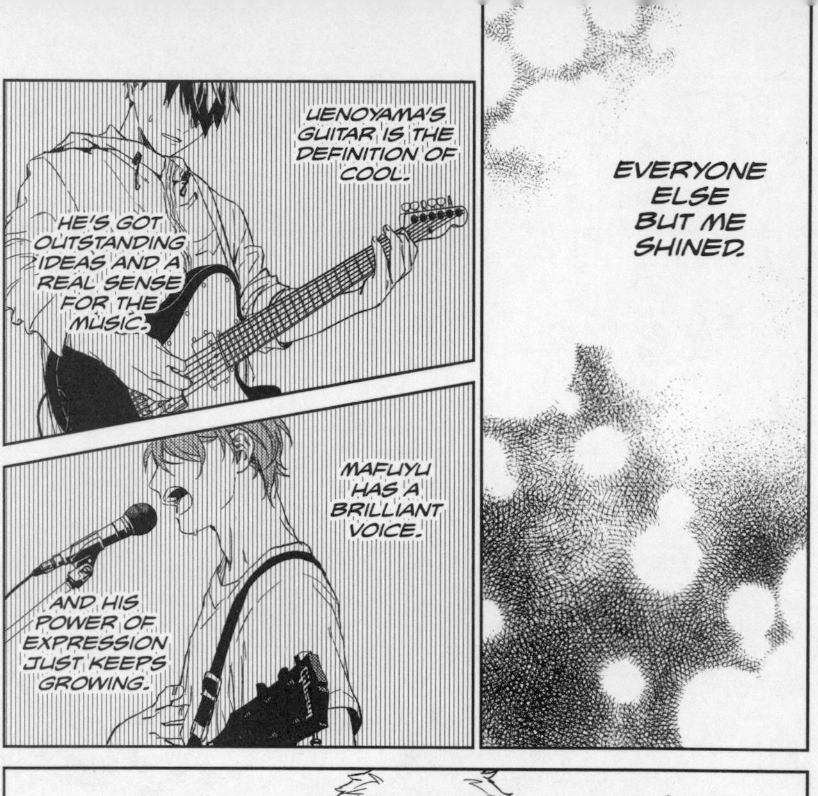
EVERYONE ELSE BUT ME SHINED.
UENOYAMA'S GUITAR IS THE DEFINITION OF COOL.
HE'S GOT OUTSTANDING IDEAS AND A REAL SENSE FOR THE MUSIC.
MAFUYU HAS A BRILLIANT VOICE.
AND HIS POWER OF EXPRESSION JUST KEEPS GROWING.
HEY!
AKIHIKO TOO...
HE CAN DO ANYTHING...
...AND MAKE IT LOOK EASY.
IT'S SO FRUS-TRATING.

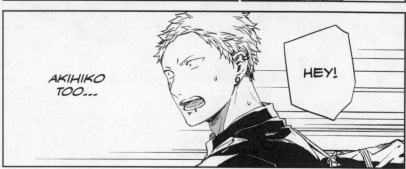

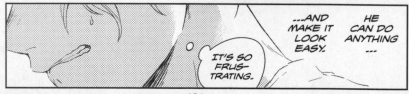

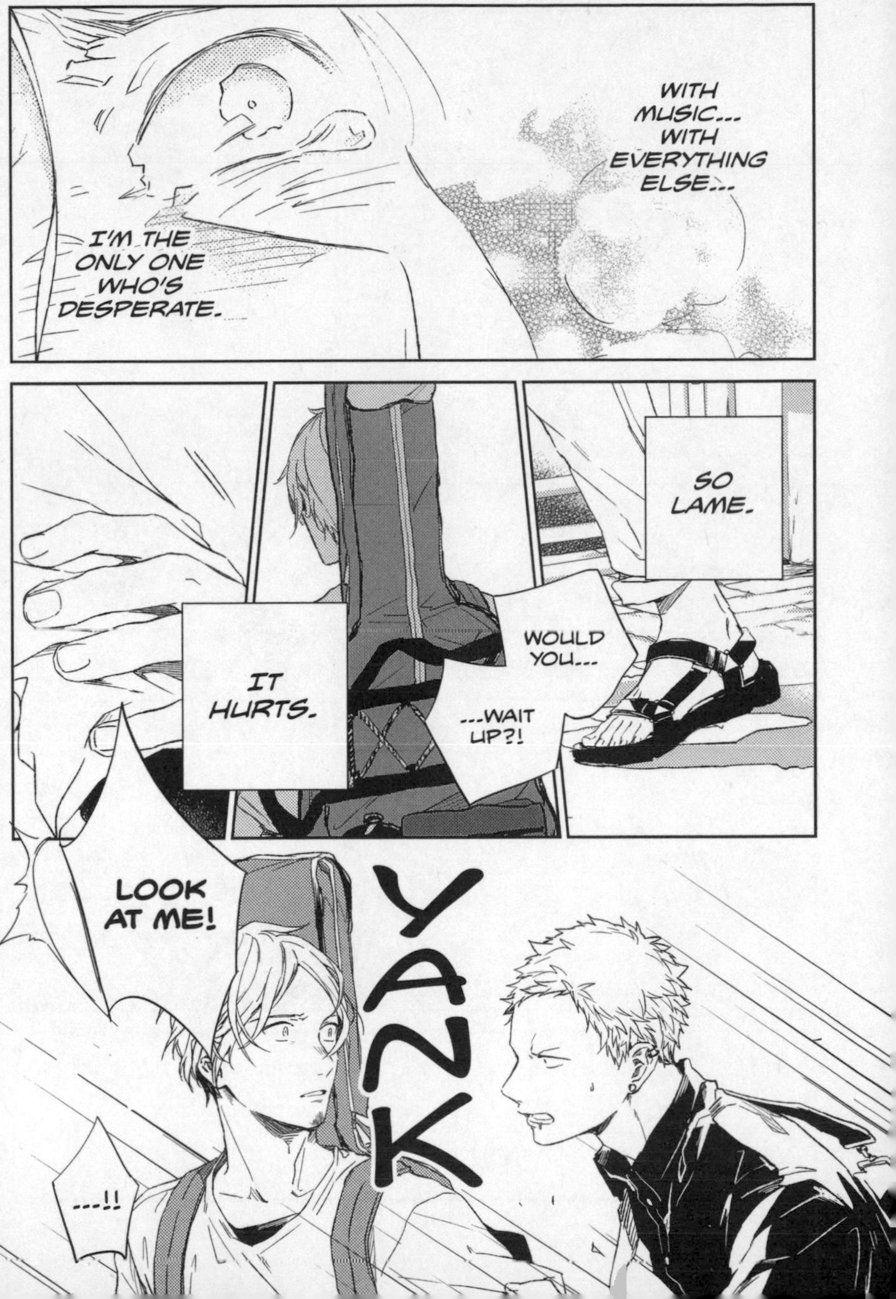
WITH MUSIC... WITH EVERYTHING ELSE...
I'M THE ONLY ONE WHO'S DESPERATE.
SO LAME.
WOULD YOU...
...WAIT UP?!
IT HURTS.
YANK
LOOK AT ME!
---!!

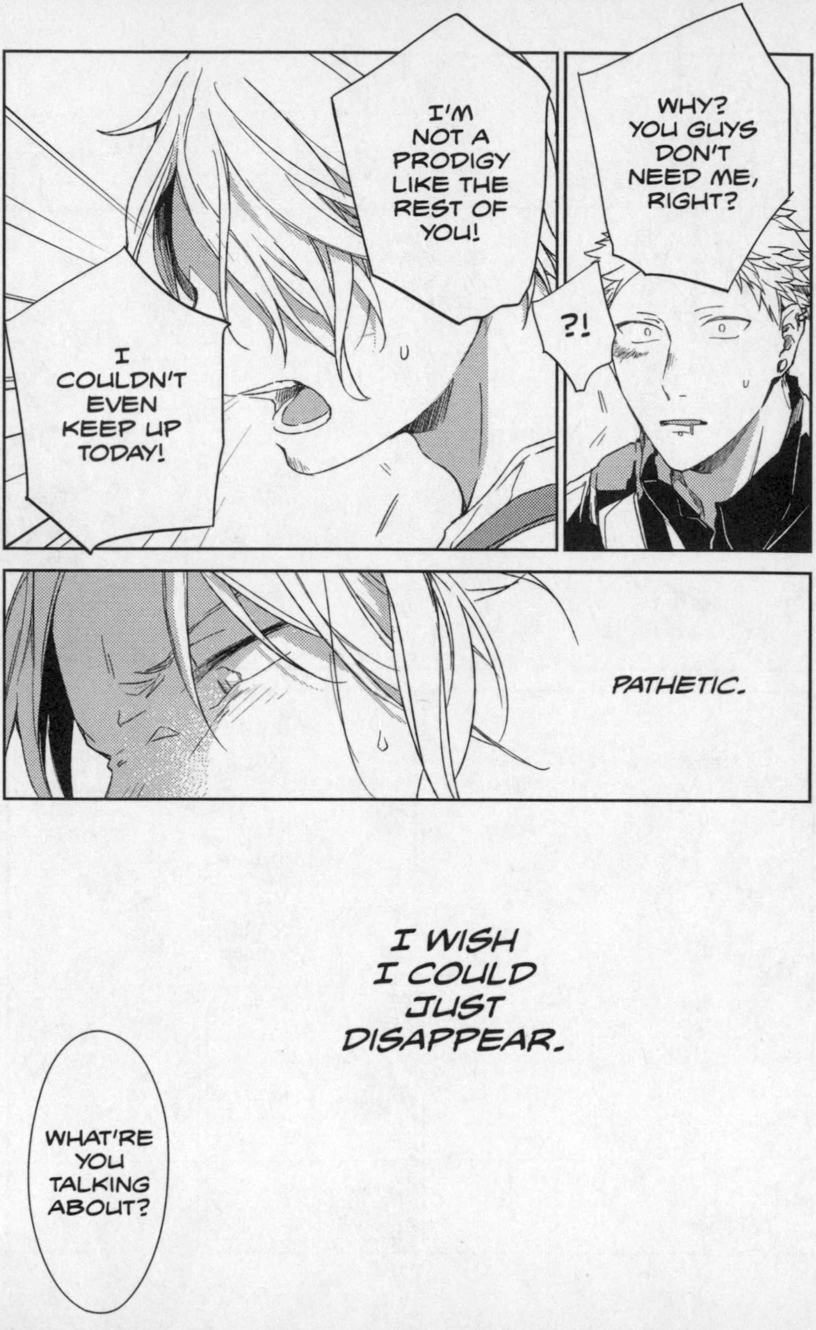
WHY? YOU GUYS DON'T NEED ME, RIGHT?
?!
I'M NOT A PRODIGY LIKE THE REST OF YOU!
I COULDN'T EVEN KEEP UP TODAY!
PATHETIC.
I WISH I COULD JUST DISAPPEAR.
WHAT'RE YOU TALKING ABOUT?

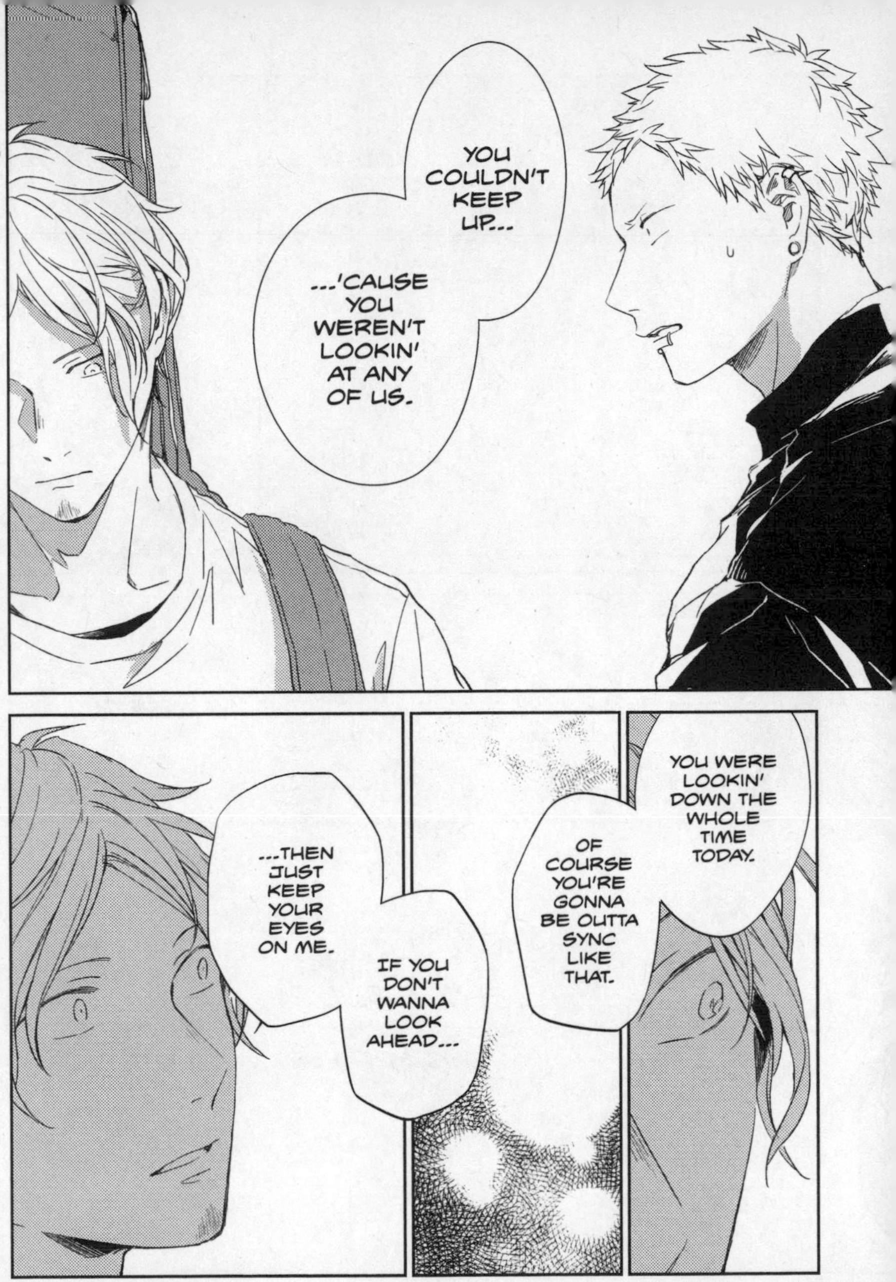
YOU COULDN'T KEEP UP...
...'CAUSE YOU WEREN'T LOOKIN' AT ANY OF US.
YOU WERE LOOKIN' DOWN THE WHOLE TIME TODAY.
OF COURSE YOU'RE GONNA BE OUTTA SYNC LIKE THAT.
IF YOU DON'T WANNA LOOK AHEAD...
...THEN JUST KEEP YOUR EYES ON ME.

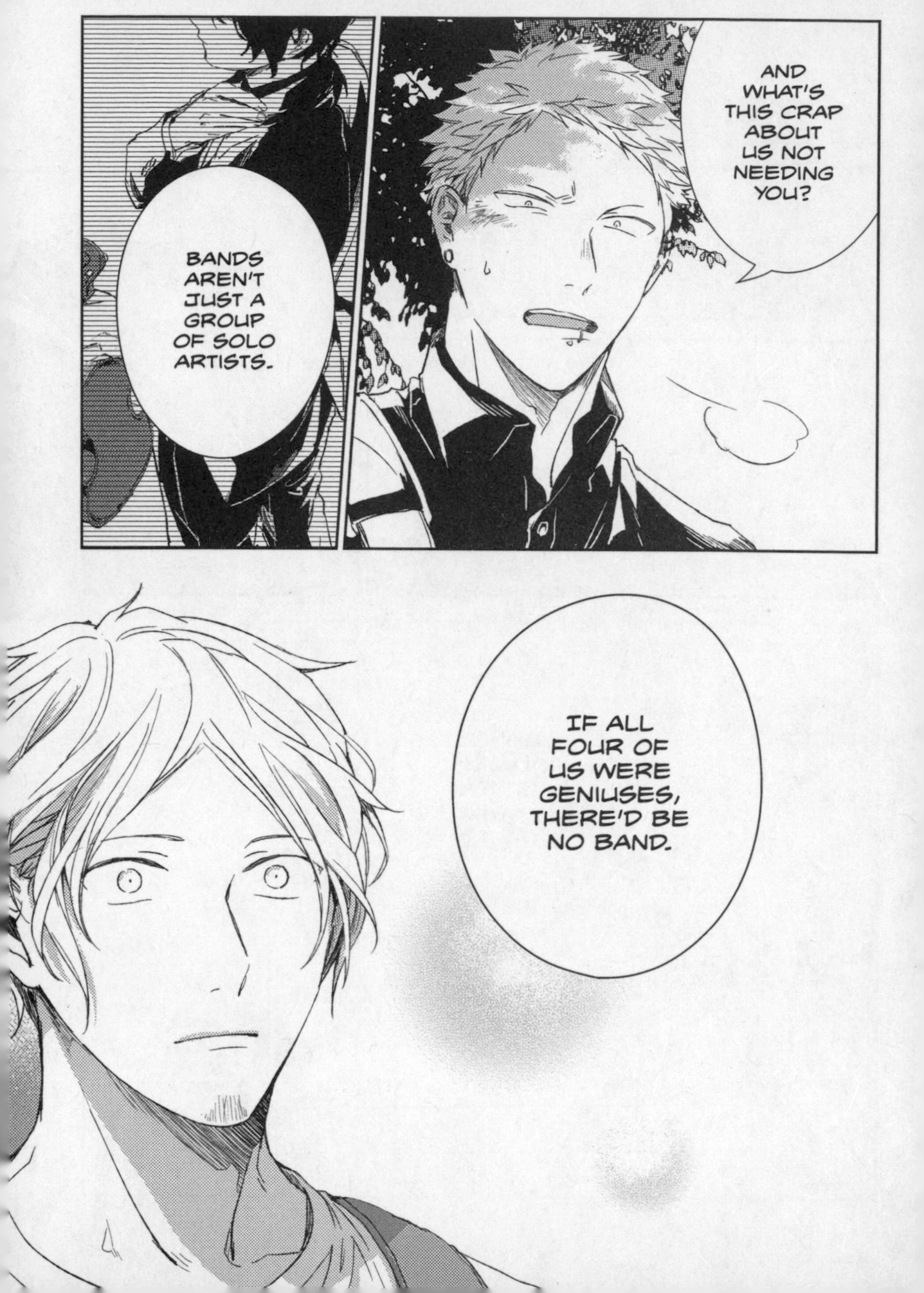
AND WHAT'S THIS CRAP ABOUT US NOT NEEDING YOU?
BANDS AREN'T JUST A GROUP OF SOLO ARTISTS.
IF ALL FOUR OF US WERE GENIUSES, THERE'D BE NO BAND.

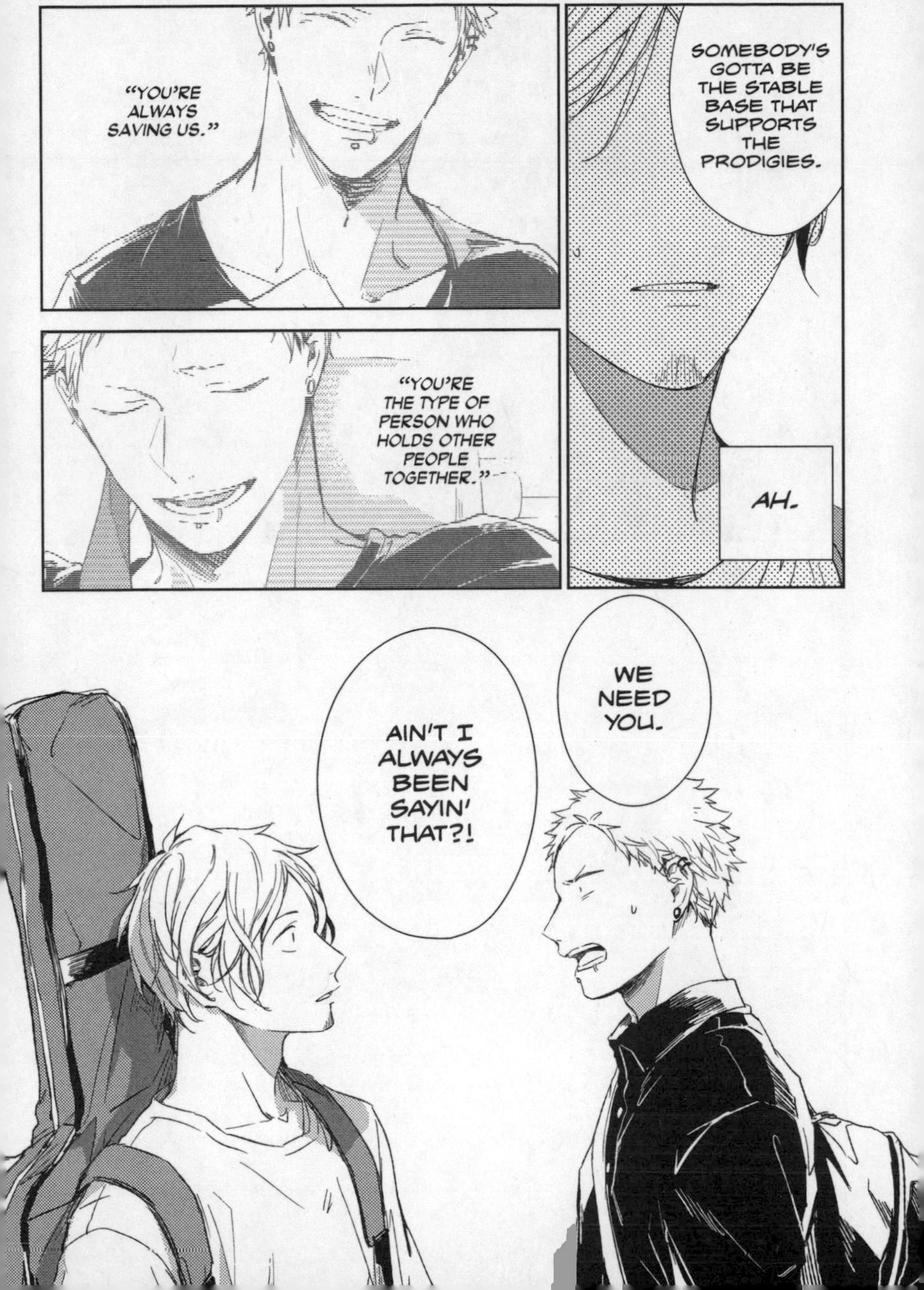
SOMEBODY'S GOTTA BE THE STABLE BASE THAT SUPPORTS THE PRODIGIES.
AH.
"YOU'RE ALWAYS SAVING US."
"YOU'RE THE TYPE OF PERSON WHO HOLDS OTHER PEOPLE TOGETHER."
WE NEED YOU.
AIN'T I ALWAYS BEEN SAYIN' THAT?!

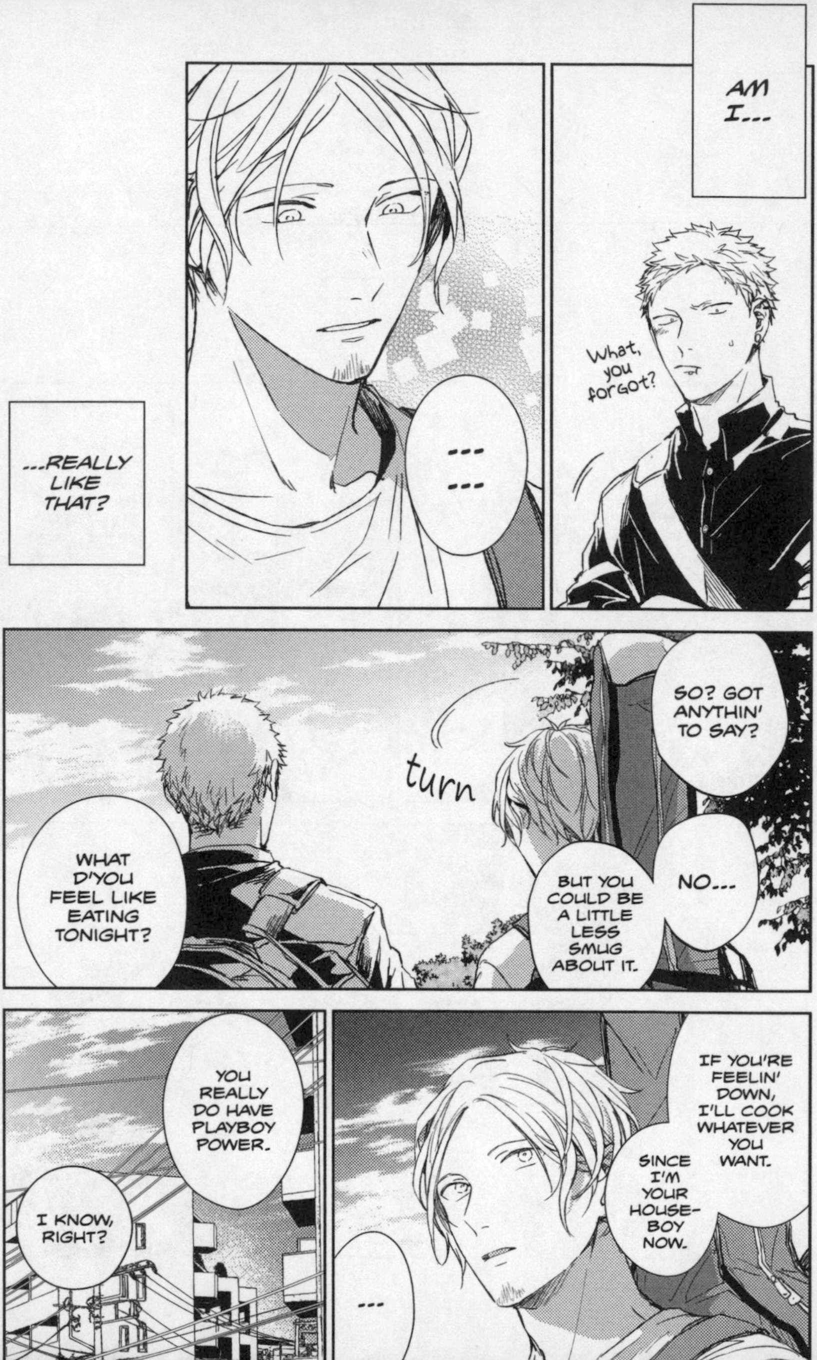
AM I...
What, you forgot?
... ...
...REALLY LIKE THAT?
SO? GOT ANYTHIN' TO SAY?
NO...
BUT YOU COULD BE A LITTLE LESS SMUG ABOUT IT.
turn
WHAT D'YOU FEEL LIKE EATING TONIGHT?
IF YOU'RE FEELIN' DOWN, I'LL COOK WHATEVER YOU WANT.
SINCE I'M YOUR HOUSE-BOY NOW.
...
YOU REALLY DO HAVE PLAYBOY POWER.
I KNOW, RIGHT?

AND SO BEGAN OUR STRANGE EXISTENCE AS ROOMMATES.
I'D BEEN PLUNGED INTO THE DEPTHS OF DESPAIR BECAUSE OF AKIHIKO.
BUT THEN AKIHIKO HIMSELF...
...HAULED ME OUT OF THAT AGONIZING PLACE.
FROM THAT POINT ON, SOME-HOW...
...MY ANGER WAS NEUTRAL-IZED, LIKE POISON DRAWN FROM A WOUND.

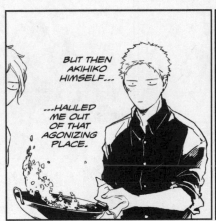

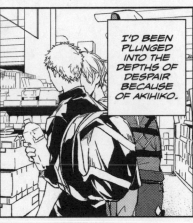

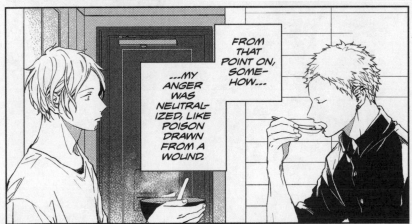

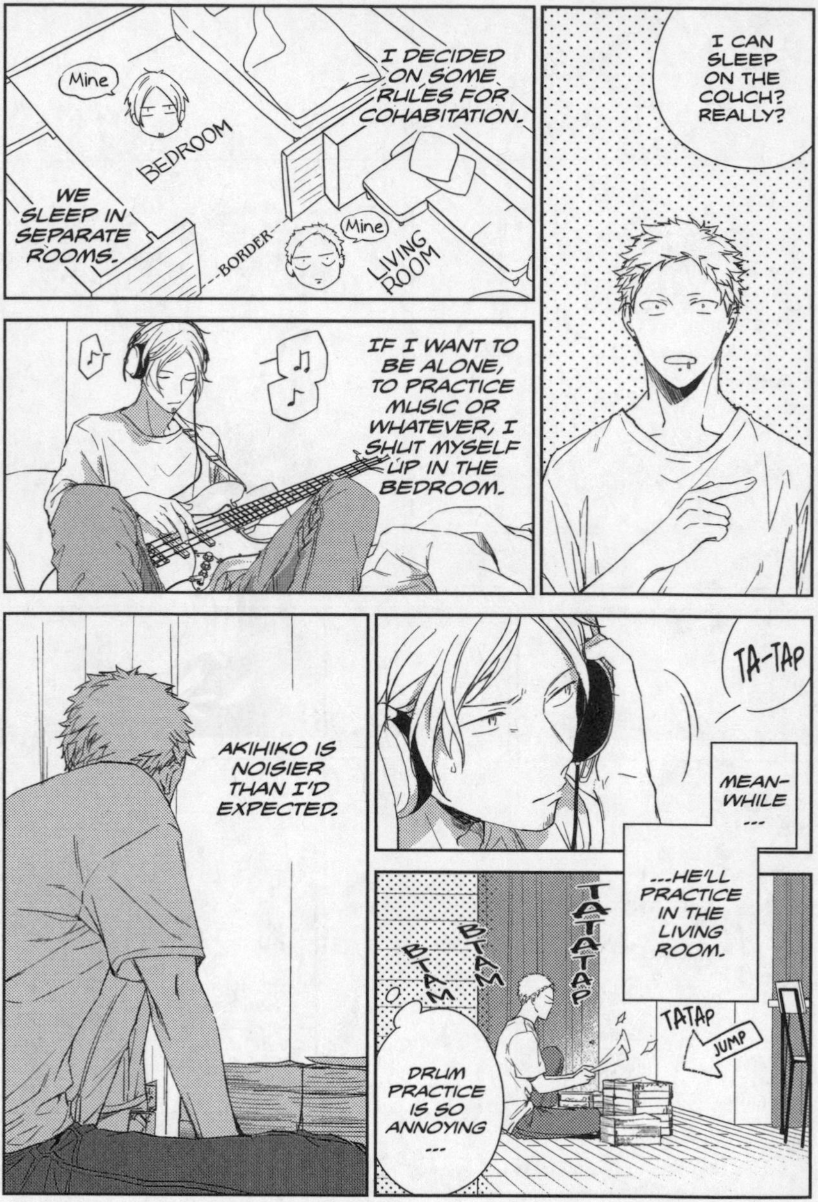

I CAN SLEEP ON THE COUCH? REALLY?
I DECIDED ON SOME RULES FOR COHABITATION.
Mine
BEDROOM
Mine
LIVING ROOM
BORDER
WE SLEEP IN SEPARATE ROOMS.
IF I WANT TO BE ALONE, TO PRACTICE MUSIC OR WHATEVER, I SHUT MYSELF UP IN THE BEDROOM.
TA-TAP
MEAN-WHILE...
...HE'LL PRACTICE IN THE LIVING ROOM.
TATATATAP
BTAM
BTAM
TATAP
JUMP
DRUM PRACTICE IS SO ANNOYING...
AKIHIKO IS NOISIER THAN I'D EXPECTED.

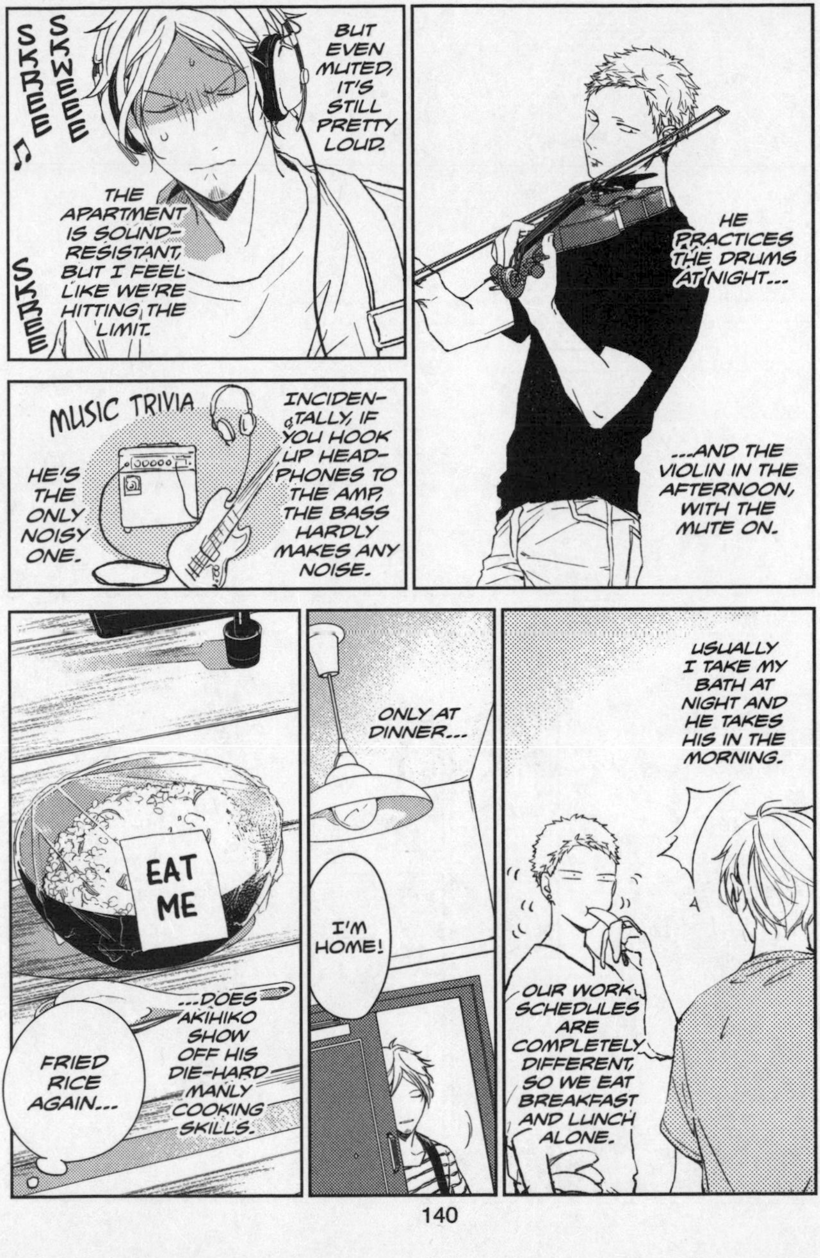
HE PRACTICES THE DRUMS AT NIGHT...
...AND THE VIOLIN IN THE AFTERNOON, WITH THE MUTE ON.
BUT EVEN MUTED, IT'S STILL PRETTY LOUD.
SKWEEE
SKREE ♪
THE APARTMENT IS SOUND-RESISTANT, BUT I FEEL LIKE WE'RE HITTING THE LIMIT.
SKREE
INCIDENTALLY, IF YOU HOOK UP HEADPHONES TO THE AMP, THE BASS HARDLY MAKES ANY NOISE.
MUSIC TRIVIA
HE'S THE ONLY NOISY ONE.
USUALLY I TAKE MY BATH AT NIGHT AND HE TAKES HIS IN THE MORNING.
OUR WORK SCHEDULES ARE COMPLETELY DIFFERENT, SO WE EAT BREAKFAST AND LUNCH ALONE.
ONLY AT DINNER...
I'M HOME!
EAT ME
...DOES AKIHIKO SHOW OFF HIS DIE-HARD MANLY COOKING SKILLS.
FRIED RICE AGAIN...

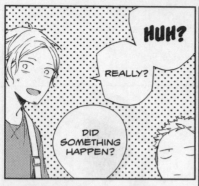

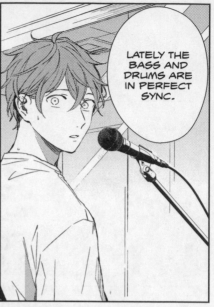

LATELY THE BASS AND DRUMS ARE IN PERFECT SYNC.
HUH?
REALLY?
DID SOMETHING HAPPEN?
NOPE, NOTHING!
AKIHIKO HAD NOWHERE TO GO, SO I TOOK HIM IN AS A FRIEND.
THERE'S REALLY...
...NOTHING MORE TO IT THAN THAT.
BUT FOR SOME REASON, I STILL CAN'T BRING MYSELF TO TELL THE OTHER TWO WE'RE LIVING TOGETHER.
IT FEELS LIKE I'M BEING DISHONEST, BUT...
TO KEEP THINGS ON THE DOWNLOW, WE LEAVE FOR HOME AT DIFFERENT TIMES AFTER PRACTICE.

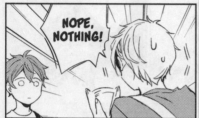

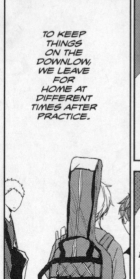

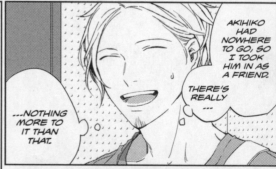

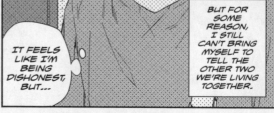

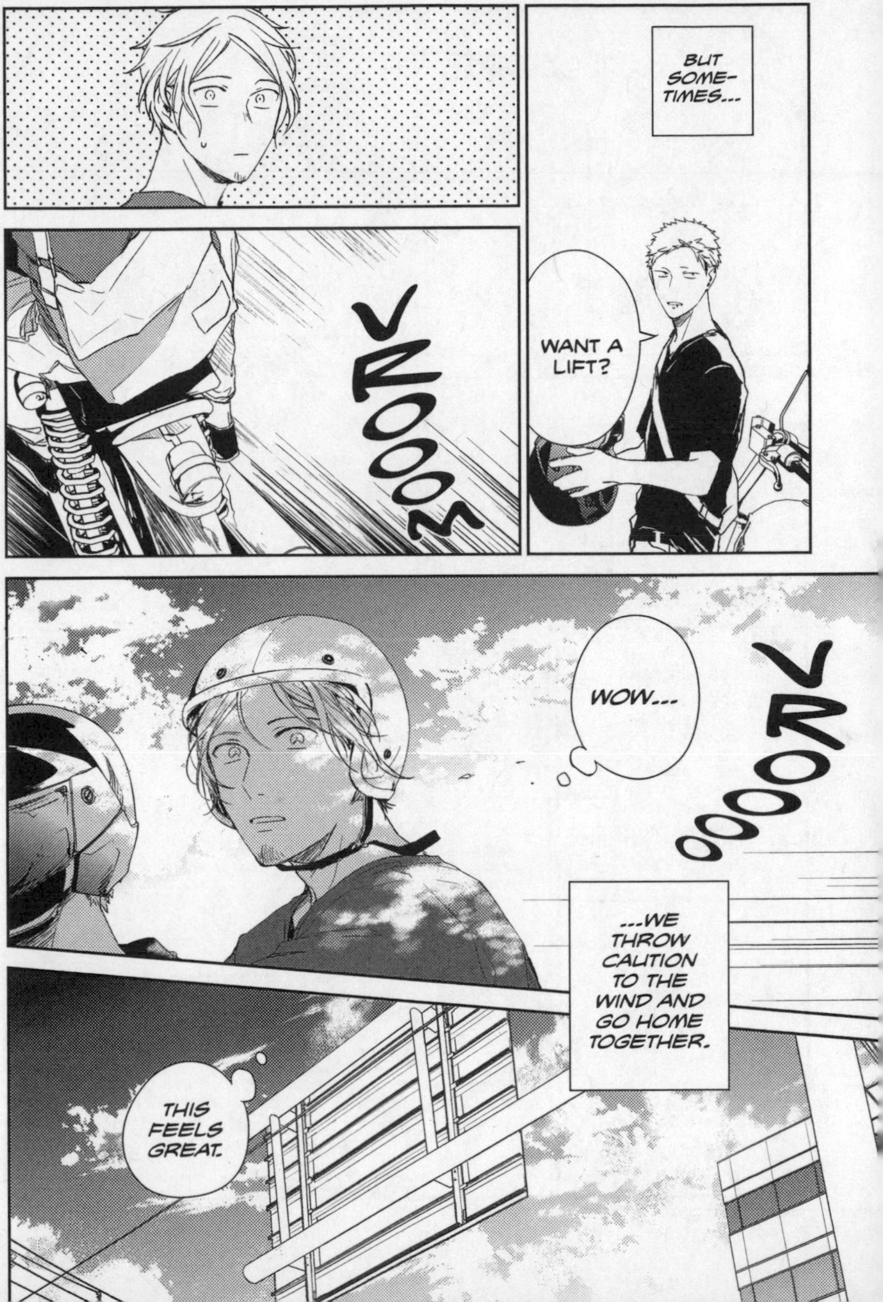
BUT SOME-TIMES...
WANT A LIFT?
VROOOM
VROOOOO
WOW...
...WE THROW CAUTION TO THE WIND AND GO HOME TOGETHER.
THIS FEELS GREAT.

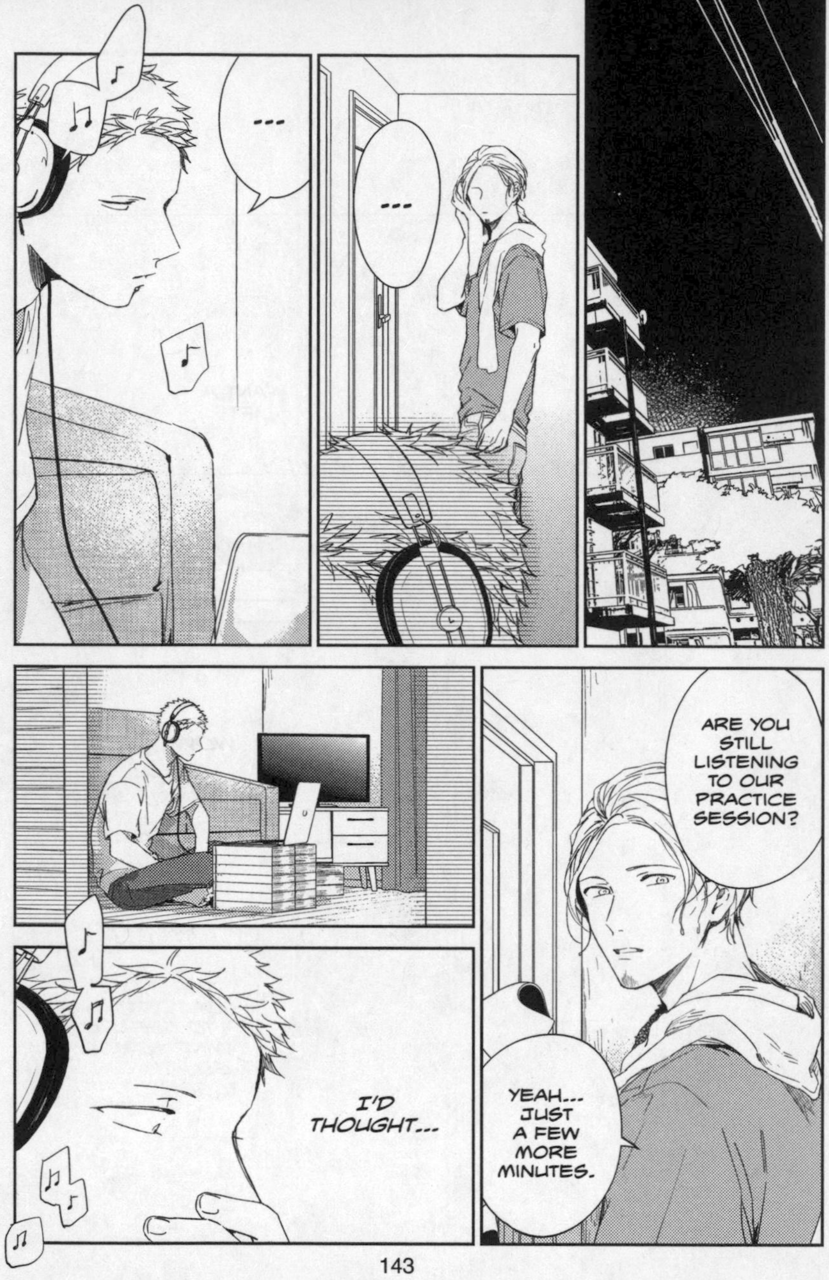
...
...
ARE YOU STILL LISTENING TO OUR PRACTICE SESSION?
YEAH... JUST A FEW MORE MINUTES.
I'D THOUGHT...

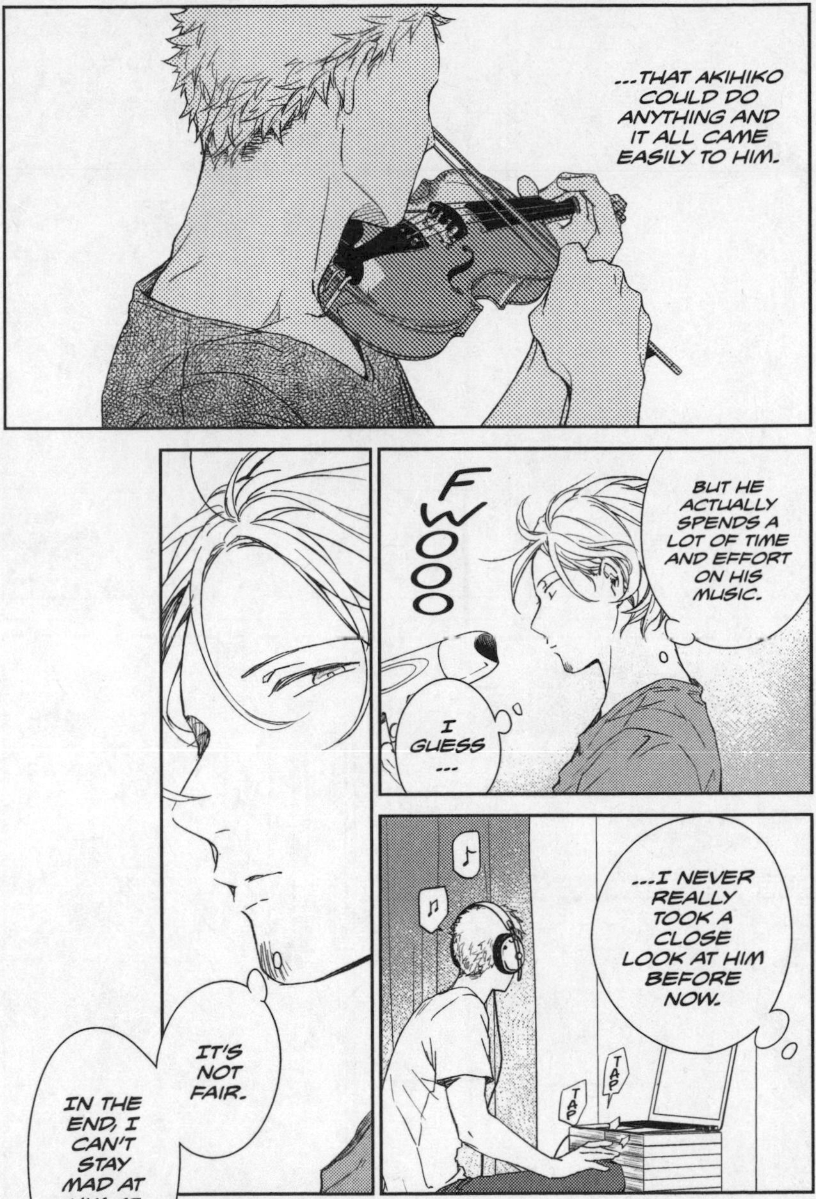
...THAT AKIHIKO COULD DO ANYTHING AND IT ALL CAME EASILY TO HIM.
BUT HE ACTUALLY SPENDS A LOT OF TIME AND EFFORT ON HIS MUSIC.
FWOOO
I GUESS ...
...I NEVER REALLY TOOK A CLOSE LOOK AT HIM BEFORE NOW.
♪
♫
TAP
TAP
IT'S NOT FAIR.
IN THE END, I CAN'T STAY MAD AT HIM AT ALL.

To Be Continued...

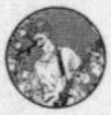

given
@given_ssn

We passed the second round of the CAC tryouts. Thank you for your support.

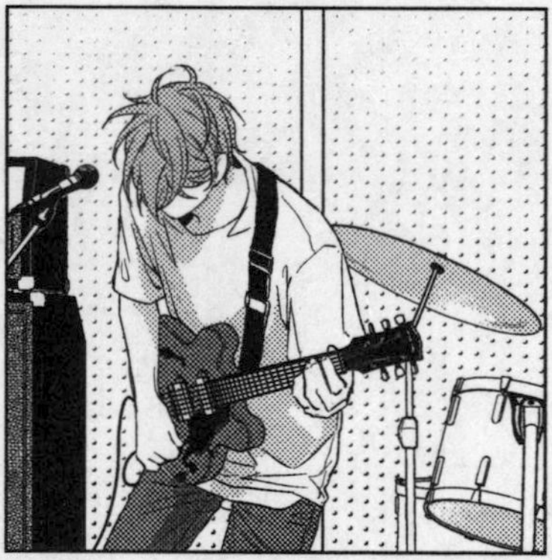

given

by Natsuki Kizu

Character Data Files 1

Kaji, Behind You!!

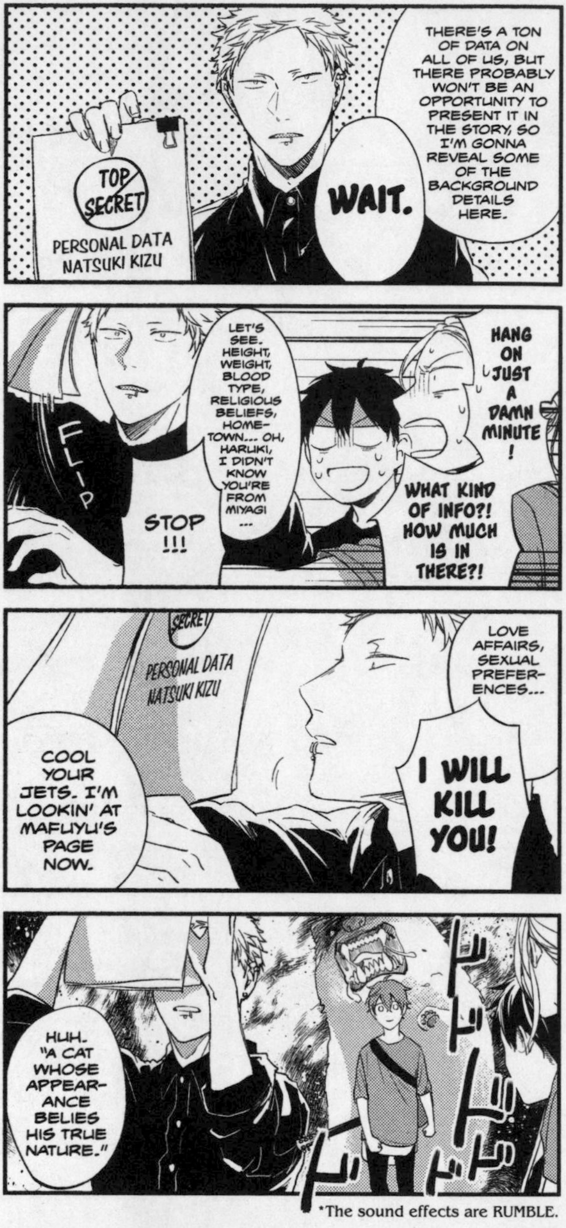
THERE'S A TON OF DATA ON ALL OF US, BUT THERE PROBABLY WON'T BE AN OPPORTUNITY TO PRESENT IT IN THE STORY, SO I'M GONNA REVEAL SOME OF THE BACKGROUND DETAILS HERE.
WAIT.
TOP SECRET
PERSONAL DATA NATSUKI KIZU
HANG ON JUST A DAMN MINUTE!
WHAT KIND OF INFO?! HOW MUCH IS IN THERE?!
LET'S SEE. HEIGHT, WEIGHT, BLOOD TYPE, RELIGIOUS BELIEFS, HOMETOWN... OH, HARUKI, I DIDN'T KNOW YOU'RE FROM MIYAGI...
STOP!!!
FLIP
LOVE AFFAIRS, SEXUAL PREFERENCES...
I WILL KILL YOU!
SECRET
PERSONAL DATA NATSUKI KIZU
COOL YOUR JETS. I'M LOOKIN' AT MAFUYU'S PAGE NOW.
HUH. "A CAT WHOSE APPEARANCE BELIES HIS TRUE NATURE."

*The sound effects are RUMBLE.

Character Data Files 2

Basic Stats

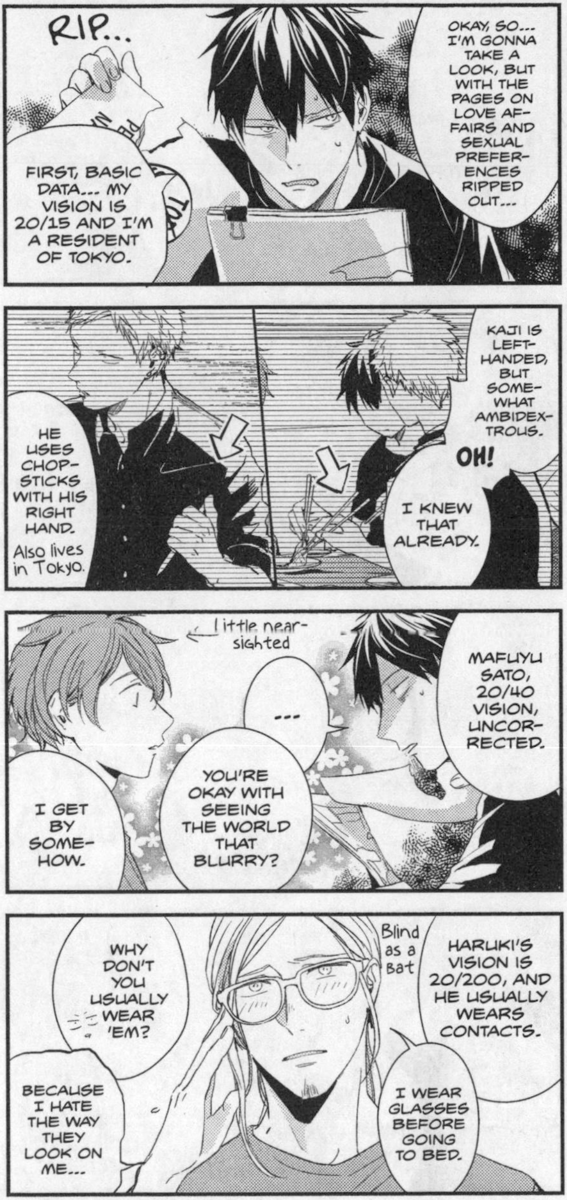

OKAY, SO... I'M GONNA TAKE A LOOK, BUT WITH THE PAGES ON LOVE AFFAIRS AND SEXUAL PREFERENCES RIPPED OUT...
RIP...
FIRST, BASIC DATA... MY VISION IS 20/15 AND I'M A RESIDENT OF TOKYO.
KAJI IS LEFT-HANDED, BUT SOMEWHAT AMBIDEXTROUS.
OH!
I KNEW THAT ALREADY.
HE USES CHOPSTICKS WITH HIS RIGHT HAND.
Also lives in Tokyo.
MAFUYU SATO, 20/40 VISION, UNCORRECTED.
...
little near-sighted
YOU'RE OKAY WITH SEEING THE WORLD THAT BLURRY?
I GET BY SOMEHOW.
HARUKI'S VISION IS 20/200, AND HE USUALLY WEARS CONTACTS.
Blind as a Bat
I WEAR GLASSES BEFORE GOING TO BED.
WHY DON'T YOU USUALLY WEAR 'EM?
BECAUSE I HATE THE WAY THEY LOOK ON ME...

Character Data Files 3

How Akihiko Kaji Got Skint

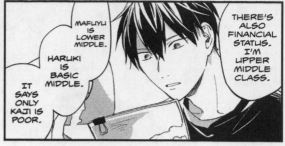

THERE'S ALSO FINANCIAL STATUS. I'M UPPER MIDDLE CLASS.
MAFUYU IS LOWER MIDDLE.
HARUKI IS BASIC MIDDLE.
IT SAYS ONLY KAJI IS POOR.
I CAN BARELY COVER TUITION, SO I HAVE TO HUSTLE, BUT EVEN SO THE MONEY'S RUNNING OUT.
HOW SO?
THAT'S BECAUSE MY PARENTS ARE FLAKES.
WHEN THEY SPLIT UP, THEY DUMPED SOME CASH INTO MY BANK ACCOUNT AND THAT WAS IT.
CLASSY.
KAJI, YOUR PARENTS DON'T GET ALONG?
OH, THEY DO.
MY DAD'S A PRO MUSICIAN IN EUROPE...
...AND MY MOM TAKES IT EASY AT HOME.
IT'S NOT THE MOST FUNCTIONAL FAMILY RELATIONSHIP, BUT THEY WEREN'T ABUSIVE OR ANYTHING.
THEY JUST NEVER SEEMED TO KNOW WHAT TO DO WITH A KID.
I DON'T EVEN HAVE CONTACT INFO FOR THEM TO BEG FOR MORE MONEY.
SO YOU WERE A NEGLECTED CHILD...
YIKES...

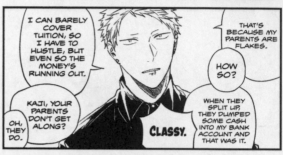

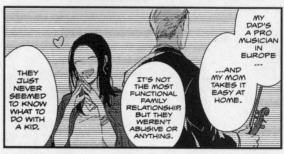

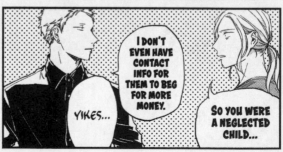

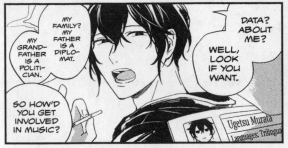

Character Data Files 4

Definitely the Kind of Kid Who Made Roly-Polies Go into a Ball and Then Played with Them

DATA? ABOUT ME?
WELL, LOOK IF YOU WANT.
MY FAMILY? MY FATHER IS A DIPLOMAT.
MY GRANDFATHER IS A POLITICIAN.
SO HOW'D YOU GET INVOLVED IN MUSIC?
Ugetsu Murata
Languages: Trilingua
WHEN I WAS A KID, I WOULD HANG OUT AT THIS OLD MAN'S FARM WITHOUT PERMISSION. I LIKED TO SMOOSH BUGS WITH ROCKS.
BAD KID!
ON THIS ONE REALLY CLEAR, SUNNY DAY, MUSIC WAS PLAYING ON THE OLD MAN'S RADIO.
THE SONG WAS PAUL SIMON'S "STILL CRAZY AFTER ALL THESE YEARS."
EVEN THOUGH I WAS A KID, I REALIZED IT WAS A BEAUTIFUL MOMENT, SO PERFECT THAT I'D BE HAPPY TO DIE THEN AND THERE.
THERE WERE OTHER SONGS TOO...
...BUT BASICALLY, I GUESS I'VE BEEN CHASING AFTER THAT DESIRE TO DIE ALL THIS TIME.
I DON'T GET YOU AT ALL.
SMOOSH
SMOOSH

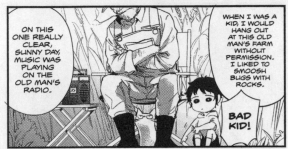

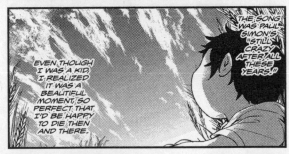

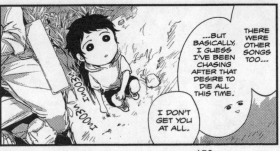

Character Data Files 5

Why Ritsuka Uenoyama Doesn't Watch Ghost Hunter Shows

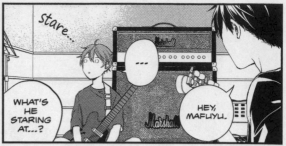

HEY, MAFUYU.
...
stare...
WHAT'S HE STARING AT...?
ACTUALLY, DID THIS ROOM SUDDENLY GET COLD?
HEY, I'VE GOT SOMETHING IMPORTANT TO TELL YOU. READY?
WHAT IS IT?
IN MAFUYU'S PERSONAL DATA FILE...
...IT SAID HE HAS SPIRIT SENSE...
...AND MAY BE ABLE TO "SEE THINGS."
AS FOR YOU...
...IT SAYS YOU HAVE SOME SPIRIT SENSE, BUT THAT...
...YOU DISMISS IT...
...AS IMAGINARY.

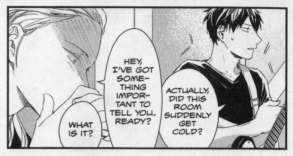

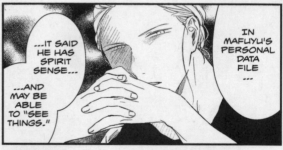

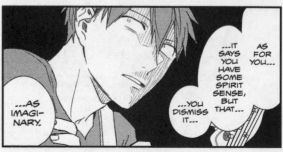

Character Data Files 6

Stand

MY STAND?
YEAH, THE ENTITY THAT APPEARS WHEN YOU'RE FIRED UP.
STAND DATA
TOP SECRET
YOU'VE GOTTA HAVE A STAND TOO, UGETSU.
THIS MASASHI...
WHAT AN INCREDIBLE STAND MASTER!
WOW... I DON'T BELIEVE IT.
SO WHAT'S YOUR STAND?
YOU WON'T LIKE IT IF I SUMMON IT IN THIS ROOM.
ARE YOU SURE?
NAH, FINE BY ME.
SEE?
stare
HUGE
PRESS

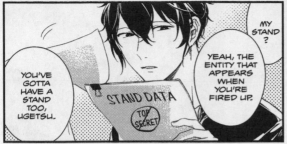

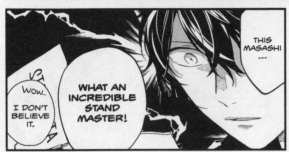

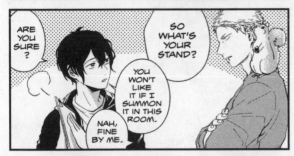

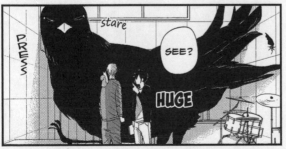

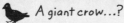

A giant crow...?

Character Spotlight! 1

Hanaoka of Hair Salon Harusame

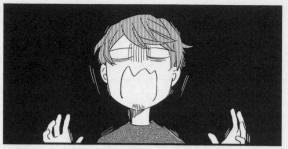

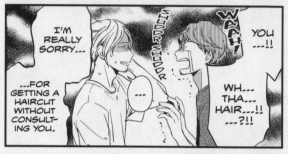

WAAH!
YOU ---!!
WH--- THA--- HAIR---!! ---?!!
SHUDDR SHUDDR
I'M REALLY SORRY---

---FOR GETTING A HAIRCUT WITHOUT CONSULTING YOU.
FORGET CONSULTING. YOU LET SOME OTHER BASTARD CUT YOUR HAIR!!!
Well, you would've refused.
DON'T TALK ABOUT YACCHAN LIKE THAT.
WHO IS THIS YACCHAN ?!
ARE YOU CHEATING ON ME?!
HARUSAME
HARUSAME

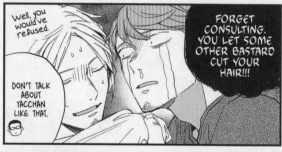

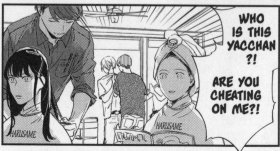

Character Spotlight! 2

High School Trio

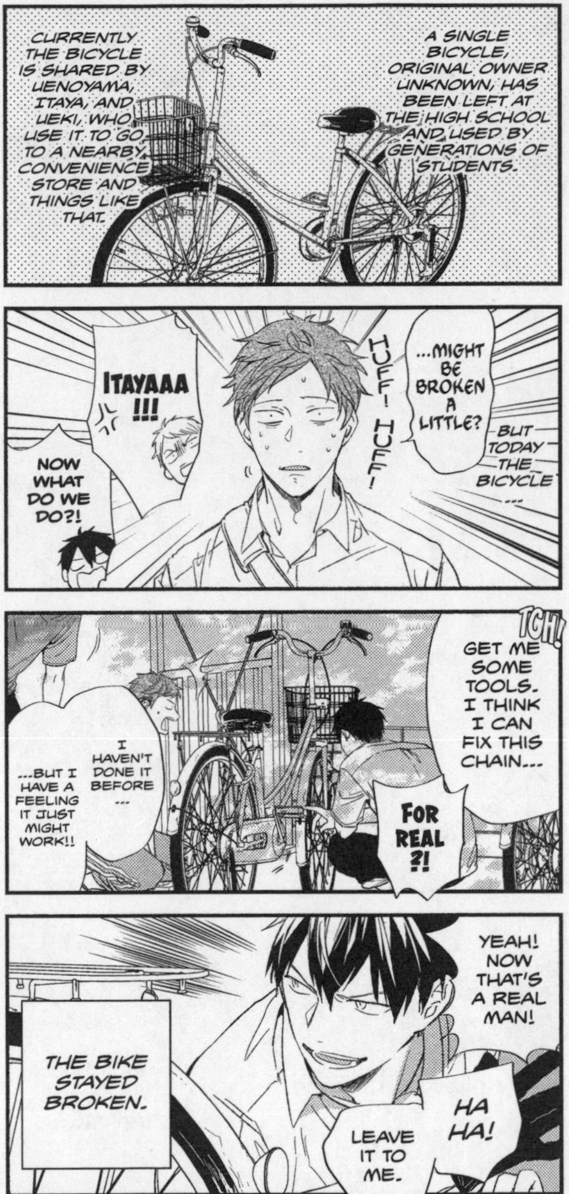
A SINGLE BICYCLE, ORIGINAL OWNER UNKNOWN, HAS BEEN LEFT AT THE HIGH SCHOOL AND USED BY GENERATIONS OF STUDENTS.
CURRENTLY THE BICYCLE IS SHARED BY UENOYAMA, ITAYA, AND UEKI, WHO USE IT TO GO TO A NEARBY CONVENIENCE STORE AND THINGS LIKE THAT.
BUT TODAY THE BICYCLE...
...MIGHT BE BROKEN A LITTLE?
HUFF! HUFF!
ITAYAAA!!!
NOW WHAT DO WE DO?!
TCH!
GET ME SOME TOOLS. I THINK I CAN FIX THIS CHAIN...
FOR REAL?!
I HAVEN'T DONE IT BEFORE...
...BUT I HAVE A FEELING IT JUST MIGHT WORK!!
YEAH! NOW THAT'S A REAL MAN!
HA HA!
LEAVE IT TO ME.
THE BIKE STAYED BROKEN.

Character Spotlight! 3

Middle School Trio

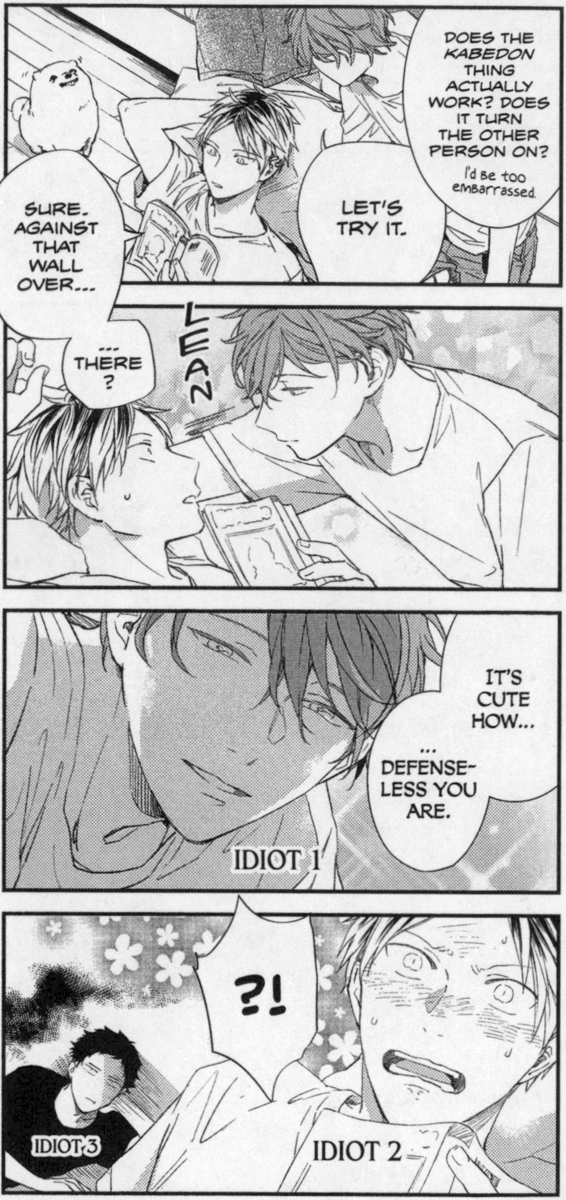
DOES THE KABEDON THING ACTUALLY WORK? DOES IT TURN THE OTHER PERSON ON?
I'd be too embarrassed.
LET'S TRY IT.
SURE. AGAINST THAT WALL OVER...
... THERE?
LEAN
IT'S CUTE HOW...
... DEFENSE-LESS YOU ARE.
IDIOT 1
?!
IDIOT 2
IDIOT 3

They have too much free time on their hands.

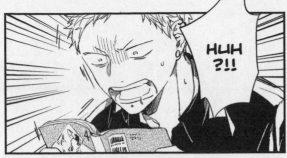

Character Spotlight! 4

Bonus Strip

HUH ?!!
...!!!
HUFF!
HUFF!
GASP...
WHAT'S WRONG?
I'VE READ THIS FAR AND REALIZED SOME-THING...
HUFF!
HUFF!
MAYBE ...
...I DON'T HAVE ANY FRIENDS ?
BOOM!!
You JUST REALIZED THAT NOW?

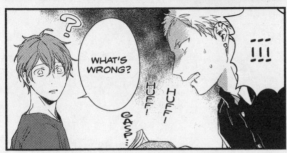

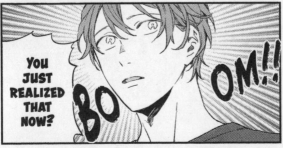

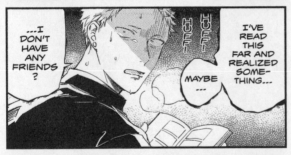

Bonus! Concept Notes and Sketches

Views of Places That Really Exist

Machida Station, Odakyu Line Area ↓

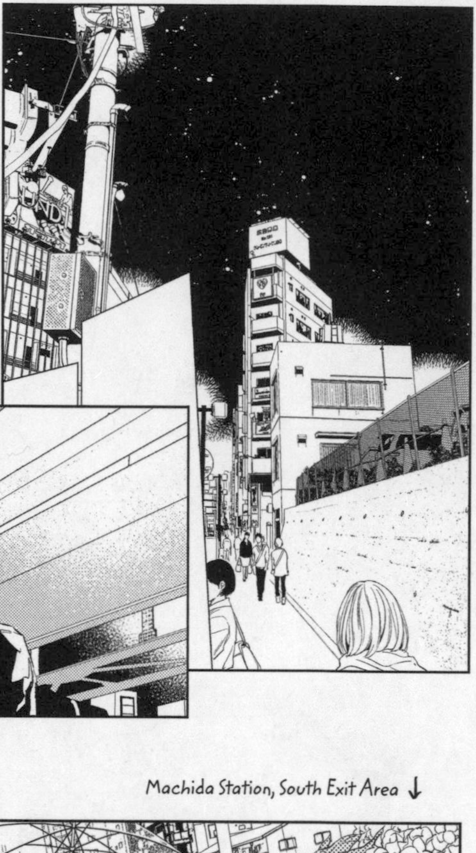

Noborito Station, Tamagawa Exit ↓

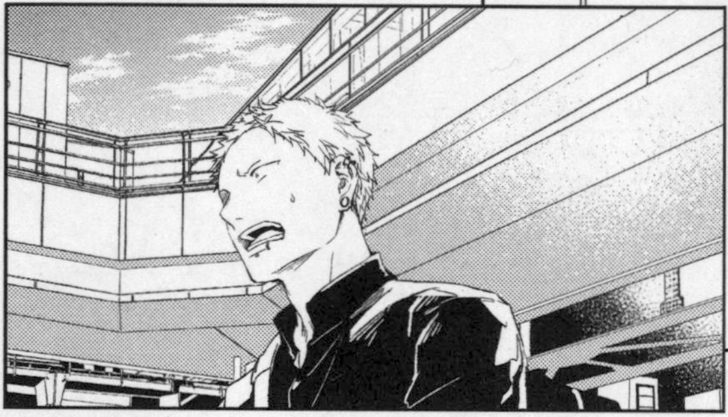

Thanks to Ayaka

Machida Station, South Exit Area ↓

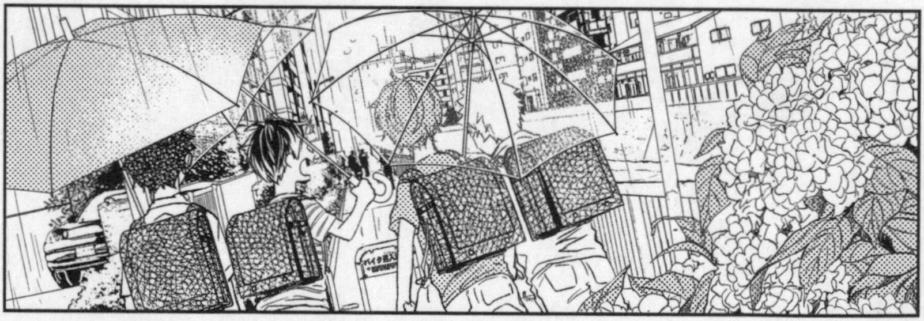

Thanks to Yoneji

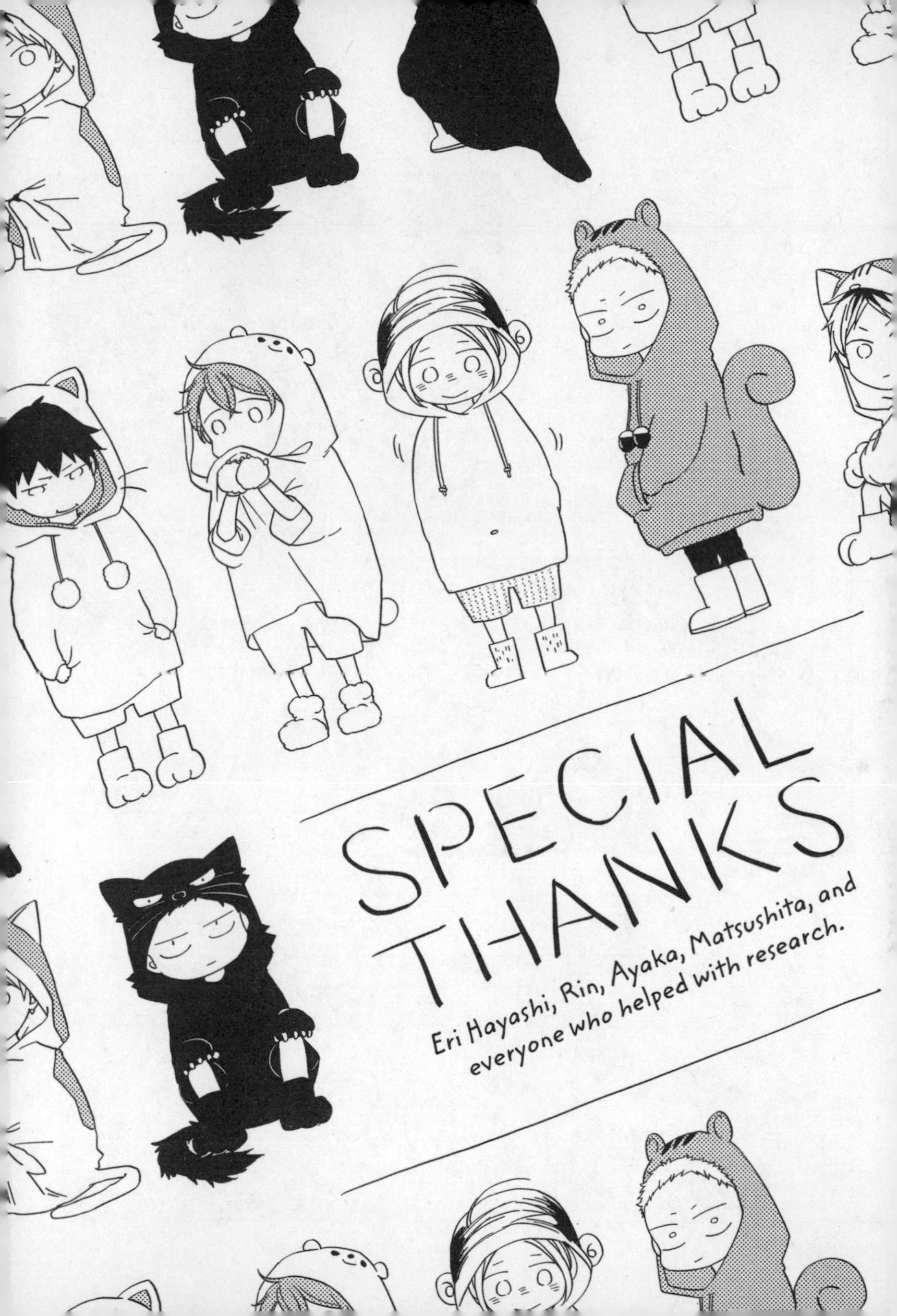
SPECIAL THANKS
Eri Hayashi, Rin, Ayaka, Matsushita, and everyone who helped with research.

About the Author

Natsuki Kizu made her professional debut in 2013 with *Yukimura Sensei and Kei-kun*, followed by the short story collection *Links* and her breakout series, *Given*, which has been adapted into drama CDs and an animated TV series. To find out more about her works, you can follow her on Twitter at **@kizu_ntk**.

Given

Volume 4
SuBLime Manga Edition

Story and Art by **Natsuki Kizu**

Translation—**Sheldon Drzka**
Touch-Up Art and Lettering—**Eric Erbes**
Cover and Graphic Design—**Jimmy Presler**
Editor—**Beryl Becker**

© 2018 Natsuki KIZU
Originally published in Japan in 2018 by Shinshokan Co., Ltd.

Printed in the U.S.A.

Published by SuBLime Manga
P.O. Box 77010
San Francisco, CA 94107

10 9 8 7 6 5 4 3
First printing, November 2020
Third printing, May 2021

PARENTAL ADVISORY
GIVEN is rated T+ for Older Teen and is recommended for ages 16 and up. This volume contains suggestive themes.